new voices
for social
democracy
Labor essays
1999–2000

Edited by Dennis Glover and Glenn Patmore
Series Editor: Gary Jungwirth

First published in November 1999 by
Pluto Press Australia Limited
Locked Bag 199, Annandale, NSW 2038
in association with the Australian Fabian Society (inc.),
PO Box 2707X, Melbourne, Vic 3001

Copyright © Dennis Glover, Glenn Patmore and 6 contributors, November 1999

Cover design by Graham Rendoth, Reno Design

Index by Neale Towart

Typeset by Chapter 8 Pty Ltd

Printed and bound by McPherson's Print Group

Australian Cataloguing-in-Publication Data

New Voices for Social Democracy, Labor Essays 1999–2000

  Bibliography.
  Includes index.
  ISBN 1 86405 097 6.

  1. Australian Labor Party. 2. Australian Greens. 3. Australian Democrats.
  4. Socialism — Australia. I. Patmore, G.A. (Glenn Anthony), 1961–
  II. Glover, Dennis. III. Jungwirth, Gary. (Series: Labor essays; 1999).

324.29407

contents

list of contributors — v

preface — vi
   by Gary Jungwirth

introduction — 1
   by Dennis Glover and Glenn Patmore

SECTION I: FUTURE DIRECTIONS — 19

1. An Australian way: a federal agenda for the ALP — 21
   by Julia Gillard

2. A green challenge to neo-liberalism — 36
   by Colin Long

3. Social democracy and citizen power: an Australian democrat's perspective — 48
   by Matthew Townsend

SECTION II: RECURRENT DILEMMAS — 61

4. Labor's Trojan Horse: the 'third way' on employment policy — 63
   by Roy Green and Andrew Wilson

5. The future of Australian unionism in the global economy — 86
   by Tim Harcourt

6. Creating the participatory society: workplace democracy for Australia? — 100
   by Glenn Patmore

7. Equality and inequality in Australia — 115
   by Rosemary Hunter

8. Welfare and redistribution in an age of risk — 129
   by Anthony O'Donnell

9. A tale of two cities: urban transport, pollution and equality — 141
   by Paul Mees

SECTION III: POSTMODERNISM AND IDENTITY POLITICS 157

10. Break-out from the giggle palace: social democracy, the postmodern economy and the prospects for political renewal   159
    by Guy Rundle

11. Mediating democracy: politics and the media in the postmodern public sphere   173
    by Catharine Lumby

12. A capitalist faggot at the end of the millennium: musings on the disappointments of politics   189
    by Christos Tsiolkas

13. Charting democracy and Aboriginal rights in Australia's psychological *terra nullius*   201
    by Larissa Behrendt

14. To praise youth or to bury it?   216
    by Tony Moore

15. Evolutionary multiculturalism and cultural diversity   233
    by Jason Yat-Sen Li and James Cockayne

16. Migration law and policy for the new millennium: building nation and community   254
    by Mary Crock

17. From here to equality: the voice of disability rights in the twenty-first century   272
    by Steve Hurd and Peter Johnston

18. Difference in an age of homogeneity: feminism, democracy and the illusion of consensus   286
    by Anne Schillmoller

endnotes   300
bibliography   312
Index   334

list of contributors

Dr Dennis Glover is an essayist, political adviser and director of research for the Australian Fabian Society. He has degrees from Monash and Cambridge universities.

Glenn Patmore is a lecturer in law at the University of Melbourne. He teaches courses in law and democracy and constitutional and administrative law. He has law degrees from Monash University and Queens University (Canada).

Series Editor *Gary Jungwirth* is President of the Australian Fabian Society.

Julia Gillard is the Federal Member for Lalor.

Dr Colin Long is a member of the Green Party and a former candidate for the Melbourne City Council. He is an expert on urban heritage and globalisation.

Matthew Townsend is a member of the Australian Democrats and a former candidate for the Senate. He is a Melbourne barrister and teaches law at Victoria University.

Professor Roy Green is from the Employment Studies Centre in the University of Newcastle. He has worked as an adviser to the British Labour Party in the early 1980s and the former Labor Federal Government. He is soon to take up a chair at the National University of Ireland, Galway.

Andrew Wilson works at South Bank University, London, and is a former adviser to the British Labour Party.

Tim Harcourt is an economist and a former research official at the ACTU.

Associate Professor Rosemary Hunter is a fellow of the Social Justice Research Centre at the University of Sydney.

Anthony O'Donnell is a fellow of the Centre for Employment and Labour Relations Law and the Centre for Public Policy at the University of Melbourne.

Paul Mees teaches transport and land use planning at Melbourne University, after spending 1997 as a research fellow at the Australian National University's Urban Research Program. He is also President of the Public Transport Users Association.

Guy Rundle is the European Editor of *Arena* magazine, a theatre critic, playwright and essayist.

Catharine Lumby is Associate Professor of Media and Communications Studies at the University of Sydney. She is the author of *Bad Girls: The Media, Sex and Feminism in the 90s* (1997) and *Gottcha: Life in the Tabloid World* (1999). She is a widely published journalist who currently writes a regular column for the *Bulletin*.

Christos Tsiolkas is the prize-winning author of *Loaded*, *Jump Cuts: An Autobiography* (with Sasha Soldatow) and *The Jesus Man*, his latest novel.

Larissa Behrendt is a post-doctoral fellow in the Law Program at the Research School of Social Sciences, Australian National University, Canberra.

Tony Moore is publisher of Pluto Press in Sydney and is completing a PhD in history at the University of Sydney. He formerly worked as a documentary maker at ABC Television.

Jason Yat-Sen Li is Youth Chairperson of the Ethnic Communities Council of NSW, Co-Chair of the Australian YES Coalition for a Republic and an international lawyer by profession. He was also a prominent contributor to the Constitutional Convention in 1998.

James Cockayne is completing an arts/law degree at the University of Sydney with honours in government, and is Co-Convenor of Young Australians for a Republic.

Dr Mary Crock is a lecturer in the Faculty of Law at the University of Sydney.

Steven Hurd and *Peter Johnston* work at the Disability Discrimination Law Advocacy Service, Victoria.

Anne Schillmoller has been a lecturer in law at Southern Cross University, Lismore, NSW, since 1991. She teaches philosophy of law, administrative law and succession.

preface

by the Series Editor of Labor Essays

Every year the Australian Fabian Society publishes *Labor Essays* as part of our commitment to encouraging debate about the future of social democracy. In past years *Labor Essays* has attempted to provide a forum for senior ALP thinkers to present practical policy issues to a predominantly Labor audience. This year we have done something slightly different, merging *Labor Essays* with a similar project by political adviser Dennis Glover and academic Glenn Patmore, to seek out new voices from across the social democratic spectrum. This special turn of the century edition is also larger than usual.

As a result of wider collaboration, *New Voices for Social Democracy: Labor Essays 1999–2000* addresses itself not just to the broad labour movement but to the centre-left in general, including supporters of all non-conservative parties, as well as to the general reader and students of Australian politics. The editors of this book have sought the views of a newer, predominantly younger set of commentators from the centre-left about the future agenda for social democracy. Our authors are a mixture of experienced policy-makers, young academics, community activists, prominent writers and future political leaders from across the centre-left, including Labor, the Democrats, the Greens and the *Arena* circle. Their essays reflect a diversity of interests, approaches and writing styles. Some essays are theoretical and academic, others more practical, programmatic and legalistic, and yet others more flamboyant and postmodernist. Essayists have been given a free hand to range as widely or as narrowly as they please, while addressing the theme of the future of Australian social democracy. The result is a stimulating and provocative snapshot of the interests, agendas and ideological assumptions of new thinkers from the Australian centre-left.

Once again the Fabian Society has teamed up with Pluto Press to publish *Labor Essays*. I would like to acknowledge the involvement of Tony Moore and Pluto for their commitment to publishing important political debates. Pluto Press is now the pre-eminent publishing house in Australia for issues concerning social democracy.

I would also like to thank our editors for their work in preparing this volume.

Gary Jungwirth
President, Australian Fabian Society
Series Editor of Labor Essays

About the Australian Fabian Society

The Fabian tradition is one of achieving social progress through research and education. Bernard Shaw and Sydney Webb began it in 1883, and generations of Fabians have placed a stamp on every facet of British and Australian society. Gough Whitlam adopted the Fabian approach from the day he entered parliament, and the seminal 1972 Whitlam policy speech was a drawing together of the threads of twenty years of systematic Fabian research and planning. Arthur Calwell before him was always proud to call himself a Fabian, and the tradition has been carried on through Bill Hayden, Bob Hawke, Paul Keating, Kim Beazley, John Bannon, John Cain, Don Dunstan, Neville Wran and Bob Carr. British Prime Minister Tony Blair is a Fabian, as were Neil Kinnock, Michael Foot, Harold Wilson, Hugh Gaitskill and Clement Atlee before him. Australia had its first Fabian society as early as 1895, and 1947 saw the establishment of the Victorian Fabian Society, which became the Australian Fabian Society in 1984. The Australian Fabian Society is the largest Fabian body ever to exist outside Britain itself. It operates nationally, with members in every State and Territory.

The society has no policy beyond that implied in a general commitment to democratic socialism, and it issues its publications as the opinions of their authors and not of the organisation. It does not admit members of parties other than the ALP. Its aim is to promote education and discussion on policies designed to further the goals of democratic socialism.

If you believe that reason, education and ideas should play a larger part in Australian politics, if you care about the quality of the society in which we live and the direction it is taking, and if you share the ethic of democratic socialism, the Australian Fabian Society welcomes you as a member.

Gary Jungwirth
President
Australian Fabian Society
Box 2707X
GPO Melbourne 3000

Acknowledgments

We would like to acknowledge the generous support and enthusiasm of the Australian Fabian Society and in particular the Series Editor of *Labor Essays*, Mr Gary Jungwirth. Special thanks must be given to Mr Tony Moore at Pluto Press for his inspired assistance in publishing *Labor Essays 1999–2000*.

We also wish to thank Mr Joe McCarthy who read material onto tape, made helpful comments and provided research assistance. His dedication and hard work was very much appreciated. We are also indebted to Miss Anna Thwaites and Mr Paul Liondas who checked and revised citations for numerous chapters. Their attention to detail and meticulous work was invaluable. We are also grateful to the Faculty of Law at the University of Melbourne who provided research funding to Glenn Patmore.

Dennis Glover and Glenn Patmore
October 1999

introduction

by Dennis Glover and Glenn Patmore

In many parts of the world today, social democracy is back in the ascendancy. In Britain, France, Germany, the European Commission and the United States, parties of the centre-left or 'the new centre' are not only in power but are winning the battle of ideas.

Although the influence of 'Thatcherism' is still evident in some of the economic and social policies of social democratic parties — in the form of a commitment to low levels of taxation and a smaller public sector — its ideological hegemony appears over. In Australia, despite holding power federally and in a majority of States and Territories, the market liberal-conservative parties have not established ideological or electoral dominance. The Coalition received less than 50 per cent of the two-party preferred vote in the 1998 Federal Election, and their neo-liberal agenda is meeting strong resistance from the left, the non-Coalition right and even from within its own ranks, particularly some sections of the National Party. The Coalition is not invincible. There is a strong possibility that social democracy will become the dominant force in Australian politics early in the new century.

What will this social democracy be like? What social, economic and political innovations will it need to address? These questions raise issues regarding the future of social democracy, which are the theme of this book.

'Social democracy' refers to a grouping of ideas and policies which have at their core the promotion of greater economic, social and political equality through various combinations of government intervention in the economy, constitutional, political and legal reform, and collective organisation by unions and other elements of civil society. Increasingly, social democratic parties are adding the promotion of a sustainable environment to this list of broad objectives.

The book is structured around three theme (section) headings: future directions, recurrent dilemmas and the identity politics of postmodernity.

Under the theme of future directions we have asked one representative from each of the Australian Labor Party, the Australian Democrats and the Australian Greens to comment on the future of social democratic politics in Australia. These essays are not official party policy statements. Rather, they are the personal perspectives of emerging thinkers from within their respective parties. While these three parties differ strongly over many issues, some obvious social democratic ground is shared by individual members.

The second theme, recurrent dilemmas, has provided authors with the challenge of confronting issues of public policy that have given rise to problems or difficulties with no apparent or straightforward solutions. These issues include employee relations, the future of unionism, workplace democracy, the role of education for citizenship and employment, the provision of welfare to enhance job opportunities and human dignity, the potential of migration policy to build families and businesses, and the importance of substantive equality in promoting social, economic, political and democratic renewal.

The third and final theme explores the dramatic changes brought about by the postmodern economy and the emergent focus on identity politics in Australia. The authors have commented on a wide range of personal and political identity issues, including:

- the new class structure of Anglo capitalist economies as a profound challenge to our conception of social democratic policies;
- the dynamic capacity of the media to shape democratic policies;
- the difficulties and the prospects for the development of an inclusive politics for women;

- sexuality and social change;
- the invisible effects of discrimination and the limitations placed on people with disabilities as participants in economic, social and political life;
- the need to adapt multicultural policy in the new social climate created by the One Nation phenomenon; and
- the Howard Government's reluctance to recognise native title rights, and other barriers limiting the achievement of social justice for indigenous Australians.

Throughout the book and cutting across the various sections and essays, it is possible to identify a number of overarching contextual themes, which permeate specific arguments and debates in contemporary social democratic thought. The contributions provide a very significant response by the centre-left to debates over 'stakeholderism', the 'third way', 'globalisation', neo-liberalism, the postmodern economy, 'identity politics', and the potential for internationalisation as a form of governance.

The challenge of market liberalism, globalisation and technological change

Underlying much of the current Coalition Government's policies in Australia is the philosophy of market liberalism, or 'economic rationalism'. Broadly speaking, this ideology aims for the reduction in the size and scope of the public sector and the power of organised labour and the promotion of market solutions for almost all social, political and cultural problems. All governments in Australia and around the world, from right to left, have wound back their public sectors since the early 1980s, but the assault on these institutions by Coalition governments in Australia in the 1990s has been more profound. Since 1995 the public service has been reduced by 16 per cent — down from 145 000 to 121 000 — through retrenchment, winding back of services and contracting out of functions to the private sector (Australian National Audit Office 1999). Sizeable portions of local, State and Commonwealth utilities that were in public hands, including gas, water, rail, telecommunications, road construction and education, have been sold, contracted out or subjected to compulsory competitive tendering (Productivity Commission 1999a). Seventy-five per cent of job growth in Australia in the 1990s has been part time, and 62 per cent casual (Productivity Commission 1999b). Trade union membership has fallen from 31.1 per cent of the workforce in 1996 to 28.1 per cent in 1998 (see Chapter 5).

Australia has also been subjected to the processes of 'globalisation', including intensified global competition and increasing global movement of capital, limiting the taxation and spending options of sovereign governments (although, as we shall see, the extent to which the options of social democratic governments are limited is disputed). The impact of globalisation is being heightened by new information technologies that are creating and destroying jobs, transforming the way government services are delivered, and homogenising national cultures (Gray 1997; Bourdieu 1998; Martin 1997).

The impact of neo-liberal policies, globalisation and technological change on Australian society is a key theme of our essayists.

Colin Long, writing as a member of the Australian Greens, has provided us with a macro-level critique of these joint processes. Long argues that neo-liberal policies are attempting to marketise and commodify virtually every area of society, leading to the degradation of the environment and increased crime and inequality. 'Citizens' are steadily being turned into 'consumers', and the process has even extended to the very building blocks of life itself through attempts by agribusiness to force genetically modified organisms onto unwilling farmers and purchasers of food. Long's emphasis on issues such as this alerts us to the emergence of new political questions outside the traditional 'left–right' divide. Long proposes a redefinition of citizenship to include social, cultural and environmental rights as a first step to empowering governments to challenge marketisation and commodification.

Recently elected Labor MP **Julia Gillard** believes that globalisation and the neo-liberal policies of the Howard Government have knocked our national and local communities off their balance. According to Gillard, neo-liberalism and globalisation are transforming the labour force and creating a society of 'winners' and 'losers', with 'information rich' and 'information poor', and a growing underclass of long-term unemployed and casualised and part-time workers who are often in geographically separated communities. Gillard also notes that the rise of non-traditional employer–employee relationships, combined with a conservative assault on unionism by the Howard Government, has effectively taken many workers outside the ambit of industrial protection. The impact of these assaults on unionism is documented by former ACTU research officer **Tim Harcourt**. Harcourt shows that despite the many strengths of the Australian trade union movement compared to union movements in other countries, union membership continues to decline both in absolute numbers and as a proportion of the labour force.

Anthony O'Donnell argues that these profound economic changes have dramatically widened disparities in wealth between families and have also reduced economic security. He believes that the Australian welfare system is increasingly under threat from attacks on progressive taxation by the Howard Government (through measures such as the GST and private health care rebates) and the growth of 'risk' in our economy — through the reduction of job security, the decline of the social safety net and the continuing demise of the extended family and even the nuclear family.

Progressive responses: 'stakeholderism', the 'third way' and the new internationalism

The changes to the world economy outlined above have challenged social democrats to come up with new solutions. Two major alternatives are currently the subject of considerable debate: 'stakeholderism' and the 'third way'.

Right throughout its history, stretching back to the mid nineteenth century, social democracy has been constantly evolving. This evolution today is more rapid than at any time since World War I. A number of tendencies have recently emerged internationally, and Australian social democratic thought and practice have played an important role in their evolution. The 'third way' emphasises the need to empower individuals and rebuild communities through 'social investment'. It challenges social democrats to think outside traditional divides of 'left' and 'right', public and private sector, and address emerging issues associated with globalisation, postmodernism and greater individualism (Giddens 1998). Participatory or 'stakeholder' democracy seeks to empower all citizens through the enhancement of individual and collective rights in the spheres of politics and the economy, as a counterbalance to the power of global capital (Hutton 1996).

Two contributions to our book endorse a participatory, or stakeholder, vision for social democracy.

Roy Green and Andrew Wilson argue for a 'stakeholder' rather than a 'third way' response to globalisation and deregulation. They believe that the influence on society of neo-liberalism has been so pervasive that it has penetrated even its opposing ideology, social democracy, in the guise of the third way. Far from being new, they claim, the third way was pioneered in Australia, but not, as is commonly thought, as a copy of the early Hawke Government period; rather, its origins lie in the latter half of the Hawke and Keating governments, after the weakening of the Accord process and the move towards greater economic deregulation. Clearly, Green and Wilson are sceptical of the third way's social democratic credentials; in fact they see it as simply the altered face of neo-liberalism.

Green and Wilson disagree that the only viable policy for social democracy in an age of globalised competition is to continue further down the path of deregulation. They believe that in fact globalisation can be managed to suit social democratic ends by a government prepared to use suitable forms of regulation to devolve power back into the community to counterbalance that of capital. They argue that the result of every election since 1993 has been an implicit rejection of deregulationist policies and they propose a number of alternatives based on the principles implicit in the original Prices and Incomes Accords of the first half of the 1980s. Essentially, these include greater public provision of services and welfare, a more supportive framework for union activity, to enable them to increase the wages of low-income workers to build social solidarity, and industrial democracy, to ensure that companies invest the increased profits created by wage moderation back into employment creation and not into speculative activity.

Glenn Patmore also argues for industrial democracy, seeing it as one way of creating a more participatory, stakeholder society. He proposes an Australian adaptation of the European model of works councils as a means of creating a positive balance between the demands of flexibility and security in the workplace. Employees must be given confidence that they will not emerge as the losers in the restructuring process being necessitated by globalisation and technological change.

A number of other authors, drawing upon the analysis of contemporary global society of Anthony Giddens, call upon social democrats to respond more positively to the changing structure of society that has resulted from globalisation and technological change. These writers lean in varying degrees towards the third way.

Julia Gillard argues that politicians must develop a unique Australian answer to these challenges. She rejects the slavish adoption of imported concepts such as the third way as symptomatic of the traditional Australian 'cultural cringe', but she concedes that some of the problems identified by thinkers such as Anthony Giddens are generic to most Western nations and should not be ignored. These include the emergence of communities blighted by inter-generational unemployment, the decline of blue-collar unionism and the changing nature of work, and the emotional insecurity caused by the decline of the traditional family. In meeting Giddens' third way halfway, Gillard proposes a new charter of government to rebuild an inclusive sense of national identity. This charter would redefine the role of government and set national priorities. It would include a commitment to provide a better education system, and it would extend industrial protection beyond traditional employer–employee relationships. Gillard argues for the deepening of national dialogue to help rebuild our sense of interconnectedness, and proposes regularly convening national forums like the Constitutional Convention to engage non-politicians in a non-adversarial environment.

Anthony O'Donnell agrees that correcting this widening social imbalance is one of social democracy's most pressing tasks. He challenges us to consider how we can rebuild economic and cultural security by looking at the opportunities offered by changing economic and social relations. Rather than be made more punitive to discourage 'welfare dependency', he believes the welfare state should be made more flexible, to provide seamless support for people as they move between unpaid, part-time and paid combinations of work in the new, riskier and more volatile economy. O'Donnell believes that the new riskier economy requires us to reconceptualise; work to spread paid work throughout the community and encourage people to construct mixes across their life cycle of paid employment, community involvement, family-rearing, education and leisure. Such a mix, he believes, would counter the division of society into the two-income work rich and the no-income unemployed, build social solidarity and enable people to enjoy a new conception of 'the good life'.

Tim Harcourt argues that rather than mourning the loss of the Cold War and the apparent victory of capitalism, social democrats and unionists should realise that there is a strong role for worker-friendly institutions in a globalised market economy, but only if unions improve their strategic management. Unions must adapt to their new environment by anticipating change and rebuilding in growth areas of the economy. They must monitor the impact of globalisation and hold its proponents responsible for their claims about its benefits. Importantly, unions must attempt to engage the generation of younger, technologically literate workers who can combine entrepreneurial talent with socially progressive attitudes.

From the Australian Democrats, **Matthew Townsend** argues for a radical approach to democratic reform at the State and federal level — one of the key themes of the third way, although he eschews the term, couching his arguments instead in the language of traditional Australian radicalism. In particular, Townsend proposes ideas to increase the representation of women in parliament, create proportional representation in State upper houses, and citizen-initiated referenda. He stresses that before the social part of the social democratic equation can be advanced, the democratic part must first be addressed.

One very important answer proposed by a number of writers is the need to tackle globalisation at the international level.

A new form of internationalism is proposed by **Colin Long**. Long claims that while we must embrace values outside commodity relationships, we cannot be backward-looking. Green social democrats, he argues, cannot ignore politics, but must fight the global market economy on its own terms — by organising coalitions of people globally, across national boundaries and within nations, by strengthening democracy and broadening our concept of citizenship to include social rights, the right to a clean environment and the right to practise traditional cultures. Long's main emphasis is on the environment, but he is careful to reject the environmental utopianism of those who argue for a return to the 'natural' world; cities and the undeveloped environment are equally part of nature. He argues that we need to manage nature through new forms of multilateral cooperation. Part of this cooperation will involve the need to improve the global and national redistribution of wealth. The inequitable distribution of wealth, Long claims, is one of the driving forces behind the never-ending drive for economic growth, particularly in developing nations. Long's argument demonstrates the awareness among new social democratic writers of the potential for international solutions to the problems and opportunities of our age.

Julia Gillard proposes the adoption of a strategy for achieving a regulatory regime at the international level that defines and supports civil, political, social and economic rights and responsibilities. Even relatively small nations like Australia, she argues, can make an impact by tackling limited and specific issues. **Rosemary Hunter** urges us to examine international means of ensuring equality by emulating the European Community's Social Chapter, as does **Glenn Patmore**, who urges social democrats to follow the example of the European Works Council Directive as one way of creating a more participatory, stakeholder society.

Social democracy and the postmodern economy

One of the big challenges facing social democracy is the rise of 'postmodernism' and the postmodern economy. This perspective has been forcefully put in Australia by a number of left intellectuals associated with *Arena* magazine. According to these thinkers, postmodernism's political significance is twofold. First, they argue, post-structuralist ideas have undermined the primacy of political and class struggle as a focus for the interest and political action of citizens, broadening the definition of what should be considered 'political' to encompass a widening sphere of contemporary culture. Secondly, they argue that capitalism has been replaced by a 'postmodern economy' characterised increasingly by intellectual labour, tertiary industries and the expansion of education and information services.

Guy Rundle, currently *Arena* magazine's European editor, argues that postmodernism has made past social democratic traditions obsolete. The changes the world has undergone in the last 50 years — which are as significant as the changes wrought by the agricultural and industrial revolutions — mean that any attempt to go back to older social democratic traditions will only serve to work against a liberating political project. Rundle argues that economic globalisation has reduced the scope for parliamentary action to succeed against footloose capital, and that the simultaneous creation of a growing pool of the permanently unemployed and an affluent, consumer-oriented working class has destroyed the hopes for developing any politically significant working-class consciousness. This set of realities, he believes, limits politics to a narrow choice between the free-market model of the United States and the social-market model of Germany — a choice he clearly finds unsatisfactory. In addition, Rundle believes that post-structuralist ideas, which deny the legitimacy of modern political structures and values and have substituted a primary interest in culture, have percolated through to ordinary citizens, undermining their belief in our political structures and the relevance of traditional ideologies of conservatism, liberalism and social democracy. For Rundle, there is no set of reforms that can ameliorate easily the impact of globalisation through social democratic means. The real political project is to encourage people to think outside the current political system and values to find ways of living meaningfully in the current age. The task for the left is to demonstrate through argument the obsolescence of existing political forms and to propose new ones.

One of the technological factors that Rundle believes is undermining contemporary political structures and values is the Internet. This theme is explored in detail by Catharine Lumby, who argues that new forms of media such as the Internet are broadening our democracy by including in public-debate issues not previously considered 'political'. Lumby calls upon the left in general to drop its suspicion of 'popular culture' and 'tabloid' forms of media, and become less elitist in its tastes and values. This argument is similar to others put recently by Mackenzie Wark (1999).

Social democracy and 'identity politics'

A recent revisionist approach to social democracy and identity politics argues for the defence of rational economic reforms and prudent fiscal management, the protection of the current welfare state and an emphasis on the economic, social and cultural priorities of the working class and lower middle class. According to this thesis, social democrats should try to appeal to their traditional base of blue-collar and routine non-manual employees and small business owners (Thompson 1999, p. x).

As many of our writers have demonstrated, class remains a key concept for understanding Australian politics, even in an age of globalisation and postmodernism. However, a surprising number of essayists challenge revisionist social democrats to take more seriously other forms of 'identity' and cultural attachment. Many of the emerging generation of social democratic writers believe that 'identity politics' — the way in which individuals identify with aspects of personal identity such as cultural interests, race, gender or sexuality as meaningful and important political issues — is now a key challenge for the centre-left. As forms of identity become more diverse, the idea of class is losing its centrality and is now considered one of many forms of analysis and identification.

According to our writers, taking identity seriously requires social democrats to develop understandings of the idea of equality that go beyond the idea of 'class'. This clearly puts them at odds with traditional pragmatic Laborists such as Thompson, who has argued that the ALP has been captured by special interest groups whose 'coercive agendas' (rather than the ALP's neo-liberal economic policies) have alienated that party's traditional electoral base (Thompson 1999, pp. ix–x).

Rosemary Hunter has proposed a means of reconciling the interests of the two camps of 'class' and 'identity' whilst implicitly rejecting Thompson's claim that 'economic rationalism' is ultimately in the interests of the ALP's working-class supporters. Hunter believes that what both the traditional working class and 'minorities' such as indigenous Australians and women have in common is their interest in policies based on substantive rather than formal equality. She argues that as a result of the changes being introduced by the Howard Government, Australians are increasingly being forced to choose between a formal equality, where all are treated on an equal footing regardless of their individual circumstances, and a substantive equality, which recognises the need to redress socio-economic inequity. Proponents of the former tend towards a flatter tax system, while proponents of the latter argue for greater progressivity in the taxation system (hence the significance in terms of equality of the continuing debate over the GST). In the field of industrial relations, the Howard Government's industrial legislation has sought to negate the substantive equality inherent in the power of trade unions and substitute a formal equality where every employee must negotiate contracts on an individual basis. Similarly, the Howard Government's refusal to apologise to the 'stolen generations', its attempts to minimise the entitlements of native people under common law through its response to the Wik case, its determination to abolish differential welfare provisions for indigenous people (in programs such as Abstudy) and its attacks on the independence of ATSIC all reflect a retreat into formal equality. Hunter demonstrates that in debates such as these, social democrats will tend to favour policies based on substantive equality and free-market liberals, formal equality. This is a significant point of common interest between proponents of class and identity politics.

A number of policy directions are proposed by our essayists to address the diverse forms of 'identity' and inequality within Australia.

A concrete example is given in an essay by **Jason Yat-Sen Li and James Cockayne**. Li and Cockayne argue that the rise of the One Nation Party was possible because while many

Australians were encouraged to tolerate other cultures, they were not encouraged to recognise the equality of all cultures within Australian society. Echoing a similar argument recently made by Ghassan Hage (Hage 1998) (also discussed by Rosemary Hunter in Chapter 7), they argue that equality can only be achieved when Australians are prepared to fully accept cultural difference and accept that cultures are mixing rapidly to produce a truly different, non-Anglo-Saxon Australian culture. They argue that Australians need to more fully accept the participation in politics of people from non English speaking backgrounds. This has implications for the preselection processes of social democratic parties. Recent problems associated with 'ethnic branch stacking' should not be allowed to derail the process of making our parties more representative of the general public. Li and Cockayne inject a further level of complexity into the concept of identity by pointing out that the cultures that make up Australia's multicultural society are themselves evolving rapidly as they come into contact with other Australian cultures — a process they call 'evolutionary multiculturalism'.

Mary Crock argues that whilst Australia's immigration policy has been relaxed and shifted from the form enshrined in early migration laws and in the Constitution itself, which were influenced by stringent Anglo-Saxon ideological and cultural norms, new restrictions by recent governments, particularly the Howard Government, are arguably as harsh. These changes to our immigration laws are coloured by new economic rationalist perceptions of the national interest. All categories of intake have been reduced, and the new points test focuses on admitting skilled migrants at the expense of maintaining family streams, and the introduction of substantially higher processing fees favours English-speaking 'first-world' migrants. Crock argues that social inclusion and belonging as well as economics should be important touchstones of our immigration policy, and that Australia should be more committed to building community organisations through reinforcing the family unit as well as through business.

The need to change the attitudes of Australians towards non–Anglo-Saxon cultures is also taken up by **Larissa Behrendt**, of the Australian National University. In her essay on post-Mabo politics, she argues that whilst the legal fiction of *terra nullius* may be over, there still remains in Australia a deep 'psychological *terra nullius*' — an inability to comprehend the real workings of Australia's system of property rights in dispossessing indigenous peoples. To provide substantive equality to Australia's indigenous peoples requires more than just equal property rights; it requires recognition of the historical context under which our current system of property ownership was imposed. Tackling this deep psychological block is necessary before Australia's indigenous peoples can be truly equal. Like Hunter, Behrendt argues that justice for indigenous Australians can only be obtained if we accept the need for substantive rather than formal equality. This requires improved outcomes in standards of living, not just the provision of identical services as for non-indigenous people, as well as effective political representation that recognises difference. One of the new nodes of tension within social democracy is the varying emphasis given to 'rights' and 'responsibilities'. Echoing recent comments by Noel Pearson, Behrendt has signalled the need for a proper balance between these two objectives by arguing not just for the recognition of substantive rights for indigenous people, but also for the devolution of more responsibility for decision-making and control of programs to indigenous communities. She also calls for alliance-building by indigenous political action to create majorities to defend and extend indigenous rights.

Writing about youth and social democracy, **Tony Moore** also notes the importance of culture in our political system. However, while he argues that we are witnessing the creation of a distinct, new, creative and 'postmodern' youth culture, he claims that young people are divided still by the older concerns of class, race and gender. Moore claims that while young people in general have been the big victims of economic restructuring, all have not suffered equally. Those who have access to quality education and employment networks have flourished and now increasingly find their skills in demand, but many others lacking these assets have gone backwards in their living standards due to the destruction of the unskilled labour market. Adults' responses to these economic pressures have reduced young people's scope for personal freedom by defining them as a separate economic category without equal rights to adults. Young people are in effect having their 'youth' extended further and further and are being made economically dependent upon their parents by changes in social support. As the generation that will inherit our society in the twenty-first century, the predicament of youth sums up many of the issues that social democracy will have to face — improved opportunities for some, further marginalisation for others. Moore adds that this process of pushing the concept of 'youth' back into a person's thirties has had a curious impact upon young intellectuals, not just working-class youth. He argues that the generation that came before 'generation X', and who are now in their thirties, have been held back by the baby boomers defending their privileges, as Mark Davis has suggested in his book *Gangland* (Davis 1997). To ensure real justice for young people — working class and intellectual — Moore believes we must now drop the concept of 'youth rights', which has marginalised young people since the 1980s, and instead regard all people, from young adulthood onwards, as equal citizens.

Steve Hurd and Peter Johnston, of the Disability Discrimination Law Advocacy Service of Victoria, argue that there is a lack of understanding in general about the need to enhance the participation of people with disabilities in society. They point out that for people with disabilities, the legislative reform agenda begun by the Hawke and Keating Labor governments has not produced equality. They propose a slightly stronger emphasis on 'rights' than for instance Larissa Behrendt, and argue that it is too early to talk about devolving responsibility for disabled people back to families. They therefore strongly criticise the disability policies pursued by the Howard Government for their emphasis on private, family-based care, and current Commonwealth disability legislation, with its non–rights-based focus. What are needed, they argue, are well-funded schemes, based on a rights approach, to promote the integration of people with disabilities back into the workforce and the community. The key is inclusion. Breaking down the psychological barriers to the acceptance of people with disabilities in mainstream society will only occur when they are able to rub shoulders on a daily basis with people without disabilities.

Author **Christos Tsiolkas** tackles the question of whether the rights of minority groups based on identity are necessarily part of a wider social democratic emancipatory project. He finds an intersection and separation between macro-globalisation politics (of economics and international relations) and minority identity politics (sexuality, gender and culture) which creates confusion in responding to political causes in a sincere and appropriate way. According to Tsiolkas, much confusion has been created about the possibilities of gay identity politics being advanced on a unified basis or commitment or at least belief; that homosexuality in itself is necessarily indicative of an egalitarian or social democratic ethics. The author has come to understand that sexual politics encompasses a range of beliefs and activisms, from conservative to reformist to radical politics. And that is true for all political positions centring on the specificity of identity — feminism, queer politics, multiculturalism. His involvement in these political spheres remains distant. Nonetheless, he still possesses a commitment to a more egalitarian society. In particular, he is concerned about the commodification of sex and sexuality through the proliferation of explicit material in the media, and particularly on the Internet. The homosexualised image is now being so rampantly used for exploitative ends that it is fracturing the sense of identity and purpose that an egalitarian gay community might otherwise achieve. The idea that gay identity politics is necessarily culturally contingent is also explored. Tsiolkas concludes that political strategies to counter the effects of the sex industry will need to be developed along cultural lines.

Anne Schillmoller confronts problems for diversity of the increasing homogeneity of globalised culture. Via processes of globalisation especially, it is argued that subcultures collide and differences diminish. She contends that the ostensible uniformity characterising homogenised culture is arguably defective and illusory. The convergence of differences is largely characterised by the dominance of Western culture and market values, and anything or anyone not fitting into this framework is therefore silenced. She pays special attention to the social and cultural exclusion of women by globalised culture and the politics of representation, and she also explores the possibilities of a truly inclusive democratic culture. Schillmoller's argument has three parts: first, how women represent themselves and other women and the perils of women speaking for all women — especially at the expense of excluding the heterogeneity of women's voices; second, the power of dominant political structures to homogenise and exclude diverse and non-dominant voices; and third, the need to develop more inclusive and open-ended democratic structures which recognise heterogeneity and diversity.

Social democracy and true environmentalism

Many of our essayists have reminded us that we are living in what is increasingly a post-industrial era. This provides opportunities to slow and reverse the environmental damage done by heavy industrialisation. **Colin Long** argues that to do this we need to go beyond the idea of environmental sustainability, which merely gives economic values to environmental concerns, such as green technology. Instead, he argues, we need to adopt a true environmentalism that leads us to consider values outside commodity relationships and regard access to a clean environment as a 'right'.

Paul Mees too provides a concrete example of how the fight for environmental values and traditional social equality issues can be combined. He argues that the creation of coordinated urban transport will not only improve air quality but also the mobility and opportunities of low-income earners, who are often unable to afford cars. Again, environmental and social policies can serve joint ends.

Conclusion

The essays in this book demonstrate how social democracy is being transformed in response to the impact on Australia and the world of globalisation, neo-liberalism, technology and postmodern thought. Taken collectively, our authors show that the next generation of Australian social democrats is cautious about the fashionable ideology of the 'third way' and opposed to the traditional Laborism advocated by writers such as Michael Thompson.

Despite their rejection of the policy prescriptions of the third way, many writers have been influenced by the analysis of post-industrial global society of writers such as Anthony Giddens. Even those such as Roy Green and Andrew Wilson, who specifically reject Giddens's analysis as a Trojan Horse for neo-liberalism, are obliged to confront his interpretation. While our writers still see class as an important source of inequality, they acknowledge that the nature of class relations is evolving rapidly. However, they see class as only one of many forms of inequality and identity.

Some authors propose enhanced democracy at the international, national, State and workplace levels as a means of promoting equality and rebuilding community in a strangely unbalanced and disconnected world. In an era when many social democrats propose a greater emphasis on 'responsibility', a number of our essayists also remind us of the continuing importance of 'rights'. It is premature, they argue, to minimise the significance of rights when many people are still denied substantive equality. Other writers affirm social democracy's continuing concern with the environment, acknowledging, however, that the new environmentalism requires an engagement with mainstream politics and a recognition that the environment encompasses the human as well as the natural world.

Interestingly, a high proportion of our writers are concerned with questions of identity and culture. This has profound implications for the future directions of social democracy. Thompson and others have argued that in recent years Australian social democracy has been hijacked by the proponents of identity and cultural politics, with disastrous electoral consequences. However, given the increasing diversity of Australian society outlined by our authors, a return to a 'meat and potatoes' social democracy would appear to fly in the face of social and intellectual trends. It could potentially alienate social democratic parties from an increasing proportion of the electorate and make it irrelevant to progressive politics in the twenty-first century. There is a danger that a philosophy or brand of social democracy that is unwilling to confront the social, economic and intellectual trends of the postmodern, post-industrial era will become a new form of conservatism.

Section I:
Future Directions

chapter 1

An Australian way: a federal agenda for the ALP
by Julia Gillard

The 1990s have been a hair-raising rollercoaster ride for Federal Labor. The improbable victory of 1993 turned to ashes in the stinging defeat of 1996. The Labor phoenix did not fully rise from the ashes in 1998, but the revival in Labor's fortunes was nothing short of stunning.

Labor polled more than 50 per cent of the two-party preferred vote in the 1998 election and is now within eight seats of becoming the government. A tiny swing of 0.92 per cent is all that is required for a Labor victory, and the number of possible Labor wins is large, with ten Coalition seats being held by a margin of less than 1 per cent and a staggering 21 being held by a margin of less than 3 per cent.

Against this backdrop, some may be tempted to conclude that Federal Labor's best electoral strategy would be to sit tight, roll itself into the smallest possible target and wait for Howard Government errors to move the tiny number of votes required to deliver victory.

But it is a temptation that needs to be resisted. There is nothing automatic about a Labor victory next time. Indeed, as one senior Liberal figure privately remarked on election night, the 1998 result for Labor may well be the equivalent of the 1984 electoral result for the Federal Coalition — a false dawn, an early revival, which heralded not an election victory but many more painful years of opposition.

The 1998 election result was achieved as a result of a sophisticated negative campaign against the GST and the attractive personality of Kim Beazley.

At its January 1998 National Conference, Labor had taken a first step towards developing a new vision for Australia. But while many in the party were wrestling with new ideas, the lack of political distance from the Keating defeat meant the electorate was not ready to switch on to positive messages from Labor.

The next election will be held in a radically different context. First, it is unlikely that there will be one dominating central negative campaign like the 1998 anti-GST campaign. Secondly, the media will undoubtedly make much of the fact that this is the first election of the new century and, as a result, will be more responsive to positive policies. Thirdly, as a government ages, the degree of difficulty in defending the record and putting forward a fresh agenda increases exponentially. By the next election, the Coalition will be struggling with that burden. As a result of these factors, it will be smart electoral politics for Labor to campaign on a positive vision at the next election.

But being prepared to articulate a new vision for Australia is much more than smart electoral politics. It is necessary to answer a deep-felt community need for more from its political leaders than empty economic babble woven through with breathless, and often meaningless, statements about globalisation and the power of new technology.

In Hugh Mackay's *Mind and Mood Study* (MacKay 1993) and in Clemenger's *Silent Majority* report (White & Cummings 1997), we find portraits of a society in which individuals increasingly feel insecure and powerless to control their lives in the face of rapid economic restructuring and social change. Most tellingly of all, parents believe their teenagers are facing a tougher world than they themselves faced.

This insecurity, pessimism and nervousness about Australia's future and the prevailing cynicism about politics is, in part, fed by a political cycle which for far too long has been limited to no more than the generation of fear of change and fear of the alternative.

In the first election of the new millennium, it is time for Labor to confidently step forward to break this political mode and answer the deeper yearnings in our society for vision, for passion and for conviction.

Through his pathway addresses, the Federal Labor leader, Kim Beazley, has already demonstrated his great capacity to generate ideas and garner support and enthusiasm for those ideas.

It is now time for Labor to build on what has already been done and to complete its vision for Australia in the next century by finding a unique Australian answer to the central issues dominating debate amongst social democrats throughout the world.

Social democracy and the third way

In recent media reporting, the emerging debate within the Labor Party about its future direction has been characterised as a debate solely about the 'third way'. The participants in the debate have been stereotyped as either third way–embracing modern reformers or traditional and backward-looking. This reporting is simplistic. Unfortunately, so too is some of the debate.

The third way, as it is understood in Australia, is the description given to the philosophy of Tony Blair and British Labour. It describes a social democratic path that rejects the solutions of the 'old left' and the 'new right', and finds a new, third way.

It is a paradigm with more resonance in the British context given British Labour's long period in the wilderness, its internal fight with ultra-leftism and the unbridled and radical nature of the new right policies followed by Thatcher.

It is a paradigm of less relevance in Australia, given that Labor was recently in government for a long period and adopted policy prescriptions throughout that period which could not in any way be described as old left.

Indeed, the current adherents of third-way philosophy seem increasingly caught in a policy straightjacket that requires the tags of old left, new right or third way to be applied to every policy issue, even when completely inappropriate in the Australian context.

Clearly, a slavish devotion to this third-way analysis model is not useful. Equally absurd is an unthinking rejection of the social democratic debates of Britain. However, the ALP is being urged by some to do so on the basis that everything tried in Britain has already been tried by Labor in government here or, even more spuriously, that to listen to British debates is to succumb to the cultural cringe.

Of course, the task for the ALP is to synthesise the best of social democratic thought from around the world and to engage in the intellectual process which has led to the discussion of the third way. In that regard it is important to note that Anthony Giddens, Tony Blair's intellectual guardian and the leading academic exponent of the third way, sees the issue as follows:

> [T]he term 'third way' is of no particular significance in and of itself. It has been used many times before in the past history of social democracy, and also by writers and politicians of quite different political persuasions. I make use of it here to refer to social democratic renewal — the present day version of the periodic rethinking that social democrats have had to carry out quite often over the past century. (Giddens 1998, pp. vii–viii)

If used in that sense, we are all engaged in the search for the third way.

In that search we need to recognise the magnitude and nature of change in our world and develop policy responses appropriate to this radically changed context.

Analysing the world in which we live

The world in which we live has been and is being profoundly altered by globalisation, new technology, a new class dynamic, a new industrial dynamic and radical changes to the nature of families. Each of these trends is analysed briefly below.

Globalisation

In the words of John Wiseman, 'Globalisation is the most slippery, dangerous and important buzzword of the late twentieth century' (Wiseman 1998, p. 1).

Certainly, our world is being remade, economically and culturally, as a result of the incredible increase in the speed of transmission of information, capital, goods and services now possible because of new transport and communication technologies.

The ramifications of globalisation are innumerable, but of most importance for social democratic parties are the following:

- the stricter limits for nation-states of economic strategy options given the greater integration of the domestic and global economy and the increasingly footloose nature of capital;
- the creation within societies of globalisation winners and losers, the information rich and the information poor; and
- the contradictory but related tendencies for globalisation to facilitate cultural homogeneity, whilst at the same time generating such insecurity that segments of the population are comforted by tribalising or, even more destructively, engaging in the politics of exclusion and hate based on race or subordinate economic position.

In the Australian context, we have already seen a variety of responses to the force of globalisation.

We hear from our Federal Treasurer that as a result of globalisation, the debate about economic alternatives is over. Indeed, it seems that all areas of policy are to be remade by globalisation, with Treasurer Costello musing as follows in relation to the issue of social policy expenditure:

> *We are becoming more conscious in Australia that we are in tax competition in our immediate region ... On average, tax revenue is around 16 per cent of GDP in our major East Asian trading partners. In Australia Commonwealth tax to GDP is around 24 per cent ... the vexing question for Australia [is] how to maintain the social security system of an advanced industrial country whilst being tax competitive in our region.*

At the same time, in the last election, we saw over a million Australians vote for a party whose answers to the complex economic and social issues posed by globalisation were little more than lashing out on the basis of race or 'welfare' envy.

In the ALP, fear, both of the perceived restriction in policy options for Labor governments and of the misery generated for globalisation losers, has been the flavour of most policy discussions about globalisation.

In designing policies for the future, Labor must find an integrated local and international approach, which tackles the positives and the negatives flowing from globalisation.

The new class dynamic

Much of traditional social democratic thinking regarding policy has been premised on the need to care for and advance a traditional working-class constituency. Such a constituency was defined by its relationship with work. The breadwinners, usually men, were in full-time, relatively lowly paid work.

Unemployment was an intermittent problem during which government assistance was needed. Government assistance was also required when life dealt a bad hand in the form of illness, injury, loss of a breadwinner and the like.

The Hawke/Keating Labor governments commenced the process of revolutionising Labor and Australia's thinking about the nature of social security with a strictly targeted approach to benefits, the introduction of forms of mutuality or reciprocal obligation and with compulsory self-provision through superannuation.

However, the nature of work and family in our society continues to change, rapidly posing new policy dilemmas for Labor.

The jobs crisis in our society remains, despite continuing economic growth. The unemployment rate is likely to stay in the range of 7 to 8 per cent and to that official count can be added discouraged job-seekers, those who have excluded themselves from the search for work because of child care, age or training issues and those who would prefer to work longer hours.

If we move beyond the official unemployment statistics and include these factors, the shortfall between available work and the demand for work is in the region of 2–2.5 million jobs.

As a product of the jobs crisis, we find a newly emerging class which has no ongoing connection with the world of work and cannot be defined through it.

In this decade, the number of long-term unemployed in Australia has almost doubled, from 115 600 people to 221 900 people. The mean period of unemployment has leapt from 36.7 weeks to 53.1 weeks. Approximately 600 000 families have no working parental figure.

It is no surprise to find that this cycle of disadvantage is concentrated in specific locations, meaning we can now identify whole communities in which being in work or living in a family supported by a worker is an uncommon experience. We are still to develop the Labor solutions to the critical needs of communities in which work plays virtually no role in shaping lifestyle or expectations.

The new industrial dynamic

Just as the concept of class is changing, so is the nature of work.

Employment is becoming increasingly casualised, even for men, who have traditionally disproportionately held permanent, full-time jobs. As employment in the manufacturing sector declines, employment continues to grow in the services sector. Outsourcing and downsizing have changed the face of many industries. As a result, employees are increasingly employed in smaller and less traditional workplaces. Increasingly, work which used to be performed by employees is now performed by micro-businesses, which have increased in number by 19 per cent since the early 1990s.

As part of the changes in the shape of our workforce, we have seen a decline in unionism and an increase in the number of workers whose relationship with their work provider is not a traditional employer–employee relationship. Combined with a conservative assault on the system of industrial regulation, these changes mean that many workers are now effectively outside the ambit of any form of industrial protection.

While these trends have been recognised and debated in the ALP, we are still to comprehensively address the policy challenges flowing from them, and to find a mechanism for building unionism, collectivity and solidarity in this new industrial dynamic.

The new family

Approximately 40 per cent of marriages will end in divorce, and in February 1999 there were over half a million single-parent families with dependent children.

It is not surprising that traditional family structures should struggle to survive in the face of increased gender equality and sexual freedom, increased expectations about the nature of relationships and acceptance of ending unsatisfactory relationships, the ability to control fertility, the stress caused by the changing nature of work and work insecurity, and community breakdown in the form of increased crime and feelings of alienation.

At the same time as the shape of the family is changing, our approach to parenting is changing. In the elegant words of Anthony Giddens:

> *Children were the raison d'être of marriage. Large families were either desired or accepted as normal. We now live in the era of the 'prized child', where children are no longer an economic benefit but instead a major economic cost. The nature of childhood and childrearing has changed profoundly.* (Giddens 1998, p. 92)

Families now not only struggle with the pure economics of child-rearing but parenting is an increasingly pressured activity as our perception of the 'prized child' and of the unsafe nature of society means children are no longer able to while away their childhood hours in largely unsupervised play activities in the local community.

It is too early to tell what will be the long-term ramifications of this change to the family and parenting in our society. What we can say is that throughout this period of change, as a society, we seem to have underestimated the raw misery that marital breakdown brings to many and the complexity of securing appropriate care arrangements for children in the face of such breakdown. At the same time we seem to have not understood that while the sexual revolution has opened the door to the possibility of a new honesty and maturity in the relationships between emotional partners, it has also opened the door to 'commodity sex', sexual exploitation, alienation and loneliness.

The Labor Party has quickly and appropriately rejected John Howard's dream of a return to the 1950s as being unrealistic and undesirable. However, we have yet to address the emotional insecurity in our society, which has led to many so fearing the future that a return to the past seems attractive.

Policies for the future

To meet the needs of the Australia of the next millennium, Labor must carve out a new vision and a new policy agenda which meets the challenges posed by globalisation, the new class dynamic, the new industrial dynamic and new family structures. That vision needs to include the following elements:

- a new spirit of optimism;
- a new definition of the role and priorities of the nation-state;
- a new approach to international relations; and
- a new approach to issues of national identity, civic leadership and community responsibilities.

A new spirit of optimism

In the United States, Bob Dole made the following declaration in his speech accepting his party's nomination for President:

Optimism is in our blood. I know this as few others can. There once was a time when I doubted the future. But I have learned, as many of you have learned, that obstacles can be overcome. And I have unlimited confidence in the wisdom of our people and the future of our country. Tonight, I stand before you tested by adversity, made sensitive by hardship, a fighter by principle, and the most optimistic man in America.

Bob Dole pitched for the presidency on the basis of optimism and lost to a younger man who spent the campaign talking enthusiastically about building a bridge to the twenty-first century and associating himself with 'ordinary people' who had won through against overwhelming adversity.

In complete contrast to America's political rhetoric of optimism, in Australia, we stand tentatively on the cusp of a new century, struggling without any visible hope or confidence with issues fundamental to national identity, and led by a man who in his dreams sees the 1950s rather than a vision of 2050.

Creating a social democratic future for Australia and cementing equity and fairness at the centre of our national life will require the electorate to give political assent to radical and fundamental policy changes. That kind of positive political assent cannot be generated unless there is a return to optimism and the belief that government does matter and things can change.

Whilst continuing to pound the Howard Government for its failures, we need to weave optimism through our campaign in the way in which resurgent Labor did in 1972 and 1983.

A new definition of the priorities and structures of the nation-state

As part of engendering a spirit of optimism and designing a vision for the future, Labor must define and affirm a role for the government of the nation-state. It is only by actively promulgating the role of government that the defeatism which has gained currency as a result of globalisation can be addressed.

Labor should draft and debate with the electorate a charter for government, which defines in simple, modern language the role of government. In doing so, Labor will need to be frank with the electorate about the limits of the powers of the nation-state and the need to determine strict priorities.

A priority area, and one in which it is clear that the actions of the nation-state can and do matter, is education.

A recently published work by Carles Boix entitled *Political Parties, Growth And Equality* contains a regression analysis of the impact of educational attainment within the population and unemployment, and concludes, for OECD nations for the period 1982 to 1990, that:

> [U]nemployment decreases a whole percentage point for each six to seven percentage points of population that have studied beyond lower secondary education. Indeed, increasingly, one of the major differences between conservative parties and social democratic parties worldwide is the attitude taken to public investment in supply side economic strategies, particularly investment in education. (Boix 1998, p. 24)

Education is also an area in which the conservatives have clearly failed, as evidenced by falling retention rates to Year 12, the looming teacher shortage crisis, the unregulated development of the private sector and the extraordinary funding cutbacks at all levels of the system.

Kim Beazley has already signalled a preparedness to consider moving to a national schooling system. In the course of exploring this policy initiative, consideration also needs to be given to TAFE and the adult education area, in order to build a truly national education system that meets the challenge of providing lifelong learning opportunities.

Despite years of rhetoric about lifelong learning, teenage lives continue to be dominated by the perception that performance in the final year of school and gaining entry to a prestige university course will make or break them. In addition, Australia still lacks a coherent and properly funded system for genuine lifelong learning.

A creative and truly national Labor plan to properly fund the education sector, to review and restructure the way in which education is provided and to give content to lifelong learning would be great public policy, with economic, employment and social advantages, and electoral appeal.

A second fertile ground for creative policy development is the area of industrial regulation. Working relationships have and will continue to diversify away from the traditional employer–employee relationship and encompass a myriad of independent contractor and labour hire arrangements. An incoming Labor government will face a system of industrial regulation which has been the subject of a concerted conservative government assault and is in need of renewal, given the policy conundrum arising from the changing nature of work.

In the same way in which the last Labor government made good use of the foreign affairs power and international conventions to extend its capacity to industrially regulate, an incoming Labor government should make use of the corporations and other powers to extend industrial protection beyond employer–employee relationships to other work arrangements.

The key aim of extending such industrial protection would be to guarantee some minimum standards, including the right to unionise and organise, in any work circumstance in which a worker is in a relationship of economic dependency with a work provider. The need to provide greater security in relation to severance entitlements for workers made redundant should be addressed as part of that minimum standards package.

Clearly, a Labor vision will go well beyond the two initiatives discussed above. However, initiatives such as these can be used as part of that vision and as a way of demonstrating the capacity of a Labor government to pursue its historic values and concerns in the new and very different century.

A new approach to international relations

Many of the policy challenges posed by globalisation can only be answered at a global level. In addition to being frank with the electorate about the role and limitations of the nation-state, Labor will need to articulate a vision for the future that includes a strategy for achieving a regulatory regime at an international level which defines and supports civil, political, social and economic rights and responsibilities.

Following the collapse of the Asian economies, which was undoubtedly worsened by the lack of prudential supervision of the international capital market, there is likely to be increased international support for exploring ways of developing such a regime. In addition, international dialogue is occurring regarding taxing international financial transactions and furthering international cooperation to ensure the integrity of national taxation regimes.

Labor needs to be a participant in these debates as well as an advocate for using international agencies such as the United Nations, the International Labor Organisation and even the World Trade Organisation to steer towards some form of international regulation of human rights, labour rights, environmental outcomes and fair trading regimes.

In addition, Labor needs to be bolstering the participation by Australian non-government organisations in the developing international entities that are dedicated to lobbying globally for the adoption of appropriate regulation regimes and charters.

In designing and pursuing this strategy, which in its very nature is long term and complex, Labor needs to engage in a dialogue with the Australian community about the importance of global regulatory regimes.

Such a process will be difficult. However, it may be possible to demonstrate to the community the possibilities open to

Australia through such a strategy by a Labor government dedicating itself to actively focusing on and achieving results in one specific area. If pursued vigorously and seen to make a difference, such a campaign could pave the way for greater community acceptance of Australian engagement on the global stage.

A new approach to issues of national identity, civic leadership and community responsibilities

What government can achieve has limits. However, there is a need to find a way of providing emotional reassurance and practical support to struggling individuals and communities.

At a broader level, our sense of interconnectedness can be furthered by the development of an inclusive sense of national identity. The current debates about the republic, reconciliation and the preamble are providing some opportunity for community debate about these vital questions of national identity.

Whatever the outcome of the referenda on the republic and the preamble, it is important that Labor finds mechanisms to continue and deepen this national dialogue. Consideration needs to be given to regularly convening forums, such as the Constitutional Convention, which engage non-politicians and move beyond a strict adversarial system, to facilitate such a debate.

In response to the increasing stress on the family unit, Labor needs to find new ways of supporting families. The support given to families with preschool children varies widely from State to State. Given the crucial importance of these early years to later development and the high stress on families at this stage, it seems time to explore developing a national standard for family support. Such a standard could deal with issues such as access to maternal and child health services, parenting programs and preschool education and development programs.

But this alone is not enough. Labor needs to find ways of enriching community life, given that community bonds will increasingly be needed to give emotional security to those whose family bonds have failed.

This need for developing new bonds between community members is most critical in the areas of entrenched disadvantage. A by-product of economic deprivation and the loss of connection with the rhythms and structures of work has been the loss of community structures. The provision of government support in the form of individualised benefits will never be enough to restore a sense of community and connectedness.

In my own community, I witnessed an amazing outbreak of community spirit and activism as we rallied to stop a toxic dump being built. That successful campaign has left behind it revitalised community structures and a feeling of belonging. It has created new community leaders and inculcated an active, rather than passive, version of citizenship.

This local example has convinced me that local communities, properly resourced and with a sense of involvement and empowerment, can be incredibly creative in working together and finding solutions to even the most difficult of community problems. A long-term investment needs to be made in working with local councils and community groups to generate that kind of involvement and empowerment, and through it to build a new vision of civic leadership, democracy and citizenship.

Clearly, it is easier to rally the community around opposition to an external threat such as a toxic dump development than to get the community involved in addressing entrenched local problems. However, Labor needs to find the mechanisms to do so.

There are no easy answers, but as part of this process, there could be some trialling of participatory democracy models that are quite different from current local government structures. For example, a targeted region in particular need could be resourced to go through an intensive neighbourhood-by-neighbourhood process of involvement to find community solutions to local problems.

Such a process might, in the first instance, involve neighbourhood public meetings and questionnaires of residents' views. This could lead to the formation of neighbourhood committees which, with appropriate support, might go on to design and implement neighbourhood projects and provide input into community-wide strategies. Such a participatory system might seem cumbersome, but such intensive effort may well be necessary to identify and develop community leaders, to build connections between people and to generate a widely accepted agenda for change.

In addition, as part of this process, some real content could be given to the notion of mutual or reciprocal obligations. Government and targeted communities could negotiate an agreed set of obligations premised on government being prepared to undertake defined obligations if matched by community self-help. This is a more productive setting for the concept of mutual or reciprocal obligations than the punitive way in which the concept is being used in respect of individual benefits.

Conclusion

It is of course no mean feat to develop a vision for society and to then endeavour to implement it.

Good policy cannot be made without openness to input from a wide variety of sources, vigorous debate and collective decision-making. The Labor approach incorporates all three of these elements.

Labor history shows Labor has been equal to the task of reinventing its vision for society while remaining true to its historic values. In the lead-up to the next election, Labor will prove it is equal to that task again.

chapter 2

A green challenge to neo-liberalism
by Colin Long

The neo-liberal, or economic rationalist, revolution has had profound effects on much of the world in the last 25 years, radically re-orienting government activity, restructuring the welfare state, undermining the security, conditions and rights of workers, and fundamentally altering the character of economic activity. The ideology of 'small government' (really, I would argue, a refocusing of government) and 'free markets' has become so overwhelmingly pervasive that many social democrats have themselves been seduced by it. The intertwined collapse of communism[1] and the moribund state of socialist thought have served to undermine the intellectual and philosophical defences of the left at a time when the attack from the right was at its most dangerous. As a result, much of the left has been left floundering, either spouting tired and irrelevant slogans or trying to demonstrate fiscal responsibility and sympathy for big business. Typically, what has been lacking are some foundational concepts with which to challenge the dominance of the free-market right, and a deep understanding of the nature of free-market capitalism at the end of the century to underpin those concepts. The purpose of this chapter is to explore such an understanding and such concepts, utilising the radical insights of the Green movement.

The neo-liberal project

The basic tenets of neo-liberalism are generally well known now: deregulation of capital and re-regulation of labour; privatisation of government enterprises; reduction in government debt; restructuring of the tax system to favour the well off; liberalisation of trade and financial flows; and an emphasis on competition and the inherent virtues of markets. Perhaps the most remarkable achievement of the neo-liberals has been their ability to confine much of the debate over these policies to questions of narrow economic efficiency. Rarely are broader issues of social equity or environmental impact, or even long-term economic sustainability, given consideration. Thus economic growth rates are talked about obsessively, uncritically, almost religiously, with no consideration given to the distribution of wealth (the trickle-down effect is implicit and treated as an article of faith), and the impact of unceasing growth on the environment. More disturbingly, the emphasis on narrow economic efficiency has successfully deflected any more in-depth critique of the profound transformations that neo-liberals are seeking to implement. And make no mistake, radical alterations to the socio-economic structure of our societies are what is sought, even if, in many respects, what we are actually experiencing is an intensification of older processes rather than the creation of new ones.

Let us be clear about what constitutes the essence of the neo-liberal project, for we need to understand this essence in order to combat it effectively. I deliberately use the term 'neo-liberal' in preference to 'economic rationalist' because of the former's connotations of the revival of old ideas, those of Adam Smith and his nineteenth-century followers. For much of the doctrine of neo-liberalism, while geared to fundamental change, relies on assumptions and ideologies that are not new. Indeed, as I have suggested, the transformations in late-twentieth-century capitalism ultimately involve an intensification of fundamental capitalist logic rather than a transformation of that logic. Capitalism, as Marx identified, is a system of commodity production and exchange. All commodities have both a use value and an exchange value. To explain these concepts, consider a rental house. For the tenant it embodies a use value: it provides shelter, somewhere to live; that is, 'it fulfils a particular want or need' (Harvey 1990, p. 100). For the owner it represents exchange value: he or she can make money by charging rent; that is, use of the house is *exchanged* for rent. 'In contrast to use value, exchange value presupposes "a definite economic relation", and is inseparable from a market on which goods are exchanged' (Giddens 1971, p. 46). Exchange is crucial to the realisation of profit, the raison d'être of capitalism.

The so-called 'communist' countries strove to fashion the 'socialist man', a person for whom the ideals, relationships and structures of socialism were second nature. These countries failed in this quest not because of the inadequacies of their citizens but because of the inadequacies of their system of socialism. But this effort to create a citizen after its own image was not unique to the failed 'communist' countries. The subtle but ubiquitous substitution of the term 'consumer' or 'customer' for 'citizen' or even 'ratepayer' alerts us to a similar process occurring in our own societies. What is occurring here is not just a matter of terminology: customers have very different relationships to the providers of services than do citizens. When the Premier of Victoria likens his Cabinet to the board of directors of one of Australia's largest companies and the voters to its shareholders, he is not just being clever. This is how he perceives governments should function: as businesses (hence his inability to understand conflict-of-interest principles and readiness to obscure government activity behind commercial confidentiality). What the users of words such as 'consumer' or 'customer' and the Premier of Victoria are trying to achieve is a naturalisation of a certain view of the relationships between people, institutions, governments and economic processes, a view which emphasises the role of markets in shaping these relationships. Ultimately, for capitalism to survive, the relationships which constitute it must be considered *normal* — this entails the occupation of the whole of social space by capitalism. This entails the 'destruction (or marginalisation) of all non-capitalist spaces and activities' (Martins 1982, p. 170) and the extension of the logic of exchange into all sectors of society, including leisure, arts, information, architecture, and so on.

User pays: effects of the neo-liberal project

This, then, is the essence of the neo-liberal project: to achieve the total 'marketisation' or 'commodification' of society, to ensure that all relationships are market-based relationships; to create the 'free-market person'. This is not just an abstract goal. Very real, practical policies that have already been implemented seek the intensification of marketisation. Privatisation removes the provision of many basic services from the political realm where considerations of social justice or environmental protection can 'interfere' with the workings of the market. 'User pays' ensures that people's access to goods and services is determined by market forces and their inherent inequalities. Competition policy and deregulation of the industrial relations system expose people in their home and work environments to the 'discipline' of the market.

The intensification of the marketisation or commodification of all aspects of society that is a hallmark of the neo-liberal project has profoundly negative consequences. Thus we notice that the imposition of neo-liberal policies has been accompanied virtually everywhere by an emphasis on law and order. This has been necessary to tackle the serious antisocial problems created by a philosophy which emphasises individual acquisitiveness over group and community wellbeing, and privatism over public or community engagement. Nothing is more bitterly ironic than the professions of horror about antisocial behaviour by the advocates of profoundly antisocial policies. Related to this, and feeding into it, is the increase in inequality both within nations and between them. Capitalism demands inequality for 'incentivation'[2] (John Hewson's term). Further, neo-liberals seem to have only one solution for unemployment — lower wages and poorer working conditions (the real meaning of 'flexible labour markets'). Combined with the restructuring of employment — with the parallel growth of high-skill, high-income jobs and low-skill, low-income jobs — that accompanies the shift to a service economy, the industrial relations policies of the neo-liberals will continue to create increasing inequality. After World War II, in particular, trade unions were remarkably successful in improving the wages and conditions of workers. They did this by insisting that workers' lives should not be subject to the 'discipline' of the market. Centralised wage-fixing, arbitration and the standardisation of conditions across industries through awards quarantined workers from the ravages of the free market, the very real dangers of which were still fresh in the minds of people who had lived through the Depression. The winding back of these hard-won benefits serves precisely to allow the market to determine wages and conditions, to achieve the marketisation of workers' lives.

The environmental implications of marketisation and commodification

We can see the implications of intensified marketisation even more clearly in two areas of particular concern to the Greens: environmental destruction and genetic intervention in food production. Timothy Doyle (1998, p. 774) has criticised the ideology of 'sustainable development', as defined by 'a dispersed array of business interests and advanced industrial nation-states', because it extends market relationships into our relationships with the environment. He cites Beder:

> *Sustainable development is not about giving priority to environmental concerns, it is about incorporating environmental assets into the economic system to ensure the sustainability of the economic system. Sustainable development encompasses the idea that the loss of environmental amenity can be substituted for by wealth creation; that putting a price on the environment will help us protect it unless degrading it is more profitable; that the 'free' market is the best way of allocating environmental resources; that businesses should base their decisions about polluting behaviour on economic considerations and the quest for profit; that economic growth is necessary for environmental protection and therefore should take priority over it.* (Doyle 1998, p. 774; the quote is from S. Beder (1994), *Sustainable Development,* Scribe Publications, Victoria, p. 8)

True environmentalism is radical because it demands that people consider values outside of commodity relationships. Note, here, that I do not argue that environmentalism demands consideration of values outside of the human relationship with 'nature': that argument is both futile and dangerous. Giddens (1994, p. 211) is right that 'Los Angeles is as much part of the environment as a country meadow' and that 'all ecological debates ... are about managed nature'. Indeed, any doubt that 'nature' can be divorced from the activities of humans should have been finally dispelled by recent developments in genetic engineering of food crops, seed patenting and cloning. And what is driving these innovations is not some biblical injunction to conquer nature, or inevitable technological 'progress', but the intensification of marketisation, so that the extension of commodity relationships has reached the very building blocks of life itself. There could be few more disturbing examples of the dangers and immorality inherent in this intensified marketisation or commodification than the patenting of seeds or the use of 'terminator' crops, plants from which farmers are unable to propagate and which lock them into subservient, reliant relationships with multinational agro-industrial companies, and through them with the free-market environment of the global economy.

For those fighting environmental degradation or the industrialisation of agriculture, the solution does not lie in seeking some kind of return to a human, romanticised nature. What is required is an acceptance of the fundamentally political character of 'nature' and the environment, and a commitment to oppose the spread of commodity relationships, to emphasise use over exchange values. The message is the same for those struggling for workers' rights or social justice: the intensification of marketisation must be fought and alternative values propagated.

Rights: a challenge to marketisation

But what methods remain open to us in this fight, in a world of globalised trade, massive and rapid shifts of capital across national borders and almost unrestrained corporate power? For a start, the left is going to have to come up with a much more sophisticated approach to the problem of globalisation than it has been able, by and large, to demonstrate so far. 'Globalisation' has become the left's most feared and reviled word, just as 'imperialism' was in earlier decades. But imperialism was a much more tangible and recognisably destructive process. Unfortunately, just as many people concerned about environmental destruction have opted to try to rediscover a virgin nature, many critics of globalisation advocate a simplified retreat into localism at the same time as 'political–economic processes (money-flows, international divisions of labour, financial markets and the like) ... are becoming ever more universalizing in their depth, intensity, reach and power over daily life' (Harvey 1990, pp. 116–17). In other words, while we think local, the free-marketeers act global.

There has been too much simplistic rejection of globalisation per se, with an emphasis on retaining power within nation-states. But this ignores the reality that some form of globalisation is necessary to rein in free-market globalisation: that is, transnational cooperation is absolutely essential for dealing with the worst effects of neo-liberal–inspired globalisation, such as unstable financial markets, environmental degradation and impoverishment of the 'Third World'. Such problems cannot be adequately tackled unilaterally: rather than a retreat into parochialism and 'localism' in the face of multinational capital, the left should be re-advocating internationalism. In the process, we in the richer countries must, of course, avoid imposing our ideologies of liberation onto other cultures. We can't go and say that we know what your problems are, and we know how to fix them — an attitude all too common in the existing multilateral agencies such as the World Bank. But we can take an active role in helping to foster frameworks and institutions both within our countries and within others that facilitate self-determination and balanced development. Crucial to this will be the promotion of a discourse of alternatives to unproblematic growth and to the unrelenting spread of commodification.

The critique of globalisation is on firmest ground when it is couched in terms of democratic rights, or rights of participation. While I have argued that some form of multinational cooperation is necessary to tackle many of the worst problems facing the planet, it is also true that, for the moment, the opportunities for democratic participation in decision-making are virtually nonexistent outside the institutional structures of the nation-state. The most insidious and destructive aspect of neo-liberal globalisation is its calculated constraints on the ability of governments to shape national policy: we are all familiar with the spectacle of federal or State treasurers citing financial market approval for their policies, or refusing to take certain actions in case of negative market reactions. Treaties such as the (for the moment dormant) Multinational Agreement on Investment and NAFTA are intended to further restrict the options of governments. Nevertheless, we can overstate this. Does a neo-liberal treasurer really feel constrained by financial markets, or does he view market approval as an objective test of the validity of his policies? The answer, I would suggest, is the latter. This should serve to remind us of a very important fact about neo-liberal globalisation: despite what its advocates would have us believe, it is not a 'natural' or 'inevitable' phenomenon. While the forces and logic of globalisation are powerful, it is a serious mistake to suppose that they are therefore beyond the control or influence of governments. Governments have made, and continue to make, decisions which shape the nature of global restructuring, which strengthen the process and condition its local impact. Globalisation, like 'nature' or the environment, is a political phenomenon.

Democratic rights and the state

This brings us to one of the foundational concepts that we must explore: the role of the state. Before turning to that, however, I want to return to the issue of democratic rights and of rights more generally. Capitalist democracies have a quite limited conception of democracy, and one that is being increasingly restricted by neo-liberal policies: one of the clear impacts of privatisation and the retreat of the state from the direct provision of services — and the concomitant marketisation of this provision — has been a reduction in democratic accountability, chiefly through the widespread use of commercial confidentiality agreements. Thus in the now largely privatised Victorian prison system we are virtually unable to ascertain the contractual arrangements between the private prison operators and the state which is depriving people of their liberty in our name. Similar lack of transparency blights many other aspects of government in Victoria, from the generation of electricity to the running of car races.

Governments are able to get away with these attacks on democratic accountability because the neo-liberals have been so successful in redefining the essence of governance and citizenship. They have sought, and largely been able, to marketise the relationship between government and its citizens: let us recall Premier Kennett's analogy between government and the board of directors of a large business.

To counter this we need to come up with an alternative definition of citizenship, which can then be used as a basis for the transformation of the state itself. Any definition of citizenship, to my mind, must rest on an emphasis on human rights broadly defined to include rights that are born of resistance to unrelenting commodification — rights to land, culture and traditions, rights to non-degraded environments, rights to a say in decisions that affect people's everyday lives, rights to shelter and to access to the means to make a decent living and rights to cultural diversity. All these rights, let me emphasise, are grounded in the challenge to marketisation and commodification. Such rights cannot be realised or protected through market processes.

One example illustrates this point well. The rights and needs of indigenous Australians have been marginalised by a philosophy which measures worth in narrowly conceived economic terms. Indeed, the Howard Government's attitude to indigenous Australians is fundamentally shaped by a nineteenth-century colonial racism based on the idea that the duty of civilised people is to 'improve' land which is otherwise being used inefficiently or inappropriately by aboriginal people. So much of the opposition to land rights and native title rights has been couched in these terms, sometimes subtly, sometimes less so, and it was no great surprise to see the extent of support for the Howard Government's ten-point Wik Plan from mining and business interests. The challenge to commodification, on the contrary, is deeply sympathetic to indigenous rights, because it recognises ways of relating to the land other than marketised ways.

These rights mentioned above are, by and large, positive rights, which, because of their widespread absence today, appear more like a set of demands. I want also to emphasise 'defensive' rights, 'human rights' which are more familiar today because they have to do largely with the defence of life and liberties, rights which have become prominent in response to the bloody nature of the twentieth century. It seems to me that the left needs to come to terms with its often unsavoury past; its support for totalitarianism in some situations still hangs like a pall over our present and our future. But it is not just the left that is guilty, of course. The truly tragic essence of the twentieth century has been the willingness of those struggling for change and those resisting change to sacrifice civil and human rights — and therefore lives — for their causes.

A rights-based agenda for social democracy

For this reason, anything that the left does must be firmly embedded within a respect for civil and human rights. The left must also finally reject the idea of rebirth through violence. In doing this, the left should actually reclaim the ground that rightfully belongs to it, but which has been claimed successfully, although fraudulently, by the right. The right's ability to claim that it represents freedom and choice has always concealed a tension within it, between conservatives and liberals, the former fundamentally committed to structure, order and hierarchy, the latter professing a freedom which is largely constrained to the realm of money-making. Of course there is a wide gulf between conservatives and liberals, historically, philosophically and politically, a point worth remembering. Indeed, they have been united largely only in their defence of capitalism, although this has historically also been nuanced.

The tensions between conservatives and liberals are amply demonstrated in Australia within the person of the Prime Minister, a profoundly conservative man, deeply wedded to structures and institutions of order, but who nevertheless preaches an economic philosophy which inexorably undermines the very order that he so wistfully seeks. Howard is one of the most dangerous types of figure that the right can throw up: a man whose economic philosophy, through its commodification of all life, is profoundly disruptive, but who tries to ameliorate this disruption by an appeal to populism, and an emphasis on an exclusive and retrogressive identity founded on myths and propaganda. Thus for those who do not fit this identity — and all such defensive identities require an 'other' against which to define themselves — such politicians are dangerous people. Howard's prolonged and intense attack on Australia's indigenous population must be seen in this context.

It is strange that the right continues to be able to portray itself as the great defender of rights and freedoms, given that its commitment to the marketisation of all aspects of existence is, as I have argued, the greatest present threat to those very rights and freedoms. A commitment to oppose this marketisation would allow the left to reclaim the ground of civil, democratic and human rights.

The state: a challenge to marketisation

Of all the broadly social democratic parties in Australia, the Greens are the most consistent opponents of the concept of limitless growth. Few people — and virtually none within the mainstream media — ever stop to ponder the environmental effects of continuous economic growth in our own country, never mind the global effects if the rest of the world wishes to attain a similar form of economic organisation and resource use as the West. Capitalism is fundamentally reliant on growth. But while governments and World Bank economists fret about maintaining and stimulating growth, the really important and challenging problem is not the creation of wealth but its distribution. Whilst the global economy is beholden to advocates of the trickle-down philosophy, more and more wealth needs to be created so that the growing numbers of the poor benefit even in the most meagre ways. While over-consumption in the rich countries needs to be challenged and the standard and quality of life in the poor countries needs to be drastically improved, the problem is not particularly a lack of wealth — it is the inequitable distribution of it.

The intensification of market processes in the last two decades has not improved the distribution of wealth. Indeed, disparities between rich and poor countries have been increasing, as have the inequalities between rich and poor within many countries. Markets distribute wealth and resources according to one's ability to exert oneself in the market process: that is, according to one's monetary resources. They do not provide a means of distribution according to principles of equity. Similarly, markets cannot provide a solution to environmental degradation. They are, indeed, a large part of the problem. The marketisation of the environment — the reduction of all environmental value to a matter of narrow economic value — is the greatest cause of environmental degradation.

If inequality and environmental degradation are two of the most pressing problems facing the world as we enter the twenty-first century, the challenge to marketisation must animate our solutions to them. And if the market plays no part in these solutions, we must look to build institutions that can intervene to ensure an even spread of economic and social benefits and the amelioration of environmental degradation. This clearly means re-examining the potential of state intervention and regulation, and strengthening the state's redistributive capabilities and functions.

The problem is that the capitalist state is fundamentally constrained by the structural relationships of capitalism, so that its interests are usually also served by the continued fostering of commodity relationships. Thus the challenge to commodification must also entail a simultaneous transformation of the state, just as the neo-liberals have been able to replace the Keynesian state with one that reinforces intensified marketisation. This transformation will be effected only in the process of the state being involved in the tackling of problems, such as those of environmental degradation and the distribution of wealth. The solutions to these problems, I have argued, fundamentally require a challenge to commodification and marketisation, and their successful negotiation will entail the state adopting this challenge. It is up to organisations like the Greens, and other activist organisations around the world, to ensure that the challenge to commodification and marketisation translates into strong governmental action to solve these pressing problems.

chapter 3

Social democracy and citizen power: an Australian democrat's perspective
by Matthew Townsend

> *Rights emerge by bargaining between the powerful and the relatively powerless; they are not simply granted, for if they were, there would be none.* (Hughes 1987, p. 310)

This essay provides an overview of various reforms to help secure the future of Australian social democracy from a Democrat's perspective.[1] I argue that much of the reform needs to occur at the State level and uses the example of Victoria to illustrate this argument, although clearly these arguments apply, with different levels of emphasis, to other States as well.

It begins with an assessment of the Victorian State Constitution; then goes on to discuss the need for parliamentary reform in that State, including proposals to increase the representation of women in parliament and introduce proportional representation; and ends with the argument for citizen initiated referenda.

I believe that creating a truly social democratic society requires renewed emphasis on the democratic aspect of social democracy, including radical reforms to the Australian Constitution at the State and federal levels. Greater social equality in Australia will only occur if citizens have a greater say in how their laws are made.

Reforming the State constitutions

It is ironic that the Commonwealth Constitution has been partly overhauled while the State constitutions have, in a number of States, received very little attention. The Commonwealth Constitution reflects world's best practice compared with the Victorian Constitution.

While the bulk of government services in Australia are delivered by State governments, the future of Australian social democracy will suffer while State constitutions receive inadequate attention. The Australian people were asked to agree to the Commonwealth political system at the time of Federation — they were asked to vote 'yes' or 'no' to the Commonwealth Constitution. But Victorians have never been asked to formally adopt the Victorian Constitution. This is surprising, given that the Victorian Constitution is nearly 50 years older than the Commonwealth Constitution, and is in far more need of attention. Consider the following:

- The Victorian Constitution can be changed without a referendum. In contrast, the Commonwealth Constitution can only be changed with the support of both a majority of voters and a majority of States.

- The Victorian constitution does not guarantee the jurisdiction of the Supreme Court. Judicial review of Victorian legislation by the Victorian Supreme Court therefore can be, and regularly is, specifically prevented by law in Victoria. In contrast, at the Commonwealth level, the jurisdiction of the High Court is entrenched and all legislation is therefore subject to High Court review.

- The State constitution does not guarantee judicial review of the action of Victorian government officials. In contrast, the Commonwealth Constitution guarantees a person's right to challenge the action of any officer of the Commonwealth.

- Victoria's constitution does not guarantee a right to fair compensation if public property is compulsorily acquired by the State Government. The Commonwealth Government, however, must pay fair compensation if it compulsorily acquires a person's property.

- The Victorian Constitution does not guarantee the right to challenge the legality of action by Victorian public officials. In contrast, the Commonwealth Constitution guarantees our right to challenge the action of any officer of the Commonwealth.
- As a result of its electoral system Victoria's upper house of parliament, the Legislative Council, has been captured by one side of politics. The Legislative Council has been controlled by conservative political parties for all but one month of its 150-year history. In contrast, the Federal Senate is rarely controlled by one side of politics. As a result, it has a far more rspectable record of scrutinizing executive government activity.

Interestingly, the need to overhaul the constitution in Victoria goes back a long way. As far back as April 1869, it was revealed that landowners had been subscribing to a secret fund known as the Victorian Fund, intended to ensure that their interests were treated favourably by parliament (Wright 1992, p. 65).

The Victorian Fund was controlled by investor Hugh Glass, a man noted for his grey horse, which was often tethered outside Parliament House or the Melbourne Club. It was estimated that in 1869 up to £80 000 had been spent to determine parliamentary outcomes through rorts, bribery and other inducements. Arguably, without an auditor-general whose independence is guaranteed in the Constitution, corruption may once again become a major factor in parliamentary decision-making.

Further in 1901 the Member for Melbourne, Edward Findley, was permanently expelled from parliament by his colleagues for printing some highly disrespectful remarks about the King. Mr Findley's electorate, however, was not asked whether they wanted him sacked. The members decided to do it themselves (Wright 1992, p. 145). Could the parliamentarians have had the power to sack their colleague without asking the electorate?

What of the power to change the electoral system? Should parliament have the power to fundamentally change Victoria's electoral boundaries without consulting the electorate?

This power has been abused in the past. In 1904, Premier William Irvine declared that because public servants were employed by the government, they were a 'special' category of voter. So he created special non-geographical electorates for them to vote in. In Queensland, more recently, a similar technique was employed when an Aboriginal community was removed from the electorate in which it was based and combined with a non-contiguous non-government seat. Techniques such as this allowed the Bjelke-Petersen Government to hold power with less than 25 per cent of the primary vote.

If State electoral laws have been abused in the past, they can be abused again. These laws should be entrenched in each State's constitution and require a referendum before amendment.

Parliamentary reform

Upper houses that work

A large part of the Australian States' democratic problems arise out of the failure of the State parliaments. They do a reasonable job of determining who shall form government, but once that is done State parliaments have little control over what the government does.

State electors therefore lack the ability to hold governments accountable between elections. A key reason for this impotence is that a number of upper houses, or Legislative Councils, do not properly represent the interests of the broader community. Indeed, they were never intended to. Victoria's, for example, was designed in the 1850s so that wealthy landowners could keep an eye on the less affluent members of the lower house, the Legislative Assembly. To vote in elections for the Legislative Council, voters had to have £5000 worth of land or an income of £500 a year (Wright 1992, p. 17).

Since then, property requirements have been removed but State Legislative Councils have not all been reformed to the point that they makes a substantial contribution to the States' political processes. This is partly why there have been consistent calls for their abolition. This would be a mistake, however, as the upper houses could become a central part of the State's political system — if they were elected in a more democratic way.

Presently, Victoria's Legislative Council is elected by a winner-takes-all system in which a party that wins 51 per cent of the vote in each electorate would win 100 per cent of the seats. On the other hand, if the Legislative Council were elected by a system of proportional representation, a party winning 51 per cent of the vote could win only 51 per cent of the seats. Not only would this be fairer, but it would reduce the chance of one party controlling the parliament.

Experience suggests that the greater number of candidates in a proportional-representation election often prevents a political party from capturing more than 50 per cent of the vote, and therefore more than 50 per cent of the seats. Reducing the potential for one party to control the Legislative Council would have a number of benefits. The first is that the government could no longer assume that the council would rubber-stamp its draft laws. Rather, it would need to convince other parties and independents of the merits of its plans. Presently, the Victorian Government can introduce and pass a Bill through the parliament before the opposition and independents have understood the proposed legislation, let alone supported or opposed it.

A second benefit of electing the council through proportional representation would be that non-government parties and independents, keen to exercise their new influence, would make the council more productive. The council could certainly do with some improvement in this area. For example, between 1994 and 1996:

- the Federal Senate, which is elected by proportional representation, sat for 229 days compared with the Victorian Legislative Council, which sat for 103 days;
- the Federal Senate amended 145 pieces of legislation, while the Victorian Legislative Council amended 25 pieces of legislation;
- the Federal Senate referred 152 Bills to its legislative committees for scrutiny, whereas the Victorian Legislative Council referred no Bills to legislative committees for scrutiny — in fact, the council does not have its own committee system to scrutinise legislation.

So how would a system of proportional representation work for the Victorian Legislative Council?

One option is to have five electoral districts of seven members each. If the entire council were dissolved at each election, a candidate would need to get a quota of 12.5 per cent to be elected. This would allow candidates from the major parties and some from the Nationals and the Democrats to be elected, but smaller parties such as the Greens might find it difficult to reach the necessary quota.

Another option, used in South Australia and New South Wales, is to have the council elected from the whole State, as one electorate. If the election of councillors were staggered to elect half every four years, as it is now, one would only need 4.3 per cent of the vote to be elected. This would increase the chances of very small parties and independents being elected. While this would make voting in the council less predictable (and create an enormous ballot paper), it would increase the proportion of voters represented in parliament. In New South Wales, up to 95 per cent of voters succeed in electing their first choice of candidates. By contrast, in Victorian Legislative Council elections, sometimes fewer than 50 per cent of voters succeed in electing their first choice of candidates.

Equal representation of women

Another important parliamentary reform would be to achieve equality for women in the State and Federal parliaments. Technically, this would be simple to achieve. For example, for Victoria's Legislative Assembly, the number of seats could be halved, with a man and a woman representing each seat. For its Legislative Council, the State could be divided into two electorates returning 22 councillors — eleven men and eleven women in each. Both houses would remain the same size. On polling day, voters would select their preferred candidates from a male list and a female list on both assembly and council ballot papers. The result would be a parliament comprised equally of men and women.

To reduce wrongly held opposition to the idea, the system could be introduced with a 'sunrise clause', or delay, of twenty years. If the system were proposed without such a delay, personal interest might prevent parliamentarians from considering the idea on its merits.

So, what are the arguments for such a change? First, there is the need for Victoria to achieve actual rather than theoretical electoral equality. In England, women such as Emmeline Pankhurst braved arrest and jail in order to win the right to vote. In Victoria, women had to run their own mock parliament to 'prove' they were politically capable, before winning the same right. This was not achieved so that for the remainder of the century winnable seats would be denied to all but a few women.

Secondly, the change would create a more diverse and representative parliament. As Joan Kirner and Moira Rayner argued in *The Women's Power Handbook*:

> *A community worth living in has to include women and reflect women's experiences just as much as men's. Women have a different view of the world: our biological, social and emotional experiences are different from men's.* (Kirner & Rayner 1994).

A third, more controversial reason is offered by Jim Carlton, a former chair of the Coalition's Policy Review Committee. He advocated a similar change for the Federal Parliament, saying women have a more consensual approach to decision-making and that a 'more balanced parliament would tend to reduce the level of conflict in politics' (Carlton, 1994).

What are the arguments *against* such a change? First, it has been said that women don't need affirmative action in order to be equally represented in parliament — they simply need to be allowed to run on their merits. As English Liberal Democrat Diana Maddock said: 'Our aim is equality of opportunity, not equality of outcome.' However, the current system, now nearly 75 years old, has created a Legislative Assembly comprising 18 per cent women; if we wait another 75 years for 'equality of opportunity', what will it reach — 36 per cent? In any event, the phrase 'affirmative action' denotes positive discrimination. Arguably, there is none here, simply a separation of the candidates to identify the most suitable from each gender. This occurs routinely in sporting events with no claims of discrimination.

A second argument against this proposal is that if we create seats for women, why don't we create seats for other under-represented groups, such as Aborigines and ethnic minorities? The answer to this is we can, providing the principle of one-vote, one-value is not breached. There are, however, few other situations in which under-represented groups can be so clearly identified.

A third argument against this proposal is that numerical equality does not provide substantive equality for women. This may be true, but what better place to test the extent to which it is true than in our most senior branch of government, the legislature?

Ultimately, the issue comes down to whether one believes parliament should reflect the communities it seeks to represent, or whether 'government of the people, for the people' can be provided almost exclusively by white, middle-aged, Anglo-Saxon men.

Citizen initiated referenda

A final suggestion for the improvement of Australian social democracy is the introduction of CIR — citizen initiated referenda. Although they are most commonly associated with right-wing political groups and politicians, I will argue, firstly, that CIR are a logical future step in the gradual devolution of power from the ruling elites to the people; secondly, that CIR would help redress a flaw in the Australian Constitution that only allows the Commonwealth Parliament to initiate constitutional change; and thirdly, that they would help engage people in the Australian political process and reinvigorate our system of representative democracy.

The idea of CIR is that citizens of a political system through their own initiative — usually through the gathering of a certain number of signatures on a petition — may force a change in a nation's constitution or to a nation's laws. Presently, the only way of changing the Commonwealth Constitution in Australia is by the passage of a Bill through the Federal Parliament; a bill that is eventually approved by a majority of voters in a majority of States. Arguably, the ability to initiate this referendum should not rest exclusively in the hands of the Federal Parliament; where necessary, the people themselves should be able to generate a referendum for constitutional change. Moreover, the people should also, in certain circumstances, have the power to directly change the nation's laws. However, this argument centres on the case for introducing CIR to change the Australian Constitution rather than introducing them to provide an alternative means of changing Australian laws.

CIR as a step in the devolution of power

First it is important to understand how power in the British and US political systems has gradually been devolved to the people over the last few centuries, and to show that the logical extension of this is direct democracy by such means as CIR.

The story begins in England during the eleventh century, with the ascension to power of the Norman kings after the Battle of Hastings. The Norman kings were an aggressive line of monarchs who ruled England in something akin to a military dictatorship (Haigh 1985, p. 66). Their feudal system relied on landowning barons to administer the land and collect taxes. Gradually, these barons came to resent the arbitrariness of the monarch's rule and made increasing demands to share in the powers of the King. This manifested itself in the signing of the Magna Carta in 1215. It was, in the words of one historian, 'legalised rebellion' (Alder 1994).

The Magna Carta limited royal rights and prevented the King from abusing the law in his favour. It made law courts generally open to free men, declared that women did not have to marry if they did not wish to, and established an elected standing committee to receive complaints against the King (Haigh 1985, p. 102).

In the thirteenth century, these councils began to meet as parliaments and demand changes to the country's laws. This tension continued for many years, and in the seventeenth century a great struggle took place between the monarchs and the parliament. The parliament eventually won, and the resulting document was the Bill of Rights of 1688, which guaranteed the supremacy of parliament by protecting parliamentarians from the excesses of the Crown (Padfield 1977). Despite establishing the parliament as the supreme legislative authority, however, the people's battle had not yet ended.

From the perspective of more recent times, Sir Isaac Isaacs, the then Attorney-General of Victoria, said at the 1898 Melbourne Constitutional Convention:

> *Since [1688], there has been a gradual but sure shifting of power from the Parliament to the people, and it was well said in the House of Commons some years ago that the people were tired of the deluge of debate, and were looking forward to the consultation of the constituencies. This is a tendency which we cannot resist.* (Reith 1994, p. 16)

Although not referring directly to CIR, Sir Isaac clearly saw the need for devolution of democratic decision-making. Certainly, there are other predictions that CIR is the way of the future. The British business magazine, the *Economist*, recently attempted to predict the events of the next 150 years. Its first claim was that direct democracy would spread through the established democracies and engender a new participatory ethic amongst the citizens of the twenty-first century (Reith 1994).

CIR address a constitutional flaw

The second argument for CIR is that they would help break the Federal Parliament's monopoly over changes to the Commonwealth Constitution. Fortunately, Australians were given the opportunity to either agree or disagree to the federal model of government at the turn of the century. It was, and still is, one of the most democratic constitutions in the world. However, the fact remains that in many ways, the people of Australia still lack the ability to take the initiative when it comes to determining how the system of government works. All we have is the ability to respond if a proposal is put to us by the Commonwealth Parliament.

The practical effect of this is that generally the only proposals put to the people are those that strengthen the position of the Commonwealth Parliament over the States, or improve the position of one political party over another. As Peter Reith (then shadow attorney-general) once remarked, the most likely explanation for the failure of the majority of referenda is that they 'have proposed more power for the central parliament. These grabs for power are not usually well received, and so the proposals have been defeated' (Reith 1994, p. 2). It stands to reason, therefore, that it would assist our system of government if the people had the power to generate proposals for change independently of the Commonwealth Parliament and, in particular, independently of the executive government of the Commonwealth. It would be a watershed measure in Australian politics if there were a proposal that had the effect of reducing the power of the Federal Government: for example, in a proposal to enact a Bill of Rights, or in a proposal to elect the head of state for an Australian Republic.

CIR as the invigorator of representative democracy

A third argument in favour of CIR is that they would help keep governments accountable between elections, and liven up our system of representative democracy. One of the failings of our present system is that people tend to feel alienated from the decision-making process that impacts upon their daily lives.

People feel as though they get one chance every three or four years to become involved in the political system, and that sometimes the choice on offer is quite limited. CIR offer a means by which people can play a far greater role in the process of government, for they offer a means by which governments can be held to account for their faithfulness to their promises between elections. As Theodore Roosevelt said in his 1912 'Charter of Democracy' speech: 'I believe in the Initiative and Referendum which should be used not to destroy representative government, but to correct it whenever it becomes misrepresentative.'

Answering the critics

One of the arguments often put by critics of CIR is that direct democracy can become hijacked by wealthy interest groups and used to persecute the disadvantaged. This must be acknowledged as a real danger. Clearly, in any voting contest, the amount of money at one's disposal is a vital factor in determining how much of a message can be communicated to the voters. The answer, however, is not to reject CIR; rather, it is to ensure that they work properly. The problem of the inequality in funding is faced also in normal elections for parliament. The Federal Government provides funding to candidates who receive over 4 per cent of the vote, and this type of funding could be provided to 'yes' and 'no' campaigns for CIR.

And there is evidence that wealthy interests do not always

win. In California, for example, tobacco companies spent nearly $17 million fighting a proposal to add 25 cents onto the price of a packet of cigarettes, with these extra proceeds going to health care for poor people, and to research into tobacco-related diseases. Even such massive expenditure did not stop them from losing (Batchelor 1992, pp. 21–5).

There are other examples to suggest that people are quite capable of seeing through the propaganda and judging issues on their merits. In 1993 a group of Swiss citizens took to the country their proposal to deny Swiss armed forces authority to buy any new military aircraft for the rest of the century. This would have saved a large amount of public money, but the Swiss citizenry decided that it was a threat to national security and it was defeated. In the same year, the Swiss agreed to a referendum that had the effect of increasing Switzerland's petrol tax, thus protecting the environment (Kernot 1994). In both cases, responsible and sensible outcomes were adopted.

Another criticism often put is that CIR may lead to the introduction of poorly drafted legislation. Once more, this must be acknowledged as a problem, but not an insurmountable one — Peter Reith's proposal, for instance, involved the Federal Court providing opinions on the legal effect of CIR proposals before they were introduced. Besides, it is not as though the existing system is perfect. It was not so long ago that an Act of Parliament that was rushed through the Victorian Parliament contained as many as 50 mistakes and provided definitions of terms that did not even appear in the Act.

A final criticism of CIR is that they may be expensive — hardly a convincing objection. The right to participate in the affairs of the nation is one of the most valuable rights we have, and something that countless thousands of people have dedicated their lives to, and on occasions sacrificed their lives for. It would be a disappointing day indeed if democracy were to be sacrificed on the grounds that it is too expensive.

For all of these arguments in favour of CIR, it must be acknowledged that the concept is not the panacea for Australia's political troubles. On the contrary, in the whole scheme of things, there are many other, perhaps more valuable constitutional reforms to be pursued. But the devolution of power from the ruling elites to the people is a historical fact, and it should be welcomed rather than resisted.

CIR are a necessary means of balancing a constitution that is too heavily stacked in the Commonwealth's favour. Without a change in the mechanism that allows for the development of our federal system, we may end up with a constitution that is too heavily focused towards the nation's capital, to the exclusion of poorer and more remote regional areas.

As Jean-Jacques Rousseau wrote in his *The Social Contract* in 1762, a 'polity' is a place where citizens practise direct democracy and where, because the people are subject to the laws, they are also the authors.

Conclusion

While State governments loom large in the lives of the Australian people, they will remain important subjects for democratic reform. This is particularly the case in places such as Victoria, where the rule book for government was substantially drafted in Napoleonic times.

Some of these reforms include the entrenchment of the State constitutions and the judiciary; the introduction of proportional representation for State upper houses; and the equal representation of women in State parliaments. At the Commonwealth level, the standard of administration would also be improved by providing the electors with the power to initiate constitutional referenda.

The most pressing reform, however, must be to provide the electorate with the opportunity to review and ratify our State systems of government. Unlike the Commonwealth Constitution, the bulk of the State constitutional framework has never been subjected to popular review or endorsement. Until this occurs, it is difficult to understand how it can be legitimately said that in Australia's State democratic systems the ultimate source of power lies with the people.

Section II:
Recurrent Dilemmas

chapter 4

Labor's Trojan Horse: the 'third way' on employment policy
by Roy Green and Andrew Wilson

This essay outlines the experience and developing policy of 'New Labour' in Britain on employment issues, the philosophy of the 'third way' associated with it, and arguments advanced to persuade the Australian Labor Party (ALP) to follow a similar course. In opposition to these attempts, we argue that 'deregulation', associated with neo-liberal ideology and incorporated also into the third way, is not suited to the Australian situation. The essay concludes with an analysis of the ALP's current flirtation with third-way policies, in particular the 'tax credits' for low-paid workers proposed by Simon Crean. The analysis suggests that this approach will compromise opposition to the proposals which were recently unveiled by Peter Reith, the Minister for Employment, Workplace Relations and Small Business, and will probably cause the ALP to lose the next election.

Introduction: contradictions of the Accord

Employment is so central to government policy as a whole that it cannot be discussed in the abstract, separately from the perspective underlying the ALP's attempt to regain power. And the fundamental question is the relationship to the 'Accord process', which sustained Labor in government for thirteen years through five election victories. A simple answer here is not possible, however, because there were a number of conflicting elements. First was the original concept, formulated in opposition and set out in the Accord document shortly before the 1983 election. Many of the individual policies were implemented to some extent, and in an attenuated form the basic concept continued throughout Labor's period in office. But almost immediately a second strand emerged, promoted primarily by the leadership of Hawke and Keating and opposed by the trade unions — economic 'deregulation'.

After Keating's 1986 'banana republic' speech, it was clear that this second strand was increasingly the preferred approach of government. From the floating of the currency in 1983 and the ensuing liberalisation of the financial system, the increasing control of Treasury over economic policy and of the Industries Assistance Commission over industry policy, 'deregulation' began to permeate industrial relations policy too. The 'two-tier' wage system in 1987 enabled the government, through choice rather than necessity, to incorporate employment policies promoted by the Business Council of Australia, causing growing strain with the trade union movement. Eventually, Keating's proposals for labour law reform in his speech to the Institute of Directors following the 1993 election brought these conflicts into the open. In the face of union hostility, the government drew back a little; however, as a partnership with the unions, the Accord was now dead (Green & Wilson 1997). From this point, the unions seemed to be obstructing rather than supporting the trend of government policy.

Following the 1996 election, Labor's move in its 1998 *Platform* to repair the breach with its traditional supporters paid immediate dividends in the election last year. More recently, however, this approach has been questioned on a number of grounds. Some have suggested that without greater emphasis on 'individualism' and a distancing from the trade unions Labor cannot win the support of 'middle-class' floating voters. More fundamentally, it is argued that a return to traditional Labor values conflicts with the needs of economic policy. In an era dominated by 'global capital', continuing the transition towards 'open Australia' begun under the Accord is inevitable. Globalisation has reduced the scope for autonomy in national policy; deregulation is therefore inescapable if Australia is to avoid stagnant isolationism. The implications for other areas of policy are not always fully spelt out by the authors, but in essence it is inviting the ALP to follow Britain's 'New Labour' Party as the pathway to power.

'New Labour': the meaning of deregulation

Employment policy in the widest sense — intersecting areas such as economics and finance, trade and industry, incomes and industrial relations, education and training — constitutes the most critical test by which government policy can be judged. Moreover, 'industrial relations', the employment relationship between capital and labour, is at the heart of the power and value conflicts of capitalist society. It conditions the public perception of what is appropriate and also what a government is able to do in fact. Election results are so closely bound up with these issues that the (non-Marxist) American political scientist Seymour Martin Lipset was prompted to describe the electoral system as a 'democratic translation of the class struggle' (Lipset 1960, p. 220). A government whose employment policy is considered successful is therefore likely to remain in office until it is brought down by a combination of other factors.

These might be exhaustion and internal division, arrogance and corruption, or inadequate public services such as health, education or transport — the factors that brought New Labour to power in 1997 after eighteen years of Conservative rule. But Labour began to water down its opposition to Conservative economic and industrial relations policies long before, after its defeat in the 1983 general election. It took another fourteen years and two heavy election defeats in 1987 and 1992, the latter in the context of a major recession, before this strategy was finally successful. Projecting itself as a 'responsible' alternative government, Labour weakened its opposition to the trend of government policy, reinforcing Prime Minister Thatcher's claim that 'there is no alternative'. Labour would oppose each new measure of restrictive union law or privatisation, but shortly afterwards undertake not to reverse it. Labour thus looked feeble, incapable of initiative, in truth a conservative party committed in its instincts to the status quo, and only grudgingly accepting reforms it conceded eventually were justified.

At last these reforms ran out of steam. They went beyond the demands of most employers, introducing unnecessary complications for the sake only of 'union bashing'. Capital was antagonised by the Tory prevarication over Europe whilst the public was exasperated by decay in public services. Then firm ground emerged from which Labour could attack the government as incompetent, countering the excesses of 'individualism' and proffering its alternative vision of a 'caring' society. But on the vital issues to business of economic and industrial relations policies Labour gave explicit commitments not to overturn the anti-union laws, or reverse the privatisation of the former publicly owned utilities and industries, or exceed prudent limits on government spending, or raise levels of taxation. More importantly, Labour promised business that unions would never again enjoy the semblance of influence they possessed during the 1970s. Labour would listen to small business and to big business, to heavy and light industry, to employers and directors, to banking and insurance, to finance and the stock market. Moreover, they would do this not surreptitiously or with bad conscience, but explicitly, as a cardinal virtue. Here is the 'new' in New Labour; its consequences are revealed in the development of employment policy over the two years since the election.

The white paper 'Fairness at Work' (May 1998) was less favourable to the unions than the election manifesto. It introduced a new requirement for 40 per cent support from all workers, including those not voting, to claim the statutory right to recognition by an employer. Worse, the white paper's proposal to allow a recognition claim without a ballot when the union had majority membership in the bargaining unit was eliminated altogether after representations from the employers. Unions were hoping for some strengthening of employment policy after the election. Instead, by progressively weakening its published proposals, the government has made a point of demonstrating its commitment to the interests of employers. When the Trades Union Congress sent a delegation to Downing Street for a lunchtime meeting with the Prime Minister, they were given not beer and sandwiches, but a stern lecture followed by an insulting press release. Where the white paper promised a 'fair balance of rights and responsibilities', New Labour is retaining and legitimating the previous legislation of the Conservatives, even though much of it has been denounced by the International Labour Organisation. New Labour claims 'to replace the notion of conflict between employers and employees with the promotion of partnership'. But where conflict as an option is difficult or impossible, it is a partnership without power for workers.

Some minimal standards strengthening legal rights for individual workers will be imposed, although most derive now from European Union legal requirements. In signing up to the Social Chapter of the Maastricht Treaty, the government made clear its intention was not to support more extensive employment rights. On the contrary, further proposals would be opposed wherever they were inconsistent with the need to promote 'competition'. True to its word, New Labour has joined with European employers in opposing the proposed directive on establishing a general framework for informing and consulting employees, issued by the European Commission last November. Within the limits established by these minimum standards, including the new national minimum wage, the intention is that employers will retain and enhance their prerogatives, free of union interference. The deregulation project aims not just to reduce state controls over capital. It also involves the continuing use of state power to weaken unions as a restriction on capital's freedom.

When the ALP lost power in 1996, it was perceived in the labour movement as politically and morally bankrupt. The vestiges of traditional Labor values seemed extirpated by Keating's drive for deregulation. Party members, who had been surprised to win in 1993, thought 'the eventual defeat had been a long time coming' (ALP 1996, p. 5). The trade union view of the Accord, for example, in *Australia Reconstructed* (ACTU/TDC 1987) was described by ACTU General Secretary Bill Kelty as 'missed opportunities' (Evatt Foundation 1995, p. vii). On the other hand, some critics of the Accord consider this standpoint delusory, because the Accord's true function was simply 'to mask the party's deregulatory agenda' (Beilharz 1994, p. xiii). Whichever view one takes here, the significant fact is that Blair gave his blessing to the Keating Government when the original Accord was in ruins, when radical interpretations, delusory or otherwise, were no longer possible.

Consequently, the concept of a 'centre-left' approach to policy has been thrown into confusion. If centre-left is defined as the position of those political parties 'left of centre' — in the United States, the Democratic Party; in Britain and Australia, the Labo(u)r parties; on the continent of Europe, the social democratic or socialist parties — to what extent can they be said to retain a defining set of principles? It is not just a matter of policy detail, which must vary from one country to another, but a question of basic 'philosophy' or vision. The hallmark of the 'left', whatever the different strands within it, has in the past been a desire to transform the existing social order. But in the 1980s the radical initiative lay with 'Thatcherism' — now termed 'neo-liberalism'. The current issue posed for the left is to what extent its basic principles preceding the neo-liberal assault remain valid. Was neo-liberalism a temporary aberration, or does it express more fundamental changes? If so, does the left have any alternative to a slightly modified version of neo-liberalism?

The philosophy of the 'third way'

These issues are squarely addressed by Anthony Giddens in his book *The Third Way: The Renewal of Social Democracy* (Giddens 1998), widely promoted as the philosophy of the Blair Government. Acknowledging the claim that 'Blair and New Labour have persisted with the economic policies of Margaret Thatcher', Giddens states his 'aim is not to assess whether or not such observations are valid but to consider where the debate about the future of social democracy stands' (pp. 25–6). Nevertheless, apropos the thesis (Bobbio 1996, p. 16) that the strategy of the left has been to 'save whatever can be saved of [its] own position by drawing in the opposing position', Giddens admits this claim is 'readily comprehensible from such a standpoint' (p. 40).

For Giddens, the third way is not an alternative to capitalism and socialism, because the latter 'is now dead' (p. 4). As it no longer occupies any political space, the concept of an alternative to it, irrelevant. As for the former, capitalism, 'no one any longer has any alternatives' (p. 43). The third way should therefore be understood as 'an attempt to transcend' both 'old-style social democracy' and neo-liberalism. The former has been undermined in part because it was 'always linked' to socialism. Keynes himself, although 'not a socialist', supposedly 'shared some of the emphases of Marx and socialism' (p. 9) and 'globalisation' has removed 'some powers nations used to possess, including those that underlay Keynesian economic management' (p. 31).

The purpose of the book is thus to legitimate a seismic shift in social democratic policy towards neo-liberalism. Social democracy, for Giddens, can only be a slightly humanised version of capitalism, which requires for its efficient functioning the economic policies prescribed by neo-liberalism. It cannot be a transition to socialism or some other qualitatively different kind of society which would enable one to speak, as Anthony Crosland did, of the 'demise of capitalism' (Crosland 1956, p. 64). Nevertheless, social democracy should retain its traditional values. 'The challenge is to make these values count where the economic program of socialism has become discredited' (pp. 1–2). Without a distinctive economic program, however, the scope is obviously limited. Can these values, on the assumptions underlying the third way, be anything more than rhetoric plastered over capitalism's neo-liberal face?

The current third-way model stems from President Bill Clinton's reinvention as a 'New Democrat' after the Republican landslide in the 1994 Congressional elections. The concept of the third way in US politics was developed by a group of policy advisers around Clinton before the 1992 election. It generated some of the most progressive ideas to appear in mainstream US politics since the New Deal, including positive economic management, labour law reform favourable to trade unions, and a publicly funded health service amongst them. The expression 'third way' obliquely referred to the Socialist International's 1951 program, which marked out a path distinct from both US free-market capitalism and Soviet communism. The employment policy element was spelt out by Clinton's first labor secretary, Robert Reich, in his study *The Work of Nations* (Reich 1991). Reich not only accepted the inevitability of 'globalisation', his book made a positive response to it. International mobility of all factors of production meant that 'the very idea of an American economy is becoming meaningless' (p. 9). The national ownership of capital was irrelevant. The only issue for national policy was therefore creation of employment. However, the original conception of the third way was swiftly destroyed by a massive conservative counterattack during the President's first two years in office.

After 1994, with Clinton's swing to the right and the departure of Reich and other liberals, the third way needed reformulation. In this context, the new Presidential spin doctor, Dick Morris, developed the theory of 'triangulation'. It involved abandoning traditional Democratic policies and absorbing Republican views, especially on welfare, enabling Clinton to stand 'between and above' both parties. The idea was then picked up by Tony Blair after abandoning his flirtation with 'stakeholder capitalism' as too radical. For capital, the only legitimate stakeholders are capitalists. Involvement of others, workers or the public, is not consistent with the free market, that is, the untrammelled prerogatives of private property. Blair's problem was how to reconcile 'old-style' Labour values with 'new-style' neo-liberal economic policies. The concept of a third way was a useful receptacle into which the new content could be poured, once it had been invented. It signified a difference both from 'old Labour' and from the Conservatives. That was the correct position, 'between and above', but the position was lacking principles and the concept lacked content.

Where Thatcher had found the philosophy of Hayek lying ready to hand, Blair needed one concocted to order. And who could be more usefully inventive here than *prince de la science* of academic sociology, Professor Anthony Giddens, recently enthroned as director of the London School of Economics? The principal aim of Giddens' book is to redefine the social democratic position on the welfare state and to undermine the libertarian element central to the social democratic tradition from John Stuart Mill to Anthony

Crosland. For Giddens, rights need to be balanced by 'responsibilities' and responsibilities need to be enforced by the state. 'Recognising the problematic history of the welfare state, third way politics should accept some of the criticisms the right makes of that state' (p. 112). These primarily concern the creation of a culture of 'dependency' and consequent 'moral hazard' — a preference to avoid working; 'dole bludging' was the common currency in Australia under the Fraser Governments of the 1970s. Accordingly, 'unemployment benefits should carry the obligation to look actively for work' (p. 65).

New Labour's welfare-to-work program and, more importantly, the 'longer-term' plans unveiled in Chancellor Gordon Brown's recent budget to replace benefits with tax credits incorporate this principle. The working families tax credit, enacted last year, is the first step towards integration of the tax and benefit systems under which credits will be allowed for all those on low incomes (*Financial Times*, 'Budget 1999', 10 March 1999). Not only does it remove the claimed 'disincentive to work' which some argue is inherent in a system of means-tested benefits; more controversially, it allows the use of greater compulsion. Benefit claimants will have to take 'advice' on how to break out of 'dependency' on the state — in effect, forcing them to take any available job.

A universal tax credit will subsidise employers, encouraging wage reductions like the wage–tax trade-offs under the Accord. Expansion of low-paid employment will allow a real reduction in the cost of unemployment benefits, not a purely notional reduction in spending caused by shifting the cost of the tax credits to Treasury. Some limit, however, must be placed on subsidisation if such a tax credit system is to work. This is the main function of the national minimum wage. Tax credits will lead to more workers being paid at or near the minimum rate, acting as a drag on the lower half of the earnings scale and increasing inequality of incomes. The alleged 'disincentive to work' is transformed into a real disincentive for employers to pay more than the rate at which tax credits begin to cut out. The compulsion to work will be legitimated by removing a possible ground for objection — that the wages offered are unreasonably low. All jobs will be deemed paid at the minimum rate, although the means of enforcement are so meagre that widespread evasion is inevitable. This will become New Labour's main employment policy and the operation of the welfare state will become subordinate to it.

On other employment issues, Giddens notes that Labour's 1987 policy review, 'the first systematic attempt to move away from classical social democracy principles', resulted in 'dependence upon the unions [being] reduced' (p. 17). Restricting trade union influence over policy is central to third-way politics, but as this has already been accomplished by New Labour it no longer requires justification. The desirability of 'family-friendly workplace policies' (p. 125), which feature in the 'Fairness at Work' white paper, is mentioned with even briefer mention of 'employee participation — a factor in democratisation' (p. 75). However, 'employee participation' is a managerial concept which does not involve any concession of influence to workers over decision-making. Giddens does not propose that workers should have any legal rights to information or consultation — Tony Blair is also completely opposed to this. Being too explicit in these areas might inhibit acceptance of the third way in countries where the trade unions retain greater power and political influence than in Britain.

The Australian setting

According to Giddens' oversimplified account, the third way was a reaction by the Democratic and Labour parties to the dominance of the Reagan and Thatcher governments. It accepted a permanent shift to the right in the boundaries of the political landscape. Thatcherism was seen by the left as primarily an ideological phenomenon, albeit with deep popular support (Hall & Jacques 1983). Now it has lost its ideological support, but it remains to haunt the left, grounded economically in the collapse of the 'golden era' of postwar capitalism and its subsequent globalisation. The ideological and moral collapse of neo-liberalism has created space for social democratic governments, but the economic imperatives continue to constrain them. In continental Europe, however, where 'neo-liberalism made less of an impact' (p. 5), the initial response of most social democrats to the third way was 'lukewarm'; they saw in it no more than 'warmed-over neo-liberalism' (p. 25).

Giddens sees Australia as another entity, along with the United States, Britain and Latin America, where neo-liberalism did have a significant impact (p. 5). This view is commonly held within Australia, too, especially on the left. John Pilger has described the ALP as 'devoted to an Antipodean version of Thatcherism' (Pilger 1989, p. 310). Similarly, Peter Beilharz seems to reject 'juxtaposition' between the new right and the Accord because the 'worm of deregulation was doing its worst within, under the auspices of the Accord' (1994, p. 184). Such views have some foundation, but they ignore the contradictory character of the Accord and reduce the real antagonism towards it. Most prominent was the new right, the archetype of neo-liberalism. However, in the Australian context, this was an ill-defined and rather marginal force, capable of much noise, but lacking really solid support in the organisation of mainstream capital. More important was the opposition from modernising forces favouring deregulation grouped around the Business Council of Australia, whose primary impetus came from the need to orchestrate pressure on the Accord. Thus the willingness of business to collaborate within tripartite Accord structures was minimal (McEachern 1991). Over time, these forces were able to shift the balance of power decisively in their direction. However, their victory was always less than complete and marked the Accord's demise, not the realisation of its true character.

The 1983 election was a victory not just for the ALP, but for the trade unions in their struggle against the Fraser Governments. Politically, capital was thrown back with its traditional groupings hopelessly split. Vicious factional struggles wracked the Liberal Party as it oscillated for years between a 'moderation' scarcely distinguishable from the government and repeated attempts to adopt a more aggressive position. The new right failed to win support from the main employers' organisations, to whom the Accord delivered wage restraint and lower levels of disputation. It failed to take over the Liberal Party and was probably counterproductive in its attempts, undermining those such as Howard who were sympathetic to its aims. Its much-trumpeted victories in a series of industrial disputes such as Mudginberri and Dollar Sweets were against smallish unions which, misjudging their own strength, broke cover from the Accord. On the whole, the Accord isolated union-busting attempts to a few firms, mainly in the resources sector, which were fought to a standstill.

Over the last two decades, the Australian electorate has rejected neo-liberal ideology, unlike in the United States and Britain. Its journalistic champions have complained of the problem within non-Labor politics of 'how to win elections on a platform of free market economics' (Kelly 1992, p. 591), confirmed by Hewson's failure in 1993. In 1996, it was a more cautious John Howard, keeping the radical right views he had openly espoused a decade earlier closely under wraps, who promised to protect the 'battlers' Labor had abandoned. Unlike Thatcher in 1979, he was given no mandate for an assault on the trade union movement. When his clandestine manoeuvring around the maritime dispute was exposed, the effect was to swing public opinion decisively behind the union. The victory of the MUA demonstrates the difference between Australia and Britain. For central to the neo-liberal project is the use of state power as a weapon against the trade unions. Within the limits defined by Accord policy, the state was supportive, enabling the unions to regroup and reorganise in a comparatively favourable political climate.

In terms of practical policy, if not of rhetoric, the Hawke/Keating governments were not greatly different from previous right-wing Labor regimes. Indeed, the retreat in office from a radical program is a common characteristic of social democratic governments everywhere. They win power when circumstances favour the basic values for which they stand. They lose it when they have so far compromised under the pressures of office as to appear weak, indecisive and ineffective — especially when they come into open conflict with their trade union partners. Thus the foundations of the Accord can be found in the final period of the Whitlam Government; the Accord's main purpose was to create a relationship capable of sustaining a centralised incomes policy without the damaging divisions which occurred under Whitlam. Even the 'shock therapy' approach to dismantling protection had its precursor in the Whitlam tariff cuts. This continuity was obscured to some extent by the mutual hostility of the chief protagonists and the predilection of some Accord critics to focus on the early period under Whitlam, the better to portray Hawke and Keating as betrayers of Labor values.

Some support for the view that neo-liberalism was a potent force in Australian politics under the Accord lies in 'deregulation' and its accompanying rhetoric. Opening a protected economy would involve major dislocations, with risks of de-industrialisation, which was also a concern in Britain during the 1980s, due to the decline in the competitive position of manufacturing industry. The Accord proposed initially to safeguard against these risks by establishing tripartite bodies and a planned approach to economic restructuring. The need to reduce protection and develop manufactured exports was accepted at an early stage, not least by the ACTU. The debate over globalisation, therefore, concerned implementation of this change in strategic perspective. *Australia Reconstructed* affirmed that the 'manufacturing sector is now facing the challenge of becoming internationally competitive and export-oriented' (ACTU/TDC 1987, p. 90). The Australian Manufacturing Council's report *The Global Challenge* (AMC 1990) set out a practicable approach for achieving it. Hence neither the ACTU's nor the AMC's position 'could fairly be accused of sentimental traditionalism. Both were arguments not for turning back but for formulating different ways forward' (Beilharz 1994, p. 143).

The arguments advanced recently by Mark Latham in *Civilising Global Capital* (Latham 1998) and by Lindsay Tanner in *Open Australia* (Tanner 1999) therefore rest upon an unconvincing logic equating globalisation with deregulation. However, protection designed to influence the location of economic activity within markets to which global capital seeks access has been used effectively by Southeast Asian economies to industrialise as part of the globalisation process. This is not equivalent to import substitution designed to establish an independent national economy, because it aims at inclusion within the globalised economy. The rational point in accepting globalisation is to forestall what would otherwise be an inevitable comparative decline, not to precipitate instant destruction hoping that something better might emerge from the ruins (Genoff & Green 1998). The burden is surely upon those equating globalisation with deregulation to explain why attempts to influence, coordinate or manage the impact of globalisation must inevitably fail.

A variation of this approach is Michael Thompson's book *Labor Without Class: The Gentrification of the ALP*. This has been misunderstood by some supporters as well as opponents of the third way. The confusion arises because at first sight Thompson's argument seems identical with critiques of the ALP and the British Labour Party from the Marxist left (Hindess 1971). Both seem to regret the loss of a 'class' perspective. The decline of traditional blue-collar working-class activism seems to confirm Lenin's view that the ALP is a 'bourgeois' party. But Thompson's position is entirely different. In arguing for a return of the party to its roots he is criticising the ALP's radical social agenda from the time of Whitlam, harking back to the Calwell period when Labor was largely under the influence of its Catholic constituency. Thompson does not, however, suggest that Labor should return to the economic policies of that era. On the contrary, Thompson believes the 'economic rationalism' of the Hawke/Keating governments is in the best interests of the working class.

The point of this strategy is not to narrow the ALP base, but to broaden it by taking in the conservative middle class and thus competing with the Liberals on their own terrain. Radicalism is made the scapegoat for Labor's election defeat:

> *It was not 'economic rationalism' that drove the working class supporters away from voting for the Labor Party in 1996 (and kept them away in 1998), rather it was the capture of the Labor Party by the special interest groups who conned Labor governments into imposing their agendas on ordinary Australians.*
> (Thompson 1999, pp. ix–x)

This is consistent with Latham's claim that the 'Keating Government was decisively defeated amid public perceptions that its policies (were) supporting the allocation of public resources on the basis of segment-of-life categories, at the expense of broader programs of socioeconomic security' (Latham 1998, p. 337). Latham believes Labor made too many concessions to 'protectionists concerned solely with the scale of trade unionism in manufacturing industries; feminists arguing for social justice solely through the prism of gender equity; and multiculturalists concerned solely with the maintenance of segment-of-life programs — the politics of segmentation and sectional interests.'

The current debate

At present, debate in the ALP over employment and industry policy is coded and confused. At the abstract level, there is a suggestion by Latham and Tanner that globalisation implies deregulation, with a straightforward choice between the 'open' economy or a return to old-style protectionism. If the latter is ruled out, there is no alternative to the deregulatory economic policies of the new right. The implicit model is New Labour in Britain, as expounded by Giddens in *The Third Way*. But this assumption is unfounded and it should be challenged. The alternative possibilities for managing the implications of globalisation for the development of economic activity in Australia, through a process involving primarily the government, trade unions and employers, must be explicitly examined.

If the approach to economic and industry policy is too abstract, the approach to employment policy is too narrow. Very specific measures, such as tax credits for low-paid workers, are being proposed, without a thorough investigation of their implications for wages policy as a whole. There is nothing objectionable about tax credits themselves. They are simply a means of providing a benefit to those in employment, as for example with Labor's proposal at the last election of a credit for parents of dependent children. Because this is based upon needs that are not shared by all workers, it cannot operate as a general subsidy to the employer. The position, however, changes when a general credit is proposed for all low-paid workers. This is effectively a payment of part of the worker's wage by the state, which will encourage a corresponding reduction of the part paid by the employer.

The position is further confused, however, by suggesting tax credits are the solution to the 'poverty' or 'unemployment' traps which result from the combination of phasing out benefits and rising rates of taxation absorbing all or most of any wage increase. This problem is inherent in any means-tested social security system, whether paid directly as benefits or indirectly, as tax credit 'allowances'. It can be ameliorated, but not abolished, by a more gradual tapering of benefits/credits and upward adjustment in taxation scales. The reason this has not been done before is simply that it is considered too expensive. It would be pleasant to think that Labor does seriously intend to alleviate the problem. In the context of the current third-way challenge to the welfare state, however, that is just plain wishful thinking. The truth is that talk of the 'poverty trap' in the current context of employment policy is nothing but spin designed to conceal the real nature and purpose of the policy.

According to Latham, the 'need for reform' of the welfare system stems from its excessive costs. 'The spread of economic insecurity and exclusion has strained the capacity of the tax/transfer system to adequately fund the welfare pool' (Latham 1998, p. 222). Means-testing and complicated entitlement criteria have been introduced increasingly in an attempt to curtail the growth in the 'income dependency ratio'. Despite this, however:

> *[E]xtensive targeting and means testing in the social security policies of the Hawke Government were only able to reduce the dependency ratio from 26 per cent in 1983 to 24.5 per cent in 1989. These gains were subsequently lost during the recession of the early 1990s and the rise of structural unemployment.* (Latham 1998)

In this context, the expressed concern of third-way advocates over the complexity of the system and poverty traps can hardly be taken as a prelude to more generous provision. On the contrary, they presage a reduction in the level of welfare, indicated by the growing attacks on the welfare lobby groups from the oracles of the third way (Latham 1999b).

This appears clearly, too, in the proposals of the 'Five Economists' (Dawkins, Freebairn, Garnaut, Keating & Richardson 1998), in which they suggest a tax credit for the low-paid in exchange for a general freeze on award rates (Watson & Buchanan 1999). A more realistic variation of the same idea would be to freeze rates for the low paid and compensate them with tax credits, in effect providing a subsidy for low-paid employment. Hopefully this would produce, according to the thesis of the economists, increasing employment in low-paid jobs, a reduction in unemployment and consequently also a net saving in benefits paid by the state. But without a reduction in wages, there can be no hope of reducing unemployment, and any subsidy would therefore be wasted as 'deadweight'. The jobs would exist anyway and the state would be increasing its expenditure by giving tax credits to no effect.

Peter Reith was therefore astute to defer further consideration of this idea until after reform of the award system (Reith 1998). The tax credit proposals to subsidise low-paid employment cannot work effectively until awards are replaced by a uniform minimum wage, as advocated in the report commissioned for the Labour Ministers' Council (Moore 1998), which defines the ultimate objective of the Reith reforms. They would be facilitated by the proposal to substitute the 'corporations' for the 'conciliation and arbitration' power as the constitutional foundation of the system, put forward in Reith's speech to the National Press Club (Reith 1999). No one doubts that 'paper disputes' and 'ambit claims' are artificial concepts from the standpoint of arbitration, serving more to create rather than settle disputes. This results from expanding the system into one of national wage regulation, beyond its original intention for resolving real interstate disputes.

If that was really the nature of Reith's problem, however, the *Workplace Relations Act* could be amended by restricting the commission's powers to the settlement of such real disputes. Its scope would be narrower than the established interpretation of the constitutional head of power allows, but it would still be based on the representative function of unions. But Reith really wants to abolish any conception of dispute resolution whatsoever so he can reduce or eliminate the access of unions to the commission. It would be left with the task of setting minimum conditions only. The functions of the Industrial Relations Commission would be drastically curtailed, similar essentially to those of the Low Pay Commission in Britain. In principle, the tax credit for low-paid workers notion is entirely consistent with where Reith wants to go — it is just a matter of timing and presentation.

That Labor's leaders appear not to have understood these issues appears evident from their uncertain response to the Reith proposals. According to the *Australian Financial Review* (19 February 1999), 'Labor seemed unsure how to handle it.' Kim Beazley conceded the paper picked up 'a bit of Labor policy' — such as tax credits for low-income earners to reduce disincentives to work — and had some 'good constructive bits to it'. He was more effective with 'an impassioned case against the moves to strip unemployed people of benefits', which he had earlier described as an 'absolute obscenity' (*Australian Financial Review*, 9 November 1998). However, Labor seems to accept, according to speeches from Simon Crean, that a significant reduction in unemployment can be achieved by giving the unemployed 'more incentive' to take jobs (*Age*, 8 April 1999) and by making the 'transition from welfare to work more attractive' (*Australian Financial Review*, 23 March 1999).

This is the theory underlying the claim that 'dole bludging' is a significant cause of unemployment, previously the exclusive preserve of the right. It justifies the use of compulsion as part of any welfare-to-work program. Compulsion is, as we have seen, explicitly part of the third way expounded by Professor Giddens and implemented by New Labour as a central element in its program. In a similar vein, Mark Latham calls for 'entrenching a sense of reciprocal responsibility throughout the work of the welfare state', supporting withdrawal of benefits when the unemployed fail to enhance their 'labour force skills and personal capability' (Latham 1998, pp. 204–6). Such ideas, he informs us, 'should not be regarded as the political property of the Right'. With even greater candour, Lindsay Tanner presents the 'challenge' inherent in this approach, wondering how to 'embrace concepts like mutual obligation without descending into the world of punitive welfare and the Poor Laws of nineteenth-century Britain' (p. 62).

There is a further reactionary implication inherent in the proposals of the 'Five Economists', deriving from their view that the right to a tax credit should be means-tested on the aggregate income of married partners. Low-paid women workers will see their wages fall without any compensation from the state. Hence, many will be driven back into the home and performance of unpaid domestic labour, reversing the postwar trend to increasing female participation in the workforce, which in turn has provided the real foundation for the advance in equality for women. Martin Ferguson, Labor's shadow employment minister, however, sees the interests of working women as predominantly the concern of 'femocrats'; he wants the 'forgotten members of our one-time heartland: women who are not in paid work' better addressed (foreword to Thompson 1999, p. vi). And in truth, there will be many more of them if the tax-credit approach to reduction of unemployment costs on the welfare state, which Ferguson has endorsed, is adopted and implemented.

Conclusion: beyond the Accord

The policy for increasing employment upon which the proponents of the third way place most emphasis is education and training (Tanner 1999, p. 156; Latham 1998, p. 232). Few doubt that this issue is indeed a central one, given the structural changes in employment which are now occurring. It forms a central plank in Robert Reich's classic analysis of the implications of globalisation for employment (Reich 1991). If unskilled industrial work is disappearing or being moved to low-wage countries then the skills and education of the workforce are the primary factor in ensuring retention of well-paid employment in the global economy. What is distinctive about the third way is not its commitment to ensuring that the state funds the creation of an adequately skilled labour force to serve the needs of capital. It is the belief, in marked contrast to previous Labor and social democratic thinking, that capital cannot tolerate and Labor governments cannot impose any restriction on capital's freedom of movement and action. The excluded restrictions are those not only imposed by the state itself but also by an influential trade union movement operating within a supportive legal and political environment.

Implementation of the third way in Australia will therefore require the ALP to distance itself from the unions both symbolically and in terms of policies. Symbolically, this will engender the confidence of business that a future Labor government will not be an instrument for strengthening the unions. The idea of partnership under an Accord-style arrangement is in principle considered undesirable by employers almost irrespective of actual policy because it legitimates the aspirations of the unions to political influence. As in Britain, it will be necessary to demonstrate on a whole range of issues, and in terms of the unions' influence over the ALP, that the idea of a trade union-based party has been abandoned. Concretely, the third way will therefore not wish to oppose Reith's 'second-wave' industrial relations reforms and will seek to ensure that the Coalition industrial relations amendments are not reversed by a future Labor government: '[I]n many respects, the industrial relations reforms advocated by the current Coalition Government have features which are entirely consistent with the Third Way' (Wooden 1999, p. 19). Nor will the third way want to abolish 'junior rates' of pay, which are consistent with the low-pay solution to unemployment. Hence, Labor's deal with the government to support legislation entrenching junior rates produced a 'major split' with the unions, but was 'welcomed by business' (*Australian Financial Review*, 26 August 1999). Kim Beazley felt obliged to give 'assurances' that 'the Labor Party would not follow its counterparts in Britain and New Zealand by distancing itself from the trade union movement' (*Sydney Morning Herald*, 27 August 1999).

Youth unemployment is of special concern to employers because the failure to introduce young people into the workforce generates well-known social problems, for which responsibility cannot easily be passed back onto the unemployed themselves. In addition, just as any long-term unemployment robs workers of even their most basic skills and faculties and renders them 'unemployable', youth unemployment reduces the usable labour pool or 'reserve army' available to accommodate fluctuations in the business cycle and restrain wage demands. To ensure that welfare-to-work programs thus promote the interests of capital, compulsion is an essential element, especially in relation to young people. In Britain, the government has boasted that its New Deal has reduced youth unemployment by 100 000. However, they have not advertised the increasing levels of coercion within their scheme (Finn 1999). According to the independent Unemployment Unit, there has been a sharp rise in the numbers punished by withdrawal of benefits, especially amongst the most socially excluded. Many are being forced to give up study designed to improve their job prospects to be 'available for work' (Working Brief 107, August/September 1999). Access to education, including higher education, which increasingly determines employment opportunities, is becoming more stratified along class lines. The scheme is designed to create a class of minimally qualified workers compelled to accept the lowest-paid jobs servicing the needs of the more privileged sectors.

The third way is concerned primarily with 'the growing number of citizens permanently excluded from the economy' (Latham 1998, p. 225), not with fairness, which is seen as incompatible with a modern market economy and should be abandoned as a goal of social democracy. What capital most desires now is a flexible workforce which can be 'churned', where insecurity and periods of actual unemployment are shared amongst workers generally. This is the vision underlying Latham's proposals for reform of income support (1998, pp. 223–31) and the 'ALP's sensible stance on youth wages' (Latham 1999a). Unjustifiably low rates for young workers in terms of their capabilities and any training offered by the employer in effect subsidise low-paid, low-skill jobs predominantly in the retail and other service sectors. They undermine adult rates of pay and create a disincentive to the employment of adults; they even encourage the eventual dismissal of the young workers themselves. But they may create, to the extent such schemes are successful, a potentially employable worker available for another low-paid job supplemented by a 'tax credit' subsidy from the state.

The shortcomings in this approach, from the standpoint of providing solutions to long-term 'structural' unemployment, which the third way assumes will continue, require policies to lower the costs of unemployment and to promote low-paid employment. Reducing social provision to the unemployed through welfare and forcing them to take low-paid jobs is therefore central to the project of the third way. Encouraging women to leave the workforce and become fully dependent upon their spouses is a second strand; undermining the arbitration system and trade union power is a third. Integration of welfare-to-work programs with state benefits through the tax credit policies with which Labor has been flirting is a relatively innocuous-looking starting point for implementation of this program. The objective is to create an acceptably subservient relationship to capital, not to court electoral popularity. On the contrary, the unattractiveness of the program to Labor supporters generates the need for spin. For example, following the decision on junior rates, a 'senior Labor Party figure' was quoted as saying: 'We're not a union bosses' party, we're a party for workers and their families and they want junior rates' (*Australian Financial Review*, 26 August 1999).

Despite these initial conflicting signals and pronouncements, Labor still has the opportunity over the next two years to retrieve its position and pursue an alternative strategy with a greater chance of electoral success. Ironically, Reith himself spells out a sound basis for opposition to his proposals in giving his reasons for not adopting the tax credit plan at this stage. He concedes it 'doesn't recognise that fairness in wages is often perceived to be about more than having access to a reasonable standard of living. It is also often perceived as being about being paid fairly for the output produced. In this context some critics may also argue that a proposal like this may have a disproportionate impact on women's wages.' The ALP, in alliance with the trade unions and other community organisations, especially the women's movement and youth groups, could campaign on this issue to defeat Reith's plan to deregulate industrial relations and institutionalise low pay. That would in turn provide a foundation for Labor, in partnership with the ACTU, to put flesh on its alternative proposals in the coming policy review.

In Australian politics, the third way is a Trojan Horse for further deregulation of the labour market. If the ALP accepts it, Reith will be able more easily to steer his proposals through the Senate. His 'leaked' strategy of 'linking Senate reform to fixing unemployment' (Reith 1998, p. 5) is a tactical feint to bounce the Democrats into accepting his plan. Senate reform is not practical politics. Reith needs to manoeuvre both Labor and the Democrats into providing at least 'critical support' for the package, creating a degree of consensus which will prevent its complete rejection. The third way will facilitate construction of that consensus. The great danger in the ALP's present approach to policy formation is that no clear choice will be made between different strategies. Instead, there are spasmodic movements towards the third way through hints and nudges. Its emergence in similar fashion in Britain took fifteen years; if the ALP follows this course, the effect will probably be similar. Internal tensions will weaken Labor's credibility as an alternative government and incoherence in the policy platform will undermine its ability effectively to oppose the government. In Australia, this strategy will probably also require fifteen years in opposition. Thus the third way is a recipe for losing the next three or four elections.

chapter 5

The future of Australian unionism in the global economy
by Tim Harcourt

At the Harvard Trade Union Program of 1999, Emeritus Professor John Dunlop asked the class of mid-career union leaders to paint a picture of where their union would be in the year 2025. This was based on a similar event in 1955, when the editor of *Fortune* magazine asked the long-serving AFL–CIO President, George Meany, where the American labour movement would be in 1980 (see Dunlop 1980). The Meany interview attracted interest because of its optimism and confidence regarding the future of American labour. Given the actual events that have occurred since 1955, with the drastic decline of trade union membership in industrialised countries, not too many optimistic scenarios are being posed in 1999. No one seems to want to emulate Meany's ill-fated forecast of 1955.

This article is written in the context of a fast-changing global economy and an overall sea of pessimism about the future role of unions in the Australian economy and society. This article does not intend to be yet another depressing account nor a desperate exercise in wishful thinking for the sake of it. Instead, this essay takes on a few issues in the debate about the future of unionism and tries to make sense of them in terms of the strategic choices that Australian trade unions can make in planning for the future.[1]

This article is in four parts. First, some data on union decline is presented. Second, some reasons for the trend in the data are discussed. Third, the comparative advantages of Australian unionism are identified to highlight our relative strengths. Finally, some basic suggestions are put forward for guiding future policy for Australian trade unions.

The facts: the decline of Australian union membership

Unions have played an important role in Australian society in terms of raising living standards for workers and advancing social justice issues. Shorter working hours, equal pay for women, improved health and safety, holiday time, superannuation, and vocational training and other facets of Australian working life are all due to enduring and forceful union campaigns. Yet despite these real-life successes, the prognosis for the Australian union movement does not look good, on the basis of the statistics alone.

Looking at the data, Australian union membership, at the end of the twentieth century, has started to fall in terms of absolute numbers and as a proportion of the labour force.[2]

Figure 1

Trade union members 1891–1996

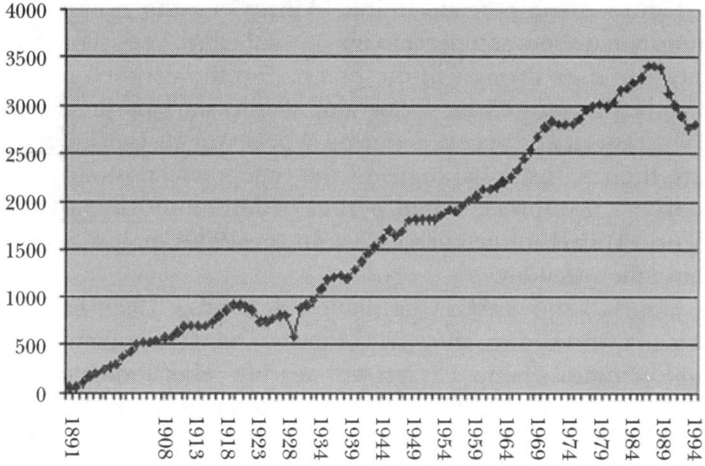

Source: ABS (1998d)

Figure 1 shows the trade union member series, which has grown throughout most of the twentieth century, despite falls during the Great Depression and in 1937. Since 1990, membership has been falling rapidly.

Figure 2

Trade union density 1911–1996
Per cent of total employees including non-financial

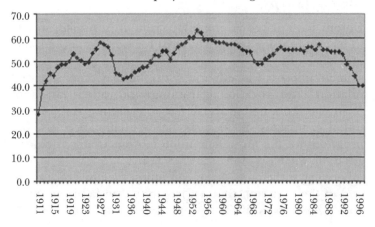

Source: Labour reports and ABS (1998d)

Figure 2 shows trade union 'density' — the number of union members as a percentage of total employees. The density rate rises strongly in the first half of the century, falls at the beginning of the 1920s and at the start of the Great Depression, and recovers during World War II. Density rates are then at historical highs in the immediate postwar years during an unprecedented period of full employment from World War II to the early 1970s. In the 1990s, union density has fallen steadily.

Figure 3 shows ACTU affiliation data since 1955. For the time period shown, the ACTU share of total Australian trade union membership has grown steadily. This indicates the ACTU's strength as a peak council in terms of coverage of Australian unions.

Figure 3

ACTU share of total union membership 1955–1995
Per cent each congress year

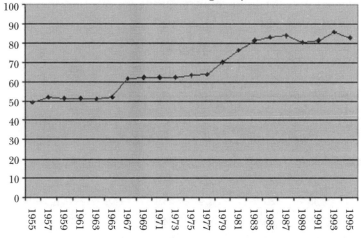

Source: ABS (1998d)

Table 1
Trade union members, 1990–98

Year	Members (millions)	Union density (%)
1990	2.66	40.5
1994	2.28	35.0
1995	2.25	32.7
1996	2.19	31.1
1997	2.11	30.3
1998	2.04	28.1

Source: ABS (1998e)

Table 1 shows a decline in union membership throughout the 1990s — from 2.66 million in 1990 (or 40.5 per cent of the workforce) to 2.04 million in 1998 (or 28.1 per cent).

Table 2 shows a reduction in union density from 1990 to 1998 in terms of gender, sector and employment status.

The decline of Australian union membership should be placed in an international context.[3] Table 3 and the accompanying Figure 4 below compare Australian union data with selected industrialised countries using various International Labour Organisation (ILO) sources.

Table 2
Trade union density by gender, sector and employment status, 1990–98

| | Union density (%) by: | | | | | |
| | Gender | | Sector | | Employment status | |
Year	Males	Females	Public	Private	Casual	Permanent
1990	45.0	34.6	66.8	30.8	18.8	45.7
1994	39.1	22.9	62.3	26.0	14.7	41.3
1995	35.7	29.1	56.4	25.1	13.9	39.4
1996	33.5	28.1	55.4	24.0	13.1	37.4
1997	33.0	26.9	54.7	23.3	13.8	36.0
1998	30.0	25.8	52.9	21.4	11.6	34.2

Source: ABS (1998e); (1998c)

Table 3
Trends in union membership, by country, 1985–95

	1985	1995	85–95
Australia	46	33	–13
Austria	50	43	–7
Canada	35	35	0
Denmark	85	85	0
France	20	15	–5
Germany	33	28	–5
Italy	42	38	–4
Japan	29	24	–5
New Zealand	44	22	–22
Spain	10	16	6
Sweden	85	83	–2
Britain	45	33	–12
United States	18	15	–3

Note: Australia's data is 1986–95 and Spain's is 1985–94.
Source: various ILO works

Figure 4

Union density in industrialised countries 1985–1995

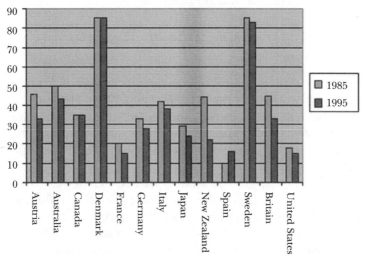

Source: various ILO works

Other industrialised countries have indeed experienced Australia's decline in union membership. In fact, for the 1985 to 1995 period Australia experienced the largest decline in union density of all surveyed countries except New Zealand. Australian density declined by 13 percentage points compared to New Zealand's 22 per cent. This worldwide trend occurred despite the fact that the Conservative Party held office in Britain (under Thatcher and then Major) and the Republicans were in power for most of that period in the United States (under Reagan and then Bush), whilst Australia had a Labor Government.

The data on trade union membership is also supported by evidence in the 1990 and 1995 Australian Workplace Industrial Relations Surveys (AWIRS) of the reduced visibility of unions in Australian workplaces (see Callus et al. 1991; Morehead et al. 1995). For example, Morehead et al. write in the 1995 survey: 'The AWIRS data confirm the decline of union membership in the first half of the 1990s. The proportion of unionised workplaces fell from 80 to 74 per cent. Most of this decline was in workplaces with 20 to 49 employees and was exclusively in the private sector' (Morehead et al. 1995, p. 158). The AWIRS survey evidence concurs with the ABS data on declining union membership.

Reasons for the decline of Australian unionism

One of the best contributions on the reasons for union decline is provided by David Peetz (Peetz 1998). He describes three main factors as causing the decline in Australian union density: structural change in the labour market; institutional factors; and the union response to new employer strategies (Peetz 1998, p. 175).

Structural change in the labour market includes casualisation, the growth of part-time work, the growth of industries and occupations where union density is traditionally low, and the growth of self-employment and alternative employment arrangements. Peetz says this explains approximately half of the decline of union density in the decade to 1992 but not a high proportion since.

Institutional factors include legislative changes that have had an adverse impact on union membership. This includes the de-collectivisation of the employment relationship and the withdrawal of union recognition. An important reason is the decline in compulsory unionism. This illustrates the dangers of unions being overly dependent on legislative provisions. For instance, New Zealand unions were very dependent on legislation and compulsory union provisions, making them vulnerable to radical legislative change.

New employer strategies and the failure of unions to respond is the final reason explaining the decline in union membership. Until recently, this has been an overlooked reason for changes in union density in Australia. Traditionally, industrial relations scholars have concentrated on unions as institutions when comparing across countries. This focus, however, ignores employer attitudes and strategies toward unions. Australian union density, for instance, may not be over twice the US density rate because Australian unions are twice as effective, it may be because US employers are more ruthless and aggressively anti-union than their Australian counterparts. According to Peetz, there have been some US-style anti-union trends in

Australian employer behaviour in the 1990s. Peetz believes that unions have been unable to counter this new Australian employer attitude and have made poor strategic choices. For instance, the concentration of Australian unions on 'market share' rather than 'expansionary' unionism can be seen as an example of poor union strategy, especially given the waste of resources when unions fight expensive coverage disputes (see Peetz 1998, p. 177).

Importantly, Peetz addresses a number of 'red herrings' in the debate that have been proposed as reasons for the decline of Australian union density. A classic example is the Prices and Incomes Accord (the 'Accord') between the ACTU and the Hawke–Keating Labor Government from 1983 to 1996. The Accord has been blamed in some circles for causing union inertia and decline (see, for example, Stilwell 1986). However, Peetz finds that the Accord 'bought a small amount of time' for the union movement during Labor's term of government to prepare itself for the onslaught when the conservatives eventually came to power (Peetz 1998, p. 177).

The Peetz analysis is also borne out in various surveys of what Australians think about unions. An example is the Australian Centre for Industrial Relations Research and Teaching (ACIRRT) survey commissioned by the Labor Council of New South Wales (Labor Council of NSW 1997). The survey found no reduction in sympathy toward unions, but did identify disenchantment with union service, particularly amongst union members.

The lesson to be drawn from both the Peetz analysis and the Labor Council survey is that there has *not* been a reduction in overall public sympathy for unions in recent years (in fact there has been a small increase in sympathy in the 1990s). However, there has been a reduction in workers' confidence in the union movement's capacity to service members. In short, the results reflect not a reduction in sympathy for unions but a reduction in confidence in the capacity of the unions to deliver service — by both unionists and non-unionists alike. This suggests that union revival is based on improving union infrastructure and strategic management.

In conclusion, structural and institutional changes that have occurred have had an adverse effect on union membership. Some of these factors are 'exogenous' or external to the union movement. There has also been evidence of a change in government and employer attitudes and strategies toward unions. However, there are also 'endogenous' factors that unions do have a say in shaping as they face the future. These 'endogenous' or internal factors include union structure, union governance, resources, human resource policies and similar factors that are part of union strategic choice. From the Peetz evidence it is clear that there is some scope for the union movement to make strategic choices in changing its internal infrastructure in order to deal with the external environment.

Reasons to be cheerful: the comparative advantage of the Australian labour movement

As an antidote to the previous section's sad tale of union decline, it is important to remember some of the comparative advantages that the Australian labour movement possesses over its counterparts in addressing its problems. If we understand some positive elements of our history, it can help us prepare for our future in the face of difficult obstacles. There are five key comparative advantages to bear in mind.

First, in assessing the economic and political change of the past two decades, the Australian labour movement has fared reasonably well. For all the criticisms put, the Hawke–Keating Labor Government was a reasonably successful and socially progressive government for an era that was economically and electorally conservative (Grattan & Gruen 1993). In industrialised countries, economic policy was drifting to the right under Thatcher in Britain, Reagan and Bush in the United States and Kohl in Germany. Financial markets were increasing their influence, as was the rest of the private sector. The electoral tide was against the centre-left. In this context, Hawke and Keating were able to provide important social and economic benefits to the labour movement. Examples include universal health coverage ('Medicare'), superannuation, childcare, targeted social payments, education and training and an overall supportive legislative framework.

Second, the Australian union movement has been able to play both an economic and a social role. All union movements, to be successful, must combine economic power or 'clout' with a strong social conscience. Strong unions in key sectors of the Australian economy have been able to maintain their bargaining strength and deliver significant gains to their members through enterprise bargaining. For example, ACTU research shows a union to non-union wage differential, or mark-up, of 14.5 per cent (or $82 per week) on average for every union member in Australia, including significant mark-ups for women, part-timers and casuals (ACTU 1998).

At the same time, Australian unions have been able to contribute to the betterment of society through arbitrated test cases that flow from union-won gains onto the rest of the labour force. Examples include the Living Wage case, pay equity, and family leave (Harcourt 1997). Australian unions have been able to socialise the gains made in bargaining through arbitration and legislation. There is no 'social unionism' versus 'business unionism' debate, as occurs in North America, as Australian unions have successfully combined traditional industrial muscle with a social conscience.

Third, as reflected in the data (Figure 3) of this article, the ACTU has been able to consolidate itself as the peak council of the labour movement. The ACTU is still considered part of Australia's political and economic structure and a key institution in Australian civil society.

Fourth, Australian unions still have the inheritance of the institutions of conciliation and arbitration. The industrial relations system, despite its critics on both left and right, has been shown to be durable and flexible in times of economic and social change in Australia. It has been able to deliver important socially progressive benefits such as equal pay and minimum wages, but incorporates economic criteria to ensure that its judgments are conducive to macro-economic performance and to a successfully functioning labour market (Isaac 1993).

Furthermore, in the context of an ever-integrating global economy, labour market institutions will become *more* necessary for economic and social distribution reasons, not less. As evidenced by Rodrik and by Garret and Lange, countries which are more open to international trade and investment tend to have stronger rather than weaker social institutions, including labour market protection (Rodrik 1997; Garret & Lange 1995). In this regard, Australia is fortunate to have well-developed labour market institutions. The globalisation era, with its uneven effects on skilled and unskilled workers, will increase the reliance Australia places on its labour market institutions for economic efficiency and social cohesion (Isaac 1998, p. 714).

Fifth, international events have assisted the Australian union movement's capacity for renewal. An example is the end of the Cold War, which, in effect, has taken the monkey off the back of the union movement. In the post-Cold War era, it is possible to be concerned about workers and inequality, without being labelled a 'communist' or a 'traitor to society'. Similarly, it has allowed those in the moderate wing of the labour movement to say that the market economy is the only game in town and change can be brought about only by parliamentary democracy. The early Australian Labor reformists have been vindicated by the events of the century, with the important defeats of fascism, communism and McCarthyism.[4]

Unfortunately, as noted by Mark Latham, the 'globalisation' debate has revived some old left ideas in new clothing. He writes: 'For 200 years, parts of the left have tried to modify or replace capitalist markets with a new system of production, distribution and exchange. For 200 years this project failed. It is likely, however, that economic globalisation will be used as an alibi for one last try' (Latham 1998, p. 389).

The real message of the globalisation debate is that there is a role for worker-friendly institutions in a market economy. Building these institutions is the important task for trade unions, rather than reverting to discredited notions of the need to 'confront capital'. Fortunately, Australian labour has a reformist tradition to build on, together with an open pluralist democracy, a major political party with union roots, a union movement with economic power and a social conscience, and well-developed labour market institutions.

Options for the future

It is almost impossible to predict the future, but you can prepare various scenarios that may come your way. As in corporate strategy, Australian trade unions need to prepare for their future in the global economy. In the final part of this article, I make some brief suggestions that will assist Australian unions in preparing for the future.[5]

First, it is important to take stock of economic and demographic changes in both Australia and the global economy. We need to know what jobs will be created in the future and which ones will go, how technology will change production and distribution, how consumer tastes will change, and so on. For instance, the Australian Bureau of Statistics population predictions for 1997–2051 suggest the strong growth of the 'Sunbelt States' of New South Wales, Queensland and Western Australia (and the Northern Territory), followed by stability in Victoria but steady decline in South Australia and Tasmania (ABS 1998a, pp. 1–3). Included in these predictions are the growth of sunrise industries, including environmental and solar technology, biomedical technology and knowledge-based industries. Unions need to prepare for these changes by using strategic planning to ensure an efficient use of resources.

Secondly, it is important to take note of the decline of ideology. Ruthven has written:

The Industrial Age contest between capitalism and socialism is nearly over. Both lost. The new order is economic rationalism to be opposed in the twenty-first century by humanism. Rationalism, in this sense, follows the dictionary definition: that which actually works; logical; sensible; moderate. The real message is that soap-box ideologies and wild-eyed fanatics have (temporarily) had their day. (Ruthven 1996)

There is no point in talking about the perils of capitalism now that the Cold War is over. Unions instead should be focusing on existing problems in the labour market, such as job insecurity, excessive working hours and wage inequality, and formulating appropriate industrial strategies. The move by the union movement to focus on working time and job security is a step in the right direction in this regard.

Thirdly, it is important to understand changes in globalisation and how nations relate to each other politically through trade and investment. There is no point in retreating into economic nationalism and trade-protective strategies.

Instead unions should play a role in changing economic institutions and providing labour market protection for those adversely affected by changes in the international economy. Trade unions can also make sure that trade liberalisation advocates are held accountable, by monitoring their claims on jobs created and the effect of trade on wages. This is a key role for trade unions to play. There is a labour movement alternative to policies of both the Pauline Hanson and the extreme free-market varieties.

Fourthly, it is important to look at the future of trade unionism as a profession and the role of human resource systems in trade unions themselves (see Weil 1997, p. 191).

Unions have untapped human resources in terms of their rank and file membership. Education and training of delegates greatly assists in this process. Educational opportunity has historically been provided by the trade union movement (through labour colleges, workers' libraries, etc.). This will be an important function of unions in the future, especially as Australia will depend on having a better-educated workforce with the rise of knowledge-based industries.

In recruiting future staff from outside the rank and file, unions should have regard to the effects of labour market deregulation on the decline in living standards of 'social justice' professionals. There are a number of social justice 'causes' which attract young, idealistic, well-educated people. Unions are competing with a number of progressive organisations that promote these 'causes', such as environmental and community groups. It is important that unions attract these people from among the alternatives on offer, by providing them with a career and 'manageable' lifestyle. It is important to have committed people working for unions, but not martyrs or fanatics. Unions should treat these employees well, provide adequate pay, benefits, career progression and reasonable working hours. There is no point burning people out and ruining their health and personal lives. On the contrary, the union movement traditionally has enabled its leaders and activists to expand their life horizons. This was especially so in the past, when educational opportunity was limited for much of the Australian workforce. Many biographies of traditional union leaders show how the movement has been a vehicle for education, economic opportunity, arts and culture, and exposure to international events and travel.[6]

Similarly, unions need to be in touch with technological developments and the rise of younger, technologically literate workers who have combined entrepreneurial talent with socially progressive attitudes. If unions cannot relate to this generation of workers, they risk locking themselves out of the mainstream workforce of the twenty-first century.[7]

Conclusion

In conclusion, unions in Australia, despite recent difficulties, have an important inheritance to draw on. Australia is an economically advanced society, it has stable political institutions, a commitment to democracy and a relatively egalitarian culture (in ethos if not always in outcome). Australian workers have made that inheritance and through their unions have passed on that inheritance to the rest of society. The Australian union movement has acted as a social movement as well as an economic one. Was the equal pay case for Aboriginal stockmen in the Northern Territory run by the North Australian Workers Union on a fee-for-service basis? No, it was argued on the important social principle of equal pay for equal work, and led to the 1967 Referendum on Aboriginal citizenship. Here, the union movement played an important social role (see ACTU 1993).

Australian unions must draw upon this rich inheritance as an agent of social change and must combine it with strategic planning and the continuing reform of union infrastructure. This will enable unions to play a progressive social and economic role in Australia in the twenty-first century.

(I would like to thank the Australian Trade Union Program at Harvard Foundation who sponsored my stay at Harvard University, where this essay was written. Thanks also to Charles Bofferding, Martin Callaghan, Michael Costa, Elaine Bernard, Richard Freeman, Dennis Glover, Gail Gregory, Tom Kochan, Glenn Patmore, Dani Rodrik, Robert Solow, Evan Thornley and David Weil for discussions I have had on some of the topics discussed in this article. Any omission or errors are mine. The views expressed in this essay do not represent the views of the ACTU.)

chapter 6

Creating the participatory society: workplace democracy for Australia?
by Glenn Patmore

As Australian citizens we have long accepted that we have a right to participate in decisions by government at the national, State or local levels. We take it for granted that we have a right to vote or stand for parliament, to speak freely, to form political organisations, and if necessary to protest and to contact our representatives.

While we understand that we have rights to participate in government decision-making, we have heard very few claims that we should have a similar right to participate in workplace decision-making. Very little public debate has taken place in our newspapers and other media regarding the extension of democratic principles to industry.[1]

In contrast to this absence of public comment, voluminous industrial relations literature has demonstrated that schemes of industrial democracy have significant benefits for employers and employees. Participation at work gives employees the opportunity to promote their interests and enhance their personal development (Finkin 1994, p. 31; Bill Kelty in Davis & Lansbury 1996, p. 15). Schemes of employee representation have also been shown to promote both productivity and efficiency (Finkin 1994, p. 32; Rogers & Streeck 1994, p. 106).

Australian employees and employers do not currently enjoy the benefits of representative consultation at work. Until recently, employee representation has been seen as the domain of unions, but with the decline in union membership,[2] union representation of employees interests has correspondingly declined. Increasingly, day-to-day, workplace-specific decisions are being left to be dominated by employers and managers.[3]

Empirical studies of workplace relations indicate that the level of joint decision-making in Australia is poor, even though case studies have shown that there are benefits flowing from employee participation schemes (Morehead et al. 1997; ACIR-RT 1994; Department of Employment, Education and Training 1995; Mitchell, Naughton & Sorensen 1997).[4] It is evident that there exists a serious gap in employee representation in workplace-specific negotiations and corporate decision-making. This is a very substantial lacuna in employee representation in Australia.

The aim of this chapter is to present the case for a new form of representative consultation in the Australian workplace. It will also argue that the extension of democratic decision-making to smaller organisations such as the workplace is necessary to create a participatory democratic society.

My examination of the potential of participatory democracy and representative consultation in the Australian workplace will be developed in three parts. The first part describes a participatory theory of democracy; the next part presents a practical example of workplace democracy, drawing on European experience; and the third part considers the possibilities of adopting a similar scheme of industrial democracy in Australia. Finally, I suggest that the European experience may provide a guide for legislative reform in the future.

The participatory theory of democracy[5]

Participation is crucial to the preservation and enhancement of a democratic society. Participation in democratic decision-making provides a means of enhancing the personal development of each individual (Lively 1975, pp. 131–2). It is only through the institutions of popular democratic government that a public-spirited and community-minded character can be fostered (Pateman 1970, pp. 29, 31; Mill 1975, p. 145).

The rationale of participatory theorists is not to ensure that the government will act in the general interest, but to emphasise the educative effect of participation. In referring to 'educative effect', theorists allude to the breadth of vision or largeness of view achieved through the practice of democracy itself (Lively 1975, p. 140; Pateman 1970, p. 31). When private individuals are involved in public functions, they are required to weigh interests not their own and to be guided by the common good. Where the school of public spirit does not exist, private persons do not owe duties other than to obey the law and to submit to the government (Mill 1975, pp. 197–8).

Given the rationale of participatory democracy, it follows that the whole people should participate in government to the greatest practicable extent. In reality, however, all cannot participate personally in most of the public business, so it follows that the 'ideal' type of good government must be representative (Mill 1975, p. 179).[6] One of the crucial problems with representative government, however, is to keep the representatives accountable to the many. Reconciling the rule of the people with accountability has been described as the 'grand difficulty in politics' (Hamburger, cited in Pateman 1970, p. 32). For a participatory theorist such as Carole Pateman, this difficulty may primarily be reconciled by maximising the number of opportunities for individuals 'to participate in political decisions so that they may develop the necessary qualities and capacities to enable them to assess the activities of representatives and hold them accountable' (Pateman 1970, p. 31).

To reiterate, participatory theorists point to the crucial link between participation and representative democracy: accountability is achieved through large-scale participation of the people in political decision-making. Three arguments can be advanced for increased participation in politics:

1. Voting and discussion are of significant educational value for all citizens. Through such participation, citizens become aware of the relationship between their circumstances and those of other citizens. Such awareness promotes community-minded citizenship (Mill 1975, pp. 272–94).

2. Citizen involvement with social justice issues and in small-scale organisations promotes the educative function of democracy (Lively 1975, pp. 140–1). The larger the scale of the organisation, the more difficult it is to make available the forms of participation necessary to the educative or personal-development function of democracy (Lively 1975, p. 141). Thus it is desirable to embrace the 'democratisation and politicisation of small-scale associations in which individuals can play a significant role' (Lively 1975, p. 141). Initially theorists identified local government (Mill 1975, chap. 15) and the jury system (Mill 1975, pp. 363–80) as channels for increasing citizen involvement in political decision-making, but later theorists have focused on the workplace as a significant locale of participation (Lively 1975, p. 143). In fact, the workplace may be considered as a site of democracy in itself. Social democratic theorists have tended to argue, not for state ownership, but rather for worker ownership and/or control: that is, worker self-management, worker cooperatives or democratic decision-making at work (see Mathews 1999; Hutton 1998; Pateman 1970, pp. 22–44; Mill 1963; Cole 1921).

3. Feminist theorists have argued that, if women are to experience the educative function of participatory democracy, it is necessary to remedy their current exclusion from political life (Pateman 1983; Phillips 1991). The focus is less on the means of participation, and more on the preconditions for participation. This has led to critiques of the practices that give rise to unequal representation of women in parliament and in the workplace.

In sum, what makes the participatory model[7] most significant is its emphasis on workplace democracy and personal development (Lively 1975, p. 143).[8] Because personal development takes place through participation in democratic decision-making, I now consider a legislative scheme of employee participation as an illustration of a rudimentary model of industrial democracy, drawing on the experience of the European Union.

A practical model of workplace democracy

The European Works Councils Directive provides a pertinent case study of an effective contemporary employee representation scheme.[9] The following section provides an outline of the directive, comments on its application, and explains its economic and democratic significance.

Outline

The European Union (EU) introduced its European Works Councils Directive (EWCD) to establish a European Works Council (EWC) or an alternative procedure for informing and consulting employees in community-scale undertakings or groups (European Works Council 1994: arts 1(1),(2)).[10] The aims of the directive are to foster and improve workers' fundamental social rights to information, consultation and participation. The EWCD has been designed to promote dialogue between management and labour and to harmonise the transnationalisation of undertakings where the functioning of the internal European market involves a process of concentrations of undertakings, cross-border mergers, takeovers and joint ventures (European Works Council 1994, recitals, art. 1(1)).

The EWCD (1994) is a form of law that applies to all member states (except Britain). States were required to implement its provisions by 22 September 1996 (European Works Council 1994, art. 14; Bellace 1997, pp. 349–50). In 1997 the directive was extended to Britain, which must implement it by 15 December 1999 (European Works Council 1997, art. 4; Barnard 1999, pp. 14–15).

The directive applies to all enterprises that employ more than 1000 people within member states of the European Union and European Economic Area, including at least 150 employees in each of two or more member states (European Works Council 1994: art. 2). The directive now extends to eighteen states (European Works Council 1994, art. 5(2)(b); 1997, art. 2).[11] Obviously the directive applies to very large enterprises, multinational or transnational corporations.[12]

The directive adopts a two-stage approach (Barnard 1999, p. 15). The first stage was designed to encourage voluntary negotiations (European Works Council 1994, art. 5; Barnard 1999, p. 15), permitting companies to create EWCs, to fashion alternative methods of satisfying the requirements of the directive, or to allow existing works councils to continue to operate (European Works Council 1994, arts 6, 12, 13; Bellace 1997, p. 351). The purpose of the second stage was to impose mandatory requirements on companies to comply with the directive. To this end, the directive requires that where no agreement can be reached between employers and employees, the 'subsidiary' provisions spelt out in the annex of the directive are to be applied (European Works Council 1994, art. 7; Barnard 1999, p. 15). The annex consists of a number of rather modest and minimal conditions regarding the composition and operating methods of EWCs (Barnard 1999, p. 15). These conditions include the following:

1. EWCs shall have between three and 30 members (European Works Council 1994, annex 1(c));[13]

2. EWCs shall have the right to meet with central management at least once per year and to consider a report drawn up by central management (European Works Council 1994, annex 2);

3. EWC meetings 'shall relate in particular to the structure, economic and financial situation, the probable development of the business and of production and sales, the situation and probable trend of employment, investments, and substantial changes concerning organization, introduction of new working methods or production processes, transfers of production, mergers, cut-backs or closures of undertakings, establishments or important parts thereof, and collective redundancies' (European Works Council 1994, annex 2);

4. EWCs are entitled to be informed and consulted where there are 'exceptional circumstances affecting the employees' interests to a considerable extent, particularly in the event of relocations, the closure of establishments or undertakings or collective redundancies' (European Works Council 1994, annex 3); and

5. The costs of operating EWCs shall be borne by central management (European Works Council 1994, annex 7; see also Barnard 1999, pp. 14–15).

The directive also imposes an obligation on central management and the European Works Council to work in a spirit of cooperation, both in relation to the operation of the EWC in general and with regard to the framework of the information and consultation procedure for employees (European Works Council 1994, art. 9).

For companies, choosing the location of central management is quite important, since significant matters under the directive are left to be stipulated by national legislation (Muller-Jentsch 1995). These matters include:

- whether representatives are elected or appointed;
- the EWCs' 'ability to engage in industrial action';
- the EWCs' 'ability to engage in wage bargaining, and the form of protection of wages and conditions of employees' representatives (European Works Council 1994, art. 10);
- the means of safeguarding confidential commercial information (European Works Council 1994, art. 8); and
- the minimum requirements of employer 'consultation with EWCs and the remedies available if employers fail to consult adequately with EWCs' (Bellace 1997, p. 357; European Works Council 1994, art. 9).

The application of the directive

While most member states had incorporated the directive into their national law by September 1996, a critical question is whether the works councils are operational (Flynn 1999). Padraig Flynn, the European Commissioner with responsibility for Employment and Social Affairs, has highlighted the success of the EWCD (Flynn 1999). Flynn stated that by April 1999 almost 600 corporations had established EWCs by means of company agreements. These agreements cover one-third of all undertakings (and about 40 per cent of employees) that fall within the scope of the directive (Conference on the Practical Application of the European Works Council Directive 1999). Given the directive's impact on larger companies and undertakings, the commission's focus has now shifted to small and medium-sized multinational companies, which need more time to conduct negotiations to achieve a result that accommodates their special features and needs (Flynn 1999).

Economic significance

Globalisation

The adoption of the directive is regarded as a vital and positive response to the economic effects of globalisation. The directive is based on the principle that employers and employees should take the lead in modernising the workplace and the workforce. The EWCD's representative consultative arrangements represent a non-protectionist response to intensified international competition, seeking to enhance the performance of transnational firms through improved cooperation between employees and management, and permitting continuous restructuring of the production process (Streeck 1995, p. 346 fn 20).

Padraig Flynn, in discussing the EWCD, drew two conclusions from recent European experience regarding the process of restructuring:

> *[First,] that constant industrial change and corporate restructuring is an inevitable part of remaining competitive in the world. The second is that, if this constant industrial change and corporate restructuring is to meet its objective — if it is to be a positive factor in our competitiveness — then it needs to engage the workforce, as an integral and as a formal part of that process.* (Flynn 1999)

Flynn maintained that if the workforce is not engaged, is not consulted in a formal way, it will create 'at worst, a culture of conflict, at best a culture of cynicism. To nurture globally productive companies and workforces, we must aspire to quite the opposite effect. We need to create a culture of anticipation, to actively engage the workforce in the process of change' (Flynn 1999).

The EWCD seeks to create a new and positive balance between flexibility and security. According to Flynn, the message is clear:

> *Mechanisms for proper worker involvement can increase the flexibility of the business environment in which firms operate. And*

they can offer workers a sense of confidence that they will not emerge as the losers in the restructuring process and that they have a stake in the future of that business. (Flynn 1999)

Flexibility[14]

Conventional debates about increased flexibility concern adaptable working hours and removal of restrictive work practices. However, flexibility as a term of art refers not only to availability and mobility of labour but also to the adaptability of management decision-making and production processes. The EWCD's promotion of flexible workplaces draws on the experiences of existing works councils in EU countries, including France, Germany, Italy, Spain, Sweden and the Netherlands.[15] These contemporary European Works Councils are a product of the structural economic change that has occurred in the last half of the twentieth century to the processes of production.

In the 1950s and 1960s there was a rapid growth in Fordist-Taylorist mass production. Decision-making was typically centralised and considerations of economic efficiency were considered to be a matter of technological expertise. Consultation with employees was passive, and was seen as a means of enhancing the information available to top management and preparing the workforce for the implementation of managerial decisions. Democratic participation or representation of interests was perceived as beyond the reach and competence of this process.

The process of consultation in conjunction with production began to change in the 1970s, with the shift from mass production to flexible production. Decision-making was decentralised and major production decisions were made, not by management or technological experts, but by workers as part of their routine work tasks. This was necessary because the frequency and speed of decision-making had increased dramatically. This change in work practices fundamentally altered the prevailing dynamic of productive cooperation and obviously required a new form of commitment by individual employees. It was recognised that deep technical and managerial knowledge could only be gained through continuous consultation or co-determination. As a result, consultation and co-determination 'between workers and management on how to increase efficiency becomes impossible to keep apart from negotiations on the mutual accommodation of interests' and views on productivity (Streeck 1995, pp. 331–2).

Therefore in continental Europe there developed a new system of workplace participation through collective bodies at the level of the enterprise or plant as well as directly on the job. The growth of works councils in European industrial relations systems in the 1970s and 1980s accomplished the joining of consultation and representation.

Efficiency

Although it is hard to make quantitative assessments of how representative consultation through works councils has contributed to economic efficiency (Rogers & Streeck 1995), participation in such bodies is thought to promote economic efficiency because it is generally believed to have positive effects on work effort and productivity.

One commentator recently summarised the number of ways in which representative consultation contributes to economic performance (Streeck 1995, pp. 344–5):

- Representative consultation is useful to firms that try to move to a flexible and decentralised organisation of work and decision-making.

- Works councils, or council-like structures, improve the flow of communication and information from the workforce to management and vice versa.

- Especially in Holland and Germany, it appears that councils improve the quality of decisions, though sometimes delaying them.

- Representative consultation facilitates the implementation of decisions.

- Participation helps firms handle worker grievances, not least by encouraging workers to come forward and speak up without fear of retribution.

- Participation provides feedback on its middle management to the top of the organisation.

Councils have been found to place pressure on firms to rationalise their human resource policies, adopt long-term strategies, and emphasise the creation and retention of high and broad skills. In this respect, works councils have been a major source of organisational innovation (especially evident in the German case of co-determination).

Democratic significance

Given the recent introduction of the EWCD, it is too early to tell if it will have a democratising effect on transnational corporations in EU countries. This is because there are no formal requirements for the domestic legislation implementing the directive to insist upon democratically elected representatives or effective enforcement of consultative mechanisms. The annex to the EWCD merely contains rather minimal requirements for consultation. The appointment or election of representatives and the remedies available if employers fail to consult adequately with EWCs depend upon national legislation.[16]

By contrast, works councils established by national legislation in EU countries are necessarily democratic institutions. These national works councils link the idea of representation with consultation. For instance, under Germany's *Works Councils Act*, consultation has been transformed into co-determination of industrial issues between works councils and management. The open nomination and elections of representatives introduces a form of democratic politics into the firm.

Towards a scheme of industrial democracy for Australia

The EWCD and works councils legislation in EU countries (such as the *Works Councils Act* in Germany) provide realistic, workable and functional legislative models of representative consultation for Australia. Nevertheless, as with any overseas model, it will be necessary to adapt them to fit in with Australia's industrial system. This task will require careful consideration and widespread consultation.[17]

Fortunately, some views about this subject have already been expressed, while others are predictable. I now consider a variety of responses to such a proposal by the major Australian political parties, unions and employers.

Employers and unions

It is likely that unions and employers will express an ambivalent attitude to any legislative employee representation scheme, since any particular proposed model will throw up many pros and cons. Various models will therefore enjoy support or encounter opposition from the key parties.

Some unions may embrace the introduction of a legislative scheme as a positive measure but also see that it has dangers. Other unions may apprehend only dangers and oppose such a scheme.

Unions may perceive a legislative scheme as dangerous if it poses a threat to their existence. Under such a scheme employers might try to exclude union-based collective bargaining by introducing new mechanisms of workplace participation that they are able to control.

On the other hand, representative consultation may be seen by unions as a positive measure in an otherwise hostile industrial relations environment. For the union movement, the status quo is no longer an option. Union membership is continuing to decline and has already dropped to its 1912 level. New and innovative measures such as works councils hold out the prospect of increasing union membership and rejuvenating the union movement.

Works councils would have the effect of providing unions with a legally guaranteed basis for workplace organisation that is highly visible at the enterprise level.[18] Having union members participate in works councils would aid the establishment and maintenance of an articulated union movement. Unions could still maintain a central coordinating role at the sectoral level, and works councils and collective bargaining could meet the needs of members in individual enterprises. Accordingly, the Evatt Foundation in its *Union 2001* publication recently proposed a system of works councils for Australia. And in *Unions@Work*, an ACTU report, it was recommended that the ACTU should initiate debate about the merits of works councils which are underpinned by industrial law.

Employers' responses to proposals for employee representation schemes will be different from the unions'. Some employers will support schemes of employee representation but express reservations about limitations on managerial decision-making. Others will resist any such limitations and will oppose a legislative scheme.

Some employers would regard a legislative scheme as an unjustified erosion of management prerogatives, and will especially resist such a scheme if it is union-based.

Other employers, however, will support representative consultation per se as a positive measure. Some might acknowledge that the current practices of unilateral management and passive forms of consultation are simply unable to provide for optimal and sufficiently flexible economic decisions. Representational consultation might take the edge out of the exercise of the management prerogative, but it is a plausible and probably necessary response to globalisation and structural economic change. Representational bodies also generate significant economic benefits.

Given these potential responses, it is possible to draw a number of conclusions. Obviously, a proposal that is not directly hostile to either unions or employers is most likely to succeed. Schemes that are neither union-based nor designed to exclude participation by union members are likely to be most acceptable to unions and employers. Where both employers and employees are likely to perceive possible benefits in a legislative works council scheme, this tends to weaken resistance to legislative action, especially as the widespread benefits are not likely to be passed on to all groups unless legislation is forthcoming.

Political parties

The possibility of legislative reform will depend manifestly upon the policies of the mainstream political parties. These policies express a range of views on this topic. The Australian Democrats' and Greens' policy statements are the most explicit in terms of promoting democratic workplaces. The Democrats state that, as a matter of principle, the party will support 'industrial democracy and the maximisation of employee representation' (Australian Democrats 1998). They have also expressed support for maximising cooperation between management and labour and encouraging employee share ownership.[19]

The Greens' policy includes as one of its goals the development of flexible and democratic workplace patterns and structures. As a short-term target, the party is committed to encouraging employee-owned or -managed businesses, or businesses with significant employee ownership or control, and to supporting processes for the participation of women in enterprises (Australian Green Party 1999).

The Liberal Party until recently opposed legal intervention, but its platform at the last election stated that it would support '(by further legislation, if necessary) the formation of enterprise unions, the disamalgamation of super unions and the creation of formal or informal workplace consultation structures' (Liberal Party 1999). In this context, it appears that the Liberals view such schemes as acting as union substitutes.[20]

By contrast, the Labor Party's current policy is the least developed. In government (1983–96), Labor adopted a voluntarist approach which involved employers choosing a participatory form of decision-making for their own workplace (Australian Government Publishing Service 1986). However, in its most recent policy statement, in which it endorsed the process of collective bargaining, Labor recognised a need for workers to 'have access to appropriate information from which to come to informed decisions' (Australian Labor Party 1999). Apart from this, nothing else is mentioned about employee participation schemes.

Conclusion

The present political climate, far from being hostile, may well be conducive to the adoption of a legislative scheme of representative consultation. The Democrats and Greens currently support proposals for industrial democracy. The Liberal Party's recent change of policy, whatever its motives, represents a very significant change of direction. Since the Labor Party adopted its voluntary approach in the 1980s, the industrial relations environment has changed significantly in Australia and globally. Given the ALP's review of policy, it would seem an appropriate time to reconsider the adoption of a legislatively mandated scheme. The Evatt Foundation's proposal and the ACTU's recent report *Unions@Work* are also significant.

The fact that the EU has acted on the belief that legislative intervention is necessary provides a persuasive political precedent for the adoption of legislative measures here in Australia. While the adoption of a legislative scheme of employee representation has remained a sleeping issue in Australian politics, if nothing else, the EWCD ought to provide us with a wake-up call.

(Special thanks must be given to Professor Richard Mitchell and to Jenny Lee, who read earlier drafts of the paper and made helpful comments. I also wish to thank Paul Liondas, Tom Clarke, Cath Button and Joe McCarthy, who read material onto tape and provided research assistance. I am also grateful to the Australian Research Council for a small grant to undertake research on this project. Any errors are my own.)

chapter 7

Equality and inequality in Australia
by Rosemary Hunter

As we approach the twenty-first century, equality and inequality are in the news in Australia. Equality issues are being hotly contested in public debates, such as those over the introduction of a goods and services tax, the content of a new preamble to the Australian Constitution, cuts to legal aid, and government policies concerning industrial relations, Aboriginal and Torres Strait Islander people and multiculturalism. What national understandings of equality do we hold, and why has equality become such a contested issue at this juncture in Australian history? This chapter addresses these questions by looking in detail at some of the current controversies over equality in a historical, philosophical and political context.

A short history of equality in Australia

In 1901, the people of New South Wales, Victoria, South Australia, Queensland and Tasmania 'agreed to unite in one indissoluble Federal Commonwealth' under a new constitution. The Australian Constitution that came into force on 1 January 1901 said a lot about the machinery of government — the houses of parliament and their powers, the executive government, the judiciary, the relationship between the new federal level of government and the States — and also included a lengthy chapter on finance and trade within the

Commonwealth. But it said very little — either descriptive or aspirational — about the machinery of Australian society. Unlike the American Constitution, for example, it did not include a Bill of Rights which defined the protections that citizens enjoyed against the power of the state (Charlesworth 1993). And it did not include any grand statements about relationships between citizens, or about how the state might protect its citizens. It was a very pragmatic, late nineteenth-century document, primarily concerned with abstract political entities (the States and the Commonwealth) rather than with the people to be governed by them. In this context, it is not surprising that the only overt reference to equality in the Constitution was section 117, which sought to ensure that States would not discriminate against residents of other States.

Of course, the late nineteenth and early twentieth centuries were not devoid of public debates about equality. The question of women's right to vote was a live topic at that time, and was inevitably linked with the question of voting on and under the new Constitution. In the federation referenda that occurred in the late 1890s, women in South Australia and Western Australia were able to vote, but women in Victoria, New South Wales, Tasmania and Queensland were not, since those colonies had not yet granted the vote to women. One issue before the first Commonwealth Parliament was that of establishing who had the right to vote in subsequent Commonwealth elections. It was eventually decided that all white women would henceforth be able to vote in Commonwealth elections, whether or not they could vote in State elections. But Aboriginal and Torres Strait Islander people were not permitted to vote in Commonwealth elections unless they had been granted the right to vote by the State or territory in which they lived. In Queensland and Western Australia, Aboriginal and Torres Strait Islander people were not able to vote in Commonwealth or State elections until 1962 (Oldfield 1992, pp. 59–66).

Two other early pieces of legislation passed by the Commonwealth Parliament were the *Immigration Restriction Act 1901*, and the *Conciliation and Arbitration Act 1904*. The *Conciliation and Arbitration Act* established a new system for dealing with major (interstate) industrial disputes, in the wake of the enormous disruption and misery caused by the Great

Strikes of the 1890s. Amongst other things, the Act gave trade unions a recognised role in industrial bargaining, on the basis that trade union representation was necessary for workers, to put them on a more equal footing with employers. Fair and reasonable relations between trade unions and employers or employer organisations were intended to replace the raw and potentially exploitative power relations between employers and individual workers (Higgins 1915; Hawke 1956; Frazer 1987; Macintyre & Mitchell 1989). Conversely, the *Immigration Restriction Act* entrenched inequality between desirable (white, generally Anglo-Saxon) and undesirable (particularly Asian) immigrants to Australia. It did not do so directly, in the manner of earlier colonial legislation restricting Chinese immigration; rather, it gave immigration officers discretion and flexibility to exclude any potential immigrant considered undesirable. It was clear, however, who were the main targets of the legislation, which for the following decades formed the underpinning of the 'White Australia policy' (Yarwood 1964; Willard 1978; Markus 1979; York 1995).

As these examples illustrate, public debates regarding the appropriate subjects of equality in various fields, and how equality should be achieved, occurred outside the framework of the Australian Constitution. The Constitution shaped the direction of the debates in a fairly limited way, by distributing legislative powers in relation to particular groups and activities between federal and State parliaments — for example, the Commonwealth could make laws concerning immigration (section 51(27)) but could not make laws for members of 'the Aboriginal race in any State' (section 51(26)) (Attwood & Markus 1997). But the Constitution did not itself provide answers to social questions about equality. Australia remains one of the few countries in the world without fundamental equality guarantees included in its constitution, and debates about equality in Australia continue to occur at the political level, outside a constitutional setting. Opinions vary considerably as to whether this is a good or a bad thing (Constitutional Commission 1988; Wilcox 1993, pp. 255–7; Morgan 1994; ALRC 1994, pp. 61–2), but it does help to explain why equality issues in Australia take the form they do. They tend to arise in the context of particular policy debates rather than in a more general way, they may not even be identified as being about 'equality' and what that might mean, and they are often resolved by means of political compromise rather than by reference to abstract principles. The closest we have come to discussing principles, or basic values, was in the debate over the proposed new constitutional preamble, which demonstrated how much difficulty we have with such an exercise.

Despite their absence from the Constitution, some identifiable basic principles informed the development of the Commonwealth of Australia: a racially homogenous society, with Asians and Pacific Islanders excluded, 'full-blood' Aborigines dying out, and 'half-castes' assimilated into white society; tariff-protected industries providing workers with a living wage; and a commitment to social egalitarianism. The welfare system that burgeoned in subsequent decades was designed to ensure that those economically disadvantaged would be adequately provided for (Watts 1987). These values have all undergone fundamental reassessment, with immigration and indigenous policies beginning to change in the 1970s, and economic and welfare policies following in the 1980s and '90s. These changes are a large part of the reason we are now experiencing a new round of equality debates, as we come to terms with a diverse, multicultural society and a globalised economy. The political solutions to these debates will have significant consequences into the twenty-first century.

The GST

The Federal Government's proposal to introduce a goods and services tax was based on the view that Australia's revenue base needed to be broadened and taxation system 'updated', to reflect and support Australia's position within the international economy. Previously, the taxation system relied heavily upon income tax, combined with a range of somewhat ad hoc sales taxes and other indirect taxes. Income tax minimisation and avoidance schemes reduced the revenue that would otherwise be available to governments for redistribution. High marginal tax rates for middle- to high-income earners also, arguably, created a disincentive to hard work, since the returns to the individual from increased earnings became smaller and smaller. A goods and services tax, together with cuts in income taxes, would provide a more secure and less avoidable source of government revenue, remove earnings-related disincentives, and make the Australian economy more internationally competitive.

On the other hand, Australia's progressive income tax system was specifically designed to generate revenue from those who could most afford to pay, and to protect those on low incomes (Krever 1991). Hence we have incremental tax brackets rather than a flat rate of income tax for everyone. The GST will be levied at a flat rate, regardless of ability to pay. In other words it is a regressive tax, having a greater relative impact on those who can least afford it. Moreover, those on very low incomes, or pensions or social security payments, will not benefit from cuts in income tax rates. They will simply be worse off. One counterargument here is that because those who are wealthier indulge in more discretionary spending on 'luxury' items, they will still pay more tax. This may well be true, but does not remove the fact that some items of expenditure are not discretionary (food, clothing, housing, amenities), and to the extent that those who are not well off spend a far greater proportion of their resources on these non-discretionary elements, they are both worse off *and* have fewer choices as to whether they spend and pay tax at all. Moreover, the gap between rich and poor in Australia is already widening, as the effects of economic globalisation — including the loss of a great deal of industrial and rural employment — are felt. Should the economically vulnerable be further disadvantaged for the sake of economic efficiency?

The GST debate is not a simple matter of 'equality' versus 'inequality', however. One definition of 'equality' in this context is to tax everyone at the same rate. This is so-called 'formal equality' — treating everybody the same, regardless of their individual circumstances. Formal equality has the great advantage of simplicity (decision-making is easy, and everyone knows where they stand), and the great disadvantage of unfairness. It is difficult to think of non-trivial situations in which formal equality is considered appropriate. We don't charge everybody the same fares on public transport: we have concessions for elderly pensioners, social security recipients and students. We don't try children charged with criminal offences in adult courts or incarcerate them in adult prisons. Even when it comes to voting, we don't expect everyone to go to a polling booth and cast their vote in the same way: we make special arrangements for people with disabilities, people unable to read English, people whose religious observance prevents them from voting on a Saturday, and people living in remote areas. Few would quibble with the need to take different circumstances into account in these instances. In the voting and public transport examples, equal *access* to the particular good can only be secured by different *treatment* — by providing something extra to those disadvantaged or, to use an unpopular term, by means of affirmative action.

Another definition of equality, then, involves taking different circumstances into account. This is sometimes referred to as 'substantive equality' or simply social or economic 'equity', and is the kind of equality that tends to be favoured by social democrats. Substantive equality is achieved if people (or more usually groups of people) come out of a process more or less equally, even if they went in unequal. The process reduces inequalities by improving (rather than leaving unchanged or exacerbating) the position of the initially worse-off. A progressive taxation system is designed to achieve substantive equality. People are taxed according to their capacity to pay, thus reducing the after-tax gap between rich and poor.

Debate over the GST, including arguments for compensation and exemptions, is hence a debate over what kind of equality we want in our taxation system — substantive or formal. The political compromise reached, to exempt food items from the GST, represents a shift away from formal towards substantive equality, and this indeed was one of the goals of the Australian Democrats in their negotiations with the government (although the extent of the shift remains to be seen in practice). The outcome of the tax debate does not provide us with a definitive, theoretical answer to the equality question, however. The vagaries of balances of power could lead to a different result next time. Nevertheless, it will have far-reaching material consequences for the distribution of wealth in Australia.

Indigenous policy and the response to Wik

The Coalition Government's policies on indigenous people, and particularly the amendments it proposed to the *Native Title Act* following the High Court's decision in *Wik Peoples v. Queensland*, raised even more complex issues of equality, involving the intersection of arguments about formal versus substantive equality with arguments about who should have the right to decide such questions.

In a different context — that of immigration and multi-culturalism — Ghassan Hage has written about the point of view shared by white racists and white multiculturalists: the assumption that they have the power to define the nation — whether as racially exclusive or as multicultural. In other words, they see themselves as 'we', the authoritative people of Australia, who have the right to determine how many of 'them' 'we' want (Hage 1998). A similar authority has traditionally been assumed in indigenous affairs, with 'us' whites assuming the right to decide what should happen to 'them' blacks. During the period of the Hawke and Keating Labor governments, however, government policies relating to indigenous people took at least some steps towards 'self-management' for indigenous people (Hand 1987), involving indigenous control over indigenous policy, including the possibility that indigenous priorities might differ from those of white Australians. Land rights, the recognition of traditional laws, protection of cultural heritage, and remedying the consequences of dispossession, as manifested in Aboriginal deaths in custody and the stolen generations, emerged as significant themes in this policy phase (ALRC 1986; Royal Commission into Aboriginal Deaths in Custody 1991; HREOC 1997), reflecting concerns that were in many respects unique to indigenous people, and that defined equality in terms of equal respect for separate histories, cultures and laws.

The Coalition Government appeared to reject self-management, and sought to shift the focus of indigenous policy back towards the old ideal of 'integration', that is, the provision of specifically targeted substantive measures to bring indigenous people into a position of equality with white Australians, according to mainstream social indicators such as health, housing, education and employment (including small business participation). This involved a reassertion that 'we' rather than 'they' knew best what was good for 'them'. Land rights and apologies were redefined as misguided pursuits.

The rise of the One Nation Party placed pressure even on this limited commitment to white-defined substantive equality for indigenous people. Pauline Hanson and her followers expressed deep resistance to the recognition and accommodation of indigenous (and ethnic) difference, and opposed *all* special measures taken to alleviate indigenous disadvantage. One Nation advocated formal equality in its purest and starkest form — everyone should be treated the same, regardless of race or history. Moreover, that same treatment should be based on the needs and interests of the white majority. Again, the resentments tapped by One Nation arose from the processes of economic restructuring, resulting in rural economic decline, and social change resulting in a more diverse population. Those who were used to being in control — of their futures and of national definitions — felt a deep sense of frustration and disempowerment. It was easier to scapegoat minorities than to locate blame in an impersonal economic system.

These policy positions provided the framework for the debate over the Wik case and its implementation in the *Native Title Act*. The High Court in Wik held that native title continued to exist (at least theoretically) over pastoral leases. In order to determine the content of native title, and hence the practical meaning of this decision, it was necessary to refer to traditional laws, and hence to consult with indigenous people. The Wik decision thus raised the twin fears of indigenous 'privilege' (on the One Nation side) and loss of control of land management by 'us' (on the integrationist side). The government's proposed amendments to the *Native Title Act* sought to 'redress the balance' (read: regain control, and minimise white resentment), by reducing the rights and entitlements of indigenous people under the common law. Significantly, in contrast to what occurred prior to the original enactment of the *Native Title Act* by the Keating Government, indigenous people were marginalised by the Coalition Government in the consultation process on the terms of the amendments, and their views were largely ignored. The political compromise brokered, on this occasion with Senator Brian Harradine, was another accident of history with far-reaching consequences.

The Prime Minister's refusal to offer an apology to the stolen generation is a further assertion of 'our' right to decide what is important. Within the integrationist mainstream, too, some special programs for indigenous people, such as Abstudy, have been dismantled in favour of the same treatment for all students needing financial assistance, regardless of the particular educational disadvantages experienced by indigenous people. Not only has 'equal respect for difference' been abandoned, but 'substantive equality' has been watered down. In the absence of constitutional protection, minorities that wield neither electoral nor economic power are particularly vulnerable to adverse policy shifts. In this situation, there is often a turning away by minorities from political lobbying towards litigation strategies in order to attempt to secure more just outcomes — for example the Mabo case (against the Bjelke-Petersen Government in Queensland), and current legal claims for compensation by stolen children. Litigants at least enjoy 'equality before the law' — they cannot be ignored or discredited simply because of who they are and how little power they have. Unfortunately, however, legal doctrine, having been developed by and for 'us', is not always equal to the task.

The preamble debate

The possibility of Australia becoming a republic has raised general questions about national identity and self-definition, and about the relevance of a constitution drawn up in the 1890s. The Constitutional Convention held in early 1998 focused largely on the question of how the head of state should be chosen if there were to be a republic, but it also, inevitably, traversed a range of more general issues, including a process for ongoing constitutional review, the Australian flag and coat of arms, and the preamble to the Constitution. The convention resolved that there should be a new preamble to the Constitution, which should contain a list of elements, including (among other things) acknowledgment of the original occupancy and custodianship of Australia by Aboriginal peoples and Torres Strait Islanders, and recognition of Australia's cultural diversity. The convention also listed matters that should be *considered* for inclusion in the preamble, including affirmation of the equality of all people before the law, recognition of gender equality, and recognition that Aboriginal people and Torres Strait Islanders have continuing rights by virtue of their status as Australia's indigenous peoples. The convention further made it clear that the proposed preamble should be seen as a statement of values or principles but should not have legal force. That is, no one should be able to make any claims on the basis of its contents, and nor should it influence the interpretation of other sections of the Constitution (Constitutional Convention 1998).

It is interesting to note that the overt references to equality in the list of items produced by the Constitutional Convention were consigned to the 'second division' — that is, those merely offered for consideration rather than agreed as essential for inclusion. It is difficult to believe that equality before the law was considered a controversial issue. Perhaps it was only included on the supplementary list because it was considered so taken for granted that it was unnecessary to spell it out in a preamble. Recognition of gender equality is a more ambivalent case. On the one hand, it may also be considered so obvious as to need no statement. On the other hand, it may be considered provocative in making the uncomfortable suggestion that gender equality does not in fact exist, and that something more may need to be done about it. Or alternatively, the majority of delegates to the Constitutional Convention may simply have lacked any commitment to gender equality. Whatever the reason, it is somewhat disturbing that the convention was unable to name gender equality as a core value or basic principle of Australian society. The distinction between recognition of indigenous 'original occupation and custodianship' in the 'first division' and recognition of continuing indigenous *rights* in the 'second division' is also noteworthy, and reflects the different — and currently dominant — definitions of 'equality' for indigenous people discussed in the previous section.

Following the Constitutional Convention, the Constitutional

Centenary Foundation embarked on public consultations on the desired content of a new preamble, via its Preamble Quest. Members of the public were invited to comment on the Constitutional Convention's recommendations regarding the preamble, and to draft their own preamble if they wished. The quest received 383 responses, expressing a wide range of views on what should be included in a new preamble. Amongst these views, four issues stood out as having clear majority support. These included acknowledgment of the unique contribution of the indigenous peoples to Australia, and 'a reference to equality, as a value which Australians overwhelmingly share' (Constitutional Centenary Foundation 1999, 'General Observations'). In both respects it appears that respondents to the Preamble Quest (who may or may not be representative of all Australians) were ahead of the Constitutional Convention delegates in being prepared to declare their commitments to indigenous difference, and to equality as a basic value.

The question begged in relation to equality, of course, is exactly what kind of equality should be referred to? Perhaps, given the largely symbolic nature of the preamble, lack of precision on this matter is not important, especially if, as determined by the Constitutional Convention, the preamble will not have any practical impact on the interpretation of the Constitution. A statement that Australians believe in and value equality is therefore sufficiently broad to encompass many different understandings of equality, and particular policy issues raising the question of equality would continue to be determined as they always have been — by a process of public debate and political compromise. On the other hand, a purely symbolic statement which is capable of multiple interpretations runs the risk of being ultimately meaningless.

The majority of respondents to the Preamble Quest also supported the inclusion of references to indigenous rights and gender equality in the preamble, although these issues attracted smaller majorities than those supporting references to the unique contribution of indigenous peoples and equality in general. Again, these positions go further than the Constitutional Convention delegates were prepared to travel, although the difference between the two levels also exactly reflects the convention's 'first division' and 'second division' concerns.

The preamble that was ultimately included in the Bill to alter the Constitution, however, was not directly based on either the recommendations of the Constitutional Convention or the results of the Preamble Quest. The first draft put out for public discussion was personally devised by the Prime Minister, in consultation with various advisers, including the historian Geoffrey Blainey and the poet Les Murray. Contrary to the recommendations and suggestions of the Constitutional Convention and the Preamble Quest, it did not include any reference to equality before the law or gender equality, nor to indigenous rights, or even indigenous prior custodianship. It did contain two statements on equality more generally: that 'the Commonwealth of Australia is constituted by the equal sovereignty of all its citizens', and that the aim of Australia's system of government is 'to preserve and protect all Australians in ... equal dignity'. While these concepts of equality were somewhat obscure, they did appear to encompass both something like formal civic equality (all Australians having the right to vote and to stand for and hold public office) *and*, in the term 'equal dignity', something like substantive equality or equal respect for difference. Preserving and protecting the equal dignity of all Australians might, for example, require a progressive taxation system, or a fair and power-balanced industrial relations system based on collective rather than individualised bargaining, or apologies for past genocidal policies and full recognition of native title rights.

Public reaction to the Prime Minister's draft preamble was generally unfavourable. While there was much disagreement as to both its content and form, the major political objections that emerged related to its assertion of 'mateship' as a core Australian value (which positively denied gender equality), and its failure to acknowledge indigenous custodianship. Another political compromise brokered with the Australian Democrats resulted in the removal of 'mateship', and insertion of a reference to Aboriginal and Torres Strait Islander peoples' 'deep kinship with their lands'. At the same time, the previous references to equality were also removed, and replaced with the statement that the Australian people are 'supportive of achievement as well as equality of opportunity for all'.

'Equality of opportunity' is an ambiguous concept, which may be taken to require merely equal treatment for everyone, or something much closer to substantive equality, depending on what kinds of opportunities are in question (the opportunity to apply for a job for which one is qualified? the opportunity to lead a fulfilling life?) (Thornton 1990, pp. 17–20; O'Donovan & Szyszczak 1988, pp. 3–6; Eisenstein 1981). It may therefore meet the need for a broad definition of equality to which many people can comfortably adhere. In the context of its juxtaposition with 'achievement', however, it appears to refer to the removal of formal barriers (such as those based on race, ethnicity or gender), in order to enable people to compete on their merits. Hence, equality of opportunity for all results in achievement for some (i.e. those who possess the greatest merit). Within this scheme there is little room to question how merit may have been acquired (through economic or social privilege, for example), or whether everyone in fact wishes to take part in the same competition. But just as significant as the final form of words regarding equality in the proposed preamble was the casual way in which varying formulations were tried and discarded. The process indicates both the lack of consensus on any particular understanding of equality, and the relative unimportance of getting the abstract concept of equality 'right' in our statement of national principles, as opposed to more immediate issues of how particular groups should be included (or at least, not excluded!).

Conclusion

By the time this book is published, a referendum will have been held to decide whether the suggested preamble will be incorporated into the Constitution. If it has, it will be interesting to see whether and how its commitment to equality of opportunity will be invoked and relied upon. Certainly, it will be specified that the preamble may not be used to interpret the other provisions of the Constitution. But equally certainly it will be raised in other contexts — political, legislative and judicial. Will it change the nature of public debates over equality issues in Australia? My prediction is that we will continue to avoid abstract theoretical arguments about the meaning of equality and continue to hammer out pragmatic, compromise solutions to particular political issues, which will affect the lives of different members of 'the Australian people' in unequal ways.

A looming danger is that international trade agreements, which bind sovereign states to particular economic and policy positions, will prevent us from doing even that. Just as commercial imperatives at the end of the nineteenth century led the Australian colonies to federate into a single Commonwealth, so similar imperatives at the end of the twentieth century are leading to supranational trade groupings such as Closer Economic Relations between Australia and New Zealand, the North American Free Trade Agreement and the European Union. The European Union is unique among these in developing an extensive social program alongside its commercial interests, and this is a model that could usefully be adopted by other groupings. It is inevitable that new global configurations will have extensive social impacts, determining new local patterns of equality and inequality. The way we choose, or are able, to respond to these developments will test any national commitment to the value of equality.

chapter 8

Redistribution and risk in the Australian welfare state
by Anthony O'Donnell

The welfare state has had its share of detractors for three decades now. The left has thought it not egalitarian enough, the right that it has been too egalitarian and bad for business. This, then, was 'the crisis' of the welfare state, 1970s-style: that in trying to please everyone, it ended up pleasing no one. Yet by the 1980s the problem was seen not so much as an excess of demands on the state as a withdrawal of support for policies promoting social solidarity. This involved the so-called 'tax revolts' that put Thatcher and Reagan into government, and saw Bob Hawke promise, in the lead-up to the 1984 election, to raise neither taxes nor government spending as a share of national income. The US right reinforced pessimism about the redistributionist agenda by arguing that welfare states have not only failed to help the poor but in fact have made them poorer (see, for example, Murray 1984).

This welfare pessimism has since infected the policies of Blair and Clinton, the kind of centrist opportunists who pass for the left nowadays, who use it to justify a search for a 'third way' and for spruiking 'the end of welfare as we know it'. Australian Federal Labor MP Mark Latham includes in his exploration of 'new thinking for Australian Labor' a tirade against the inadequacies of the social democratic welfare state. In language reminiscent of Margaret Thatcher, he rails against 'welfare dependency' and 'social democracy's embrace of a centralised, over-administered, nanny state', without bothering to examine any of the empirical studies that tell us what welfare states actually do (Latham 1998, p. 254). All this is a far cry from the glory days of the postwar Keynesian settlement, when the welfare state was the jewel in the social democrat crown and British Labour MP Anthony Crosland crowed that successive governments — including Conservative governments — were unlikely to dismantle the welfare state. 'The national shift to the left', he wrote in 1956, 'may be accepted as permanent' (Crosland 1956).

I want to argue that to a large extent this welfare pessimism is misplaced, its logic flawed. The redistribution effected by the welfare state to tackle poverty remains one of the great achievements of social democratic politics. This is not to say that the welfare state does not face some very real economic, social and political challenges. But to a large extent these challenges need to be met within the terms of a redistributive agenda, not through the abandoning of it. The welfare state retains a limited but vitally necessary role to play in securing well being.

What welfare states do: the story so far

First, however, it is worth examining the role that the welfare state plays in the distribution of income. At the beginning of the 1980s, Australia recorded a poverty rate of 11 per cent, falling to 9.5 per cent in 1989–90. Recent Australian Bureau of Statistics (ABS) figures show this has remained relatively stable, with a rate around 10 per cent in 1996.[1] By international standards, Australia's record of poverty alleviation appears good, particularly when we consider the countervailing forces of increased unemployment, rising wage inequality and an ageing population. Furthermore, Anthony King discusses the 'depth' of poverty or how far people's incomes fall below a poverty line (in his example, the Henderson poverty line) and draws the favourable conclusion that 'The overwhelming majority of income units below the poverty line are clearly in the income range closest to the poverty line and increasingly so' (King 1998, p. 79). As well as indicating a rise in the living standards of the poor, this also means people's chances of escaping poverty are greater, making persistent deprivation less likely.

Despite the relative stability of the poverty rate, changes in the composition of the poor are apparent. People of working age now constitute a major group amongst the poor population. The rise in the poverty rate of households headed by people of working age can probably best be explained by the dramatic increase in unemployment over the past twenty years. There seems little evidence of an increase in the number of households with a head in full-time employment who are in poverty: the figure has stayed fairly constant at around 2 per cent (Gregory & Sheehan 1998). This is partly due to our institutional commitment to modest but regular increases in the minimum wage, which serves — unlike in the United States and Britain — to make employment a buffer against poverty. How long such a situation will last is unknown, given John Howard's ominous pronouncements in 1997 that Australia's 'cultural' commitment to such a safety net is supposedly inhibiting a return to full employment.

Importantly, though, Australia's containment of poverty is also due to our social security system. That is, over the course of the 1980s and early 1990s, government benefits substantially improved the income of the bottom 20 per cent of households, with sole parent benefits, family payments and rent assistance all substantially boosted in real terms. This means, in effect, that despite the increasing inequality of wage income — including the decline in real wages for the bottom 30 per cent of full-time male workers, and a fairly steady proportion of unemployed with no wage income — government benefits worked to contain inequality in disposable income (that is, income retained after paying tax and receiving any government benefits), and to keep the disposable income of the poorest at a steady level (Harding 1997). This represents, depending on your perspective, either a major achievement in difficult times, in contrast to the United States or Britain, where disposable income inequality rose markedly, or else slim pickings for thirteen years of a supposed social democratic government that ended up giving with one hand and then, thanks to its deregulatory spasms, taking away with the other.

What welfare states do not do

I do not want to sound overly boosterish about the operation of the Australian welfare state, because 10 per cent living below an austere poverty line is hardly acceptable, especially to the extent that this figure indicates persistent deprivation rather than short-term low income, and particularly when the amount of government money required to lift them above it would not be all that great in the scheme of things. But my discussion does show that as a redistributive tool, a properly designed welfare state is capable of working as advertised, through what is, at essence, a 'Robin Hood' strategy of taking money from well-off households and giving it to poor households, taking money from households with no children and giving it to households with children, and taking money from working-age households and giving it to aged households.[2]

Although the welfare state clearly can play a significant role in ameliorating inequality and improving the living standards of the poor,[3] the predominant welfare pessimism sidesteps this insight in favour of cultivating two influential arguments. One is fairly new: economic globalisation and the imperative of international competitiveness limit the scope for domestic measures of social protection. The other is quite old, but has recurred spasmodically over the last 400 years: the dangers of welfare 'dependency' and the moral hazards of the welfare state. Let's look briefly at each in turn.

First, there appears to be no consistent meaningful relationship between welfare state spending, economic growth, productivity and gross domestic product (GDP) per capita (Pfaller, Gough & Therborn 1991). In fact, there is some evidence that an economy's increasing insertion into world trade and capital flows is linked to greater, not less, welfare spending (Garrett & Mitchell 1995).[4] This suggests that the sustenance or, conversely, the gutting of the welfare state is a political choice, not an economic fait accompli.

Second, let's be clear about what we mean by 'dependency'. Obviously, some forms of economic dependence are seen as normal or even positive: wage labour, family relationships, rents, investments, even age pensions (McIntosh 1998, p. 5). Today, many people have moved from being dependent on spouses or parents to looking for work themselves, while drawing a welfare benefit in the process. Or they have found work while their spouses or parents have lost theirs. Or they have been able to set up independent households, supported by government benefits. All this indicates not an unprecedented rise in forms of economic dependency, but a shift from intra-family or private dependency to social dependency. Over the past twenty years, the share of Australians in work has remained relatively constant and it is this group which continues to support the rest, just as it did before the rise in 'welfare' dependency (Freeland 1993).

In any case, we are only talking about economic dependency. The fact that many 'working' men display a singular inability to cook, wash or iron clothes and to generally attend to the practical and emotional organisation of households suggests that, in terms of day-to-day functioning, many men are actually dependent on women. If we are concerned about scroungers and layabouts, perhaps it is to this group of freeloaders that we should be directing our attention.

The problem is that welfare dependency, as opposed to other forms of dependency, has emerged as a kind of 'post-industrial pathology' par excellence (Fraser & Gordon 1994). Overall, the social welfare system seems to discomfit people by bringing to light dependency — or, more precisely, inter-dependency — as an inescapable aspect of the human condition. How we organise the forms of this interdependency is a matter for continued discussion; it cannot be willed away by tough talk of moral rearmament.

New inequalities: some real challenges for the welfare state

It is difficult to find any evidence of welfare 'pathologies' beyond the anecdotal or the tabloid moral panic. Yet the constant reiteration from both sides of the political spectrum of the failures of the welfare state does work to undermine the postwar consensus around the state's capacity for redistribution and the provision of welfare services. I would argue that this creates the real political risk that the state will only provide minimal or precarious welfare to those who need it most. This political hazard now joins emerging economic and social hazards posed by the new economy.[5]

The economic hazard arises from a radically restructured labour market. As well as the risks posed by the rise in unemployment and part-time work, men and women are more likely today to see their hold on a job as precarious. This is partly because, with a growing number of casual and short-term jobs, many workers do lack security of tenure. In total, a quarter of the Australian workforce is employed casually, in both full-time and part-time positions, a dramatic rise from around 17 per cent only ten years ago, and again very high by world standards. Most jobs described as casual carry few of the benefits, including training and career prospects, that attach to more tenured positions. Similarly, the pool of unemployed serves as a reminder to workers of the possibility of retrenchment, and if the future of employment lies in part-time and casual jobs, then retrenchment carries the very real risk of failing to find a new job as good as the last (Froud et al. 1997, p. 366). John Burgess and Iain Campbell have used wider measures of 'precariousness', looking at uncertainty of job duration or span of hours, irregular or inadequate income, lack of standard benefits, and unprotected status, to conclude that, due to current labour-market practices, over half of the jobs in Australia are precarious in one or other respect (Burgess & Campbell 1998, p. 15).

A substantial number of low-wage, intermittent and precarious workers live in high-income families. This means that in couple households, household wellbeing is becoming less a function of the work status and occupational standing of a male breadwinner than it had been under the old postwar order. Instead, it is now linked to having multiple earners within a household, one preferably in secure or at least skilled employment in a growing white-collar or 'non-smokestack' sector, with a partner in full-time or part-time employment at various stages over the life cycle, and perhaps some other household members in employment (Pahl 1988, p. 253). In effect, the amount of employment within a household is an important determinant of the place of a household in the distribution of income. Over a ten-year period to 1994 there has been increased workforce participation in high-income households, but the bottom 40 per cent of households have seen declining rates of workforce participation (Dawkins 1996, p. 281). 'Work-rich' households — provided at least one of the earners is a full-time worker — enjoy increased income, a lesser risk of poverty, access to home purchase and further education (see Saunders 1998). The tail end of the income distribution, however, shows a remarkably different pattern and while the number of dual-earner households has increased, so has the number of no-earner households. In fact, in world terms Australia has a very high level of worklessness among households, at nearly 14 per cent of households with a head of workforce age. When children are taken into account, the situation is bleaker, with 18 per cent of couple and sole parent families with dependent children being worker-less in 1997 (ABS 1999). We are seeing what David Goldblatt refers to as the 'scission of economic growth and the good life', the realisation that economic growth no longer translates into generalised affluence, and even for those for whom the nexus between growth and affluence is maintained, this does not translate into security or wellbeing, overlaid as such affluence is with a general sense of precariousness (Goldblatt 1997).

These figures also point to a further social hazard that compounds economic and political risk: if appropriate combinations of earnings and forms of work 'pooling' within households are the key to getting ahead in the new labour market, then the break-up or dissolution of households and families is a pretty sure way to fall behind — this at a time when family relations, like work relations, are becoming increasingly contingent and serial (Froud et al. 1997, p. 365). Not only has the number of single-person households risen, but over one-third of marriages ends in separation, mostly leaving women to care for children. While women's part-time work contributes positively to the standard of living in many couple households, and works to decrease inequality substantially between households, it leaves them financially vulnerable on break-up. As part-time and often low-wage workers, or without recent labour-market experience, on divorce they are likely to fall into poverty (Shaver 1998, p. 284).

Future directions

One policy prescription that attempts to surmount the political risk I outlined earlier is to ask the welfare state simply to do more of the same: that is, to use income transfers to compensate or 'top up' the incomes of those bearing the brunt of the new economic hazards. In other words, if trends in work and householding are generating increasing levels of market inequality, as I have suggested, then the welfare state just has to pedal faster and harder to undo this inequality. But this ignores the fact that, in John Myles's words, once the genie of wage inequality is let out of the bottle, it is very difficult to put it back again (Myles 1997, p. 39).[6]

Put another way, we need to recognise that the context in which the Australian welfare state operates has changed. Our welfare state was always seen as leaner and meaner than its Western European counterparts, but our social security system operated in conjunction with a commitment to full employment, centralised wage-fixing, award coverage and widespread home ownership, amounting to what was, by world standards, a surprisingly comprehensive system of social protection. However, as Professor Ronald Henderson discovered in the early 1970s, it was a system of protection which managed to exclude the usual suspects: Aborigines, newly arrived migrants, the aged, single mothers, all those who could not rely on the market or intra-family transfers, anyone who was not — or was not able to attach themselves to — an able-bodied pale male. In the two decades following Henderson's Commission of Inquiry into Poverty, which reported in 1975, the welfare system was substantially upgraded, with regard to coverage, the removal of some, but not all, of the moralism that informed certain eligibility rules, and substantially improved benefit levels, tested against more rigorous notions of need and adequacy. Over the same period, alas, those other pillars of the postwar social settlement — a buoyant labour market and centralised wage-fixing, the nuclear family, latterly home ownership — have all, for better or worse, taken a battering.

In this new context welfare is being asked not to work as a supplement to other forms of social protection but as a substitute. In fact, the main argument made to justify wage 'top-up' proposals is that labour-market deregulation — and particularly a fall in the real minimum wage — is necessary to reduce unemployment by pricing the low-skilled unemployed back into the market. The use of some form of welfare payment or 'guaranteed minimum' to offset the rise in working poverty that would result from falling wages has received renewed attention recently in the Australian context (see, for example, Dawkins (1996)) but is not a particularly new idea. John Myles traces it to Milton Friedman's work of the early 1960s, and low-wage top-ups in the form of earned income tax credits have operated in the United States since 1975 (Myles 1997). In fact, the idea goes back further: late-eighteenth-century Poor Laws were mobilised to similar purpose under the 'Speemhamland System' in Britain. Historians Eric Hobsbawm and George Rudé summed up the experience as:

> [A]n emergency measure ... designed to hold off mass unrest, but which had the advantage of doing so without raising the market rate of wages ... the traditional social order degenerated into a universal pauperism of demoralised men who could not fall below the relief scale whatever they did, who could not rise above it, who had not even the nominal guarantee of a living income since the 'scale' could be ... reduced to as little as the village thought fit for a labourer ... farmers were encouraged to pay as little as they could (since wages would be supplemented by the parish) and used the mass of pauper labour as an excuse for not raising their productivity. (Hobsbawm & Rudé 1969, pp. 50–1)

I am not against the provision of 'in-work' benefits, such as our current system of family payments. The old dichotomy that underpinned our welfare state, that a person was either in full-time work or out of work and hence on welfare, is clearly no longer sustainable. People are following increasingly diverse trajectories as they negotiate transitions between education or training and employment; domestic work, especially parenthood, or private activities and paid employment; part-time work and full-time work; unemployment and employment; and full-time work and retirement (Schmid 1995). The social security system needs to support these transitions rather than impose transaction costs on those who negotiate them, such as waiting periods for benefits, stringent means and assets tests and inadequate payment levels. Nevertheless, a problem with a US-style tax credit scheme for those in low-paid work is that non-working adults — including those who, for various reasons, cannot work — are not helped at all in the immediate term, merely told that new job opportunities will arise in the future as a low-wage labour market blooms.

In fact, government transfers under such schemes end up acting as a de facto subsidy to employers, absolving them of any responsibility to maintain a 'living wage' (and allowing them to compete solely on the basis of real wage-cutting, a dubious strategy). And, if there is little or no mobility between the growing pool of low-wage jobs thereby created and better paid employment, the risk is that such a policy will create a fairly permanently marginalised claimant class. An important element of redistribution should first be effected through labour market measures such as setting and maintaining a floor of minimum standards for wages and job security (Deakin & Wilkinson 1991). And if pundits are genuinely concerned with the poverty traps and 'making work pay', then there is no better incentive to work than a high minimum wage.[7]

The role that remains for welfare in the context of a comprehensive floor of labour market rights is, first, to meet a range of specific costs, such as those to do with raising children or coping with chronic illness or disability and, second, to finance people's withdrawal from the labour market for specific purposes, whether for caring for children or other relatives, training and education, or periods of transitional unemployment. There is no reason for these life cycle transitions to be occasions for poverty.

As well as increasing the value of payments so that they are adequate to meet needs (for a start, payment for the long-term unemployed could be increased to pension levels and indexed in the same way), there is a need to construct a more seamless form of income support as people move in increasingly individualised and volatile patterns between unpaid work, part-time work and full-time work. Administratively, it requires the reduction of benefit waiting periods, the liberalisation of assets and incomes tests, a more imaginative and flexible approach to the activity test, and so on, allowing for easy transitions as well as combinations of part-employment and part-benefit receipt at different times in a person's life cycle. For example, under the Keating Labor Government, an earnings credit scheme for benefit recipients allowed income from employment in one payment period to be offset against credits attained during payment periods when the recipient undertook no paid work. Similarly, determining eligibility for benefit through the use of an income test based on a period longer than a fortnight — say, six or twelve months — would focus on medium-term stability of income, rather than penalising those who endure weekly or fortnightly fluctuations of income from paid work.

Culturally, it calls for a reconceptualising of work, and hence arguing for a more equitable distribution of that work, in particular an equitable reduction of paid working time and the recognition and support of currently unpaid work.[8] The idea of any 'guaranteed minimum income' needs to be understood not in terms of locking people into low-paid jobs in a deregulated labour market, but in terms of people gaining access to their desired mix of paid and unpaid work across their life cycle, with an adequate income secured against fluctuations. The recognition of different forms of social participation and activity — full-time or part-time paid employment (or availability for paid employment), caring for children or dependent adults, community work, sustaining neo-traditional forms of land use, education and training — widens the concept of citizenship to recognise the value of different contributions through the life course.[9]

Reasons to be cheerful?

There are perhaps few reasons to be cheerful about the prospects of maintaining a redistributive welfare state in Australia, or for its extension along the lines I have just outlined. Current Coalition Government initiatives are running in the opposite direction. These include, on the one hand, tighter income-testing for young adults, tighter asset-testing that requires beneficiaries to run down their savings, less opportunity to combine benefits with market earnings, extended waiting periods for immigrants, increased surveillance regarding the work test. The principal aim seems to be to cut costs to government incurred by increased social dependency, by reinforcing both market dependency and private dependency. On the other hand, the new tax package means lower-income and middle-income earners will pay a higher share of Australia's tax, while upper-middle-income earners will pay less, a prospect John Howard describes as 'political pleasure of the most exotic kind'. Squeezed from both ends, the very idea of a progressive tax-transfer system seems a thing of the past.[10]

In this context, it is perhaps little wonder that progressives feel tempted to 'move on' from the old social democratic agenda. Much of what parades as 'new thinking' about welfare from the left does contain valuable ideas about the role of training and education, social investment, the provision of in-work benefits, and so on. Yet it also tends, I think, to overstress the integrative function of paid work (ignoring the perils of either precarious employment or long and unsocial hours of work) and to underplay the importance of unpaid work. And politically, these new ideas are more often than not used to displace rather than supplement basic redistributive methods that ease the immediate poverty and aid the day-to-day functioning of the least well off.

Again, rebuilding an ethic of collective provision and reciprocal relations does seem a hard task in a world where personal autonomy realised through the consumption of ever-increasing numbers of commodities has been elevated to the level of cultural quest. Transformations of the deep structures of social and personal life, brought about by communications and biotechnologies that dis-embed us from the constraints of time, place and even bodies, might explain why welfare policies based around 'market' and 'contract' models resonate more than any call for a new ethic of social solidarity.

Seen in this light, the defence of redistribution and the instigation of a genuine safety net that is both adequate and flexible appears a particularly mundane task. It may, in fact, not prove a sufficient response to wider concerns, but it remains a vitally necessary step. It is necessary for giving us the collective security and hence the room to manoeuvre, the social spaces that might allow for new ways of being and the development of truly radical initiatives and politics.

chapter 9

A tale of two cities: urban transport, pollution and equality
by Paul Mees

When Don Dunstan died early in 1999, tributes flowed from all sides of politics and many corners of public life. Dunstan was lauded for reform in areas as diverse as urban conservation and gay rights, not to mention marvellously memorable gestures like his public defiance, at the end of Glenelg Jetty, of a so-called psychic's prediction that Adelaide would be engulfed by a tidal wave.

But the obituaries were strangely silent on the issue that, more than any other, brought South Australian Labor to power in 1970, inaugurating the 'Dunstan decade'. According to Leonie Sandercock (1975, p. 134), Labor won office largely on the strength of public anger over the 1968 Metropolitan Adelaide Transportation Study (MATS) report, a massive US-style freeway plan prepared by American consultants. The Dunstan Government's urban transport policies were the most radical in Australian history: the freeway network was scrapped, the rail system was extended, private bus operators were banished and services upgraded. Adelaide was the first Australian city to have a multi-modal ticketing system, with free transfers between different modes of public transport (a measure that, three decades later, residents of Sydney and Brisbane are still waiting for); it was the only Australian city where public transport patronage increased during the 1970s, both absolutely and on a per capita basis. Adelaide is the only Australian city without an urban freeway, and has had the slowest rate of growth in car usage since the 1970s.

Dunstan's policies provided a model for those of the Whitlam Government, which withdrew federal support for contentious inner-city freeways, and commenced funding urban public transport. Dunstan and Whitlam recognised that urban transport is a critical issue for social democrats because of its centrality to any attempt to improve access and equity for urban Australians.

A quarter of a century after Don Dunstan's famous election victory, there was a change of government in another Australian State in which public concern over freeway building played a major part. But this time, in Queensland in 1995, it was a Labor administration that lost office, with the National Party the unlikely beneficiary of a green backlash over the Goss Government's proposed tollway between Brisbane and the Gold Coast. One of the defeated MPs, who was also the environment minister, was quoted in the *Australian* of 17 July as saying: 'The Government had looked for an alternative to the tollway, but all the figures on estimated future traffic showed it was the responsible decision to make.'

The transport professionals told the Queensland Government that there was simply no alternative to the proposed road, in exactly the same way that the US consultants had told Don Dunstan that there was no alternative to a freeway network in Adelaide. In both cases, the experts were wrong, since neither freeway proposal eventuated, but the world did not come to an end. But across Australia (with the partial exception of Adelaide), transport planning continues to be based on the freeway networks designed in the 1960s, and continues to be justified using the analytical techniques used to develop those plans. Meanwhile, the share of travel made by public transport, on foot or by bicycle continues to decline, despite substantial capital investment programs. And increasingly it is green parties and — at least until their 1999 GST backdown — the Democrats who are seen as the advocates of 'green' transport policies of the kind Dunstan and Whitlam made Labor famous for.

Why are current Labor governments more prepared to

swallow the 'expert' advice of road engineers than Don Dunstan was? What happened to the urban transport vision that seemed so much a part of Labor's success in the 1970s? And can urban transport regain its former place as a key element of a reformist social democratic platform?

Why urban transport is important

Transport in Australian cities is, to a greater extent even than in the 1970s, dominated by the car. Mass motorisation has brought advantages, including increased mobility for those with access to cars, particularly in rural and remote areas. Most of us are attracted by the freedom of the 'open road', but when large numbers of people want to drive cars in confined areas like cities, freedom of movement may be diminished, rather than enhanced. In the 1960s, concern was directed to 'urban efficiency' issues like traffic congestion and parking problems, but the 1970s saw new concerns emerge, from depletion of oil reserves to social justice for the car-less. In the two decades since, these problems have become more, not less, acute, especially in the environmental area.

Environmental problems

Transport is implicated in a range of urban environmental problems. Emissions from cars, buses and trucks are the major source of health-damaging urban air pollution, now that environmental regulation and improved technology have reduced contributions from traditional sources like industry and home heating. Motor vehicles emit lead (which causes brain damage), benzene (a proven carcinogen), photochemical smog and particulates (which cause a host of human health problems). Some pollutants, such as lead, are being reduced through improved technology, but others continue to increase. In addition to local pollutants, motor vehicles contribute to the greenhouse effect: transport is the second-largest source of greenhouse gases in Australia (after electricity generation), but the fastest-growing (NGGIC 1996, pp. 16, 17, 22).

Technological change may ameliorate some of the problems, but the scope for doing so may have been overstated. For example, the average fuel efficiency of the Australian passenger vehicle fleet was 11.4 litres per 100 kilometres at the time of the Australian Bureau of Statistics' first Survey of Motor Vehicle Usage in 1963. By 1995, the figure had actually increased marginally, to 11.5, as more fuel-efficient engines were offset by ageing of the car fleet, larger vehicles (e.g. four-wheel drives) and increased use of accessories such as air conditioning. Meanwhile, the volume of travel by motor vehicles in urban areas had quadrupled. Improved technology is a necessary, but not sufficient, condition for making urban travel more environmentally sustainable: something must also be done about demand.

Equity issues

Social equity problems caused by transport have not gone away either. And equity would remain an issue even in the unlikely event that a non-polluting car could be invented. The car has increased mobility for those who can avail themselves of it, but the car-dominated city is actually less accessible for those without private vehicles. Land-use patterns are arranged to suit the automobile, with dispersed activities (fewer, and larger, shops, schools, hospitals, etc.) and wide roads and large car parks, which make walking impractical and cycling positively dangerous. Meanwhile, public transport is generally of such poor quality that, for most trips, it might as well not exist. Only eight bus routes in the whole of Melbourne operate at all on Sunday evenings, with none serving the area east of Warrigal Road, home to more than a million residents.

Analysts tend to underestimate the number of people affected. The cars-to-persons ratio in Australian cities is about 0.5, meaning that up to half the population are without cars at least some of the time. As well as the old, the poor and the disabled, the young tend to be car-less. And one consequence of this is the increasing conscription of adults, particularly women, as unpaid chauffeurs. It has recently become fashionable in some quarters to argue that the car is the ideal transport mode for women because of their greater propensity than men to make short local trips. But much of this local travel is made simply to ferry another person to a destination: the number of trips of this type grew from 9 per cent of all trips in 1964 to 18 per cent in 1994. It is not clear that this is really a matter of liberation for women at all.

There is also some evidence that the lack of alternatives is forcing many families of modest means, particularly in outer suburbs, to buy more cars than they can really afford (this is one reason for the high, and increasing, age of Australia's car fleet). Many of these households are headed by women. The poorest municipality in Sydney, Wyong, had in 1991 an average household income of $27 619, compared with Mosman's $58 621. But car ownership in Wyong was actually higher, at 1.27 vehicles per household to Mosman's 1.23, and public transport was used for only 4.4 per cent of non-work trips, compared with 14.6 per cent in Mosman (Battellino 1997, p. 233). It is hard to avoid the conclusion that the main reason for this pattern is that public transport in Mosman is of much higher quality than in Wyong.

This perverse situation is one reason for the apparent popularity of freeways among residents of outer urban areas. This popularity is frequently used as a rationalisation by State Labor politicians for policies which focus on roads to the virtual exclusion of other options like public transport (thus guaranteeing the perpetuation of the trend). But it should not come as a surprise that outer-urban residents presented with the alternatives of a new freeway or nothing will opt for the freeway. Not since Dunstan's time have outer-urban residents been presented with a real choice.

Transport and economic efficiency

Environmental and equity concerns are reason enough for social democrats to care about urban transport policy, but traditionally these have been allied to concerns about efficiency. Unfortunately, it is usually at this point that policy consistency comes unstuck. There are many reports which claim that traffic congestion imposes enormous financial costs on the community: for example, a study of 'transport externalities' by the Victorian Environment Protection Authority estimated the annual cost of traffic congestion in Melbourne to be $2031 million, compared with $86 million for road noise and $45 million for illness and deaths due to cancers caused by vehicle emissions (EPA 1994, pp.10–16). The corollary is that new roads, by reducing congestion, can confer similarly dramatic financial benefits.

Where do these figures come from? Their origin lies in

the 1950s, when road engineers sought a fair way of comparing different road schemes to see which deserved to be funded first. Notional travel time savings were estimated by multiplying the vehicle hours 'saved' by the new road by some hourly rate, and compared with the cost of the road to give a 'benefit–cost ratio'. The road with the highest ratio 'won'. Nobody pretended that the travel time savings really flowed through to the general economy: they were simply a device for comparing investment options. But soon less cautious engineers and economists began to claim that the travel time savings were real, and the road lobby eagerly supported these claims. Thus was launched the whole process of constructing completely bogus 'economic benefits' from road projects.

The problem is that when real-world evidence supporting these economic benefits is sought, it cannot be found. The Standing Advisory Committee on Trunk Road Assessment, the British Government's official advisory body on road schemes, reviewed the evidence and found no causal relation between investment in urban roads, or even traffic speeds, and economic growth (SACTRA 1998). Thus, road-rich Glasgow is outperformed economically by road-poor Edinburgh, just as traffic-choked Sydney wins investment ahead of Melbourne, where road conditions are much freer. One reason why this may be the case is the fact, verified in an earlier report by SACTRA (1994), that, as with any other product, improving roads generates more demand for them, reducing if not negating the supposed travel time and congestion benefits of the investment. But none of the road studies carried out in Australia, from the 1960s to the present day, has taken this 'induced traffic' into account.

The whole exercise is so intellectually dubious that Martin Mogridge, a leading British transport economist concludes that 'the cost of congestion is an invalid concept in an urban area' (Mogridge 1990, p. 281). Indeed, it is possible to have too little congestion, rather than too much — as the authors of Vancouver's 1993 transport strategy note:

> *Congestion is usually considered an evil; however, allowing congestion to deteriorate for single-occupant vehicles is a practical method of promoting transit and carpools. More congestion*

> *for single-occupant vehicles would magnify the impact of some travel demand management. For instance, buses/carpools in high occupancy vehicle lanes will gain an edge since the relative time saved by escaping lineups will be greater.* (GVRD 1993, p. 26)

No city in the world has completely eliminated congestion, so the issue here is how much is appropriate given the limited funds available, the partially self-defeating nature of new road-building, and environmental and equity imperatives.

And the show goes on

Although it is widely acknowledged that they have been intellectually discredited, the transport planning techniques developed in the 1950s, and the inappropriate extensions of cost–benefit analysis developed in the 1960s, are still the basis of road planning in every Australian city. And, with the partial exception of Adelaide, the original road plans developed using those techniques are the templates from which current transport proposals are drawn, although in some cases the names have been changed to protect the guilty. Thus, Brisbane's currently mooted City Valley Bypass is actually the Central Freeway from the 1965 Brisbane Transportation Study prepared by US consultants Wilbur Smith & Associates, while Sydney's M4 Motorway extension can be traced back to the County of Cumberland Main Roads Plan of 1947. Why is this so?

Melbourne as a case study

To answer this question, I will take Melbourne as a case study (an excellent outline of a similar history in Sydney is provided by Ball (1996)). Melbourne's grand freeway plan was released in 1969, after a six-year study in which the US firm Wilbur Smith & Associates had worked closely with a team of local engineers. Only three and a half years later, the freeway network was severely pruned by Premier Hamer just prior to the 1973 State election. Hamer had taken his cue from Dunstan and won the election easily. But Hamer's 1973 changes were an unhappy compromise between the road-driven logic of the 1969 plan and Dunstan's more radical approach, which moved away from freeways. The most controversial sections of the Melbourne freeway were simply dropped without any analysis of the likely effects, leaving a whole series of freeways ending apparently in the middle of nowhere, which have created problems to the present day. Hamer's press release stated that 'a greater emphasis on public transport' would fill the role of the deleted freeways, but this did not happen, for reasons outlined below.

In 1980, a new transport minister was directed by the Legislative Council to hold an inquiry into the proposed closure of a rural rail line. The Minister responded with an inquiry into all aspects of the Victorian land transport system and appointed a retired General Motors executive, W.M. Lonie, to conduct it. There was public protest at Lonie's perceived bias, but this diverted attention from the real author of the report, Robin Underwood, the chief planner of the Country Roads Board (predecessor to VicRoads), and one of the authors of the 1969 freeway plan. The Lonie report recommended sweeping cuts to public transport and the revival of most of the freeways cancelled in 1973.

The Lonie report was one factor behind the defeat of the Liberal Government in 1982. But the new Labor administration was, like Hamer after 1973, gradually worn down by the persistence of the bureaucratic road lobby, rising road traffic and public transport deficits, and the apparent absence of alternatives to new freeways. Labor's 1987 metropolitan plan, 'Shaping Melbourne's Future', simply incorporated the main freeway routes from the 1969 plan without any analysis at all. And in 1992, the Kirner Government called tenders for the construction and financing of a private sector road that Jeff Kennett, who inherited the project, called 'City Link'.

It used to be popular for social democrats to attribute the road-dominated nature of transport policy to a road lobby comprising car and oil companies, motorists' organisations, and so on. While this lobby certainly exists, it hardly needs to: the core of the road lobby is actually the corps of road planners employed by State and local governments. No conspiracy theory is needed to explain this road lobby's success. As the Melbourne example illustrates, it has a long-term plan, laid down in the 1960s, and has worked doggedly to pursue it.

Public transport in the doldrums

One reason for the continuing success of the road lobby is the apparent failure of alternative policies, particularly those designed to promote public transport. Substantial capital investments were made during the 1970s, largely thanks to funding inaugurated by the Whitlam Government, but, with the exception of Adelaide, without stemming the decline in patronage. In Melbourne, following Hamer's 1973 freeway policy shift, investment in new rail and tram rolling stock and construction of the city underground railway was accelerated. But patronage continued to fall, and deficits mounted.

Public transport's key weakness

The reason, as I have argued elsewhere (Mees 1999), is that the capital investment, while often needed, did not address the real weakness of Melbourne's public transport system: poor service quality and lack of integration, arising from a lack of overall planning. Historically, Melbourne's public transport was a mess of competing, uncoordinated operators and routes, with dozens of small private bus companies and two public corporations, Victorian Railways and the Melbourne and Metropolitan Tramways Board, that acted as if they were privately owned by competing against one another. The weaknesses of this model had been identified as early as the 1950s, by the city's planning authority, the Melbourne and Metropolitan Board of Works:

> *[I]n the inner suburbs where the population has been constant [over the last 15 years], railway bookings have declined by 26.5% ... the reason is not competition from private cars, but from trams ... there are about 100 routes operated by privately owned buses ... A few of the private buses run to and from the city, but in most cases they act as feeders to rail and tram services ... On account of infrequent service and poor co-ordination the saving in walking time by use of a feeder bus is largely offset by waiting time ... there are relatively few who can save much time by using these services.* (MMBW 1953, vol. 1, pp. 192, 184)

New rolling stock, and even new lines, could not address this fundamental problem. What was required was a planned integration and expansion of services to create a comprehensive network providing access across the whole city at a range of times. The fact that this would have worked can be confirmed by comparing Melbourne with similar cities which followed such an approach. It is precisely what was being provided in metropolitan Toronto at this time, as the Toronto Transit Commission took over private bus services and integrated them into its network, which was based around a new rail system expressly designed for easy transfer to and from trams and buses. Between 1950 and 1990, per capita public transport patronage in metropolitan Toronto actually increased, from 292 trips to 325 (GVRD 1993); Melbourne, which initially had much lower car ownership, started with a higher figure of 449 trips, but by 1990 this had plummeted to 97.

The difference between the two cities is not the result of differences in infrastructure: because Toronto started building urban railways a century later than Melbourne, its network is much smaller, and so is its tram system. Rather, the explanation lies in service differences, as can be seen the comparison of two typical suburban bus services in Table 1.

Table 1
Suburban bus service levels and patronage, 1991

	Melbourne	**Toronto**
Bus route (no.)	888/9	37
Suburb served	Springvale	Etobicoke
Length of route, excluding branches (km)	16	16
Distance from CBD (km)	17–23	13–23
Gross residential density of catchment (per hectare)	23	25
Average service frequency (minutes):		
peak period	20	4–5
off-peak (daytime)	20	7–8
evening	no service	10–12
Saturday morning	60	10
Saturday afternoon	120	10
Sunday	no service	12
Last bus on weeknights	6.06 p.m.	24-hour service
Weekly patronage	10 000	120 000
Weekly service (no. of departures)	400	2000

Source: see Mees (1999)

Integration: the path not taken

So why did this happen in Toronto, but not Melbourne? The Melbourne and Metropolitan Board of Works, which had recognised the problem in the 1950s, could not resolve it directly because, while it had responsibility for metropolitan roads at the time, it did not have control over public transport. The board suggested that a new organisational structure was needed, and that 'it should not be beyond the imagination of the appropriate authorities to devise suitable and adequate machinery' (MMBW 1953, vol. 2, p. 105).

History shows, however, that the task did prove beyond the imagination of those responsible. It was not until 1983 that a single authority was established to run public transport, and this body never even attempted to integrate the different modes of transport, let alone expand services to deprived outer suburbs. Nor, by and large, have authorities in other Australian cities. Perhaps the most extreme case is Brisbane, where decades of rivalry between Queensland Railways and the Brisbane City Council (which runs most bus services) is literally being set in concrete with the construction of a billion-dollar network of express bus-ways parallelling rail lines. Meanwhile, thanks to a lack of feeder services and the absence of fare integration, only 7 per cent of Brisbane rail passengers travel to the station by bus, compared with 76 per cent in Toronto (IRTP 1997; Mees 1999). The closest Australian equivalent to the service integration and expansion seen in Toronto (and other Canadian cities) was the Dunstan reforms in Adelaide in the 1970s, but even these were largely reversed in the following decades, as successive governments from both parties succumbed to helpful advice from 'economic rationalists'.

Why has the task of providing integrated public transport proven beyond the imaginations of those charged with it? Viewers of 'Yes, Minister' might have anticipated that public-transport bureaucrats would be as anxious to expand their 'turf' as their counterparts in the road sector. But in practice their attitude has been quite different. Managing and justifying decline have, for public transport planners, frequently proven more attractive — or perhaps less difficult — than overseeing expansion.

Thus, in Perth, the Fremantle rail line, closed under the Court Government, was reopened by the Burke Labor administration. Subsequently, the whole rail system was electrified and a new line built to the northern suburbs along a freeway median. Patronage has skyrocketed and cost-recovery is the highest for any urban rail system in Australia. But the policy was fought every step of the way by the public transport bureaucracy of the time (Newman 1991). The Industry Commission excoriated the northern suburbs line in its 1994 report on Urban Transport, while a Canberra-based study criticised the decision to reopen the Fremantle line, citing the view of unnamed bureaucrats:

Railway officials commented somewhat ruefully after this episode that the government should have waited a little longer, ended passenger and freight service simultaneously, and torn up the line so that restoration of passenger trains would have been impossible. (Stevenson 1987, p. 108)

Similarly, in Adelaide, the bureaucracy has retained a constant anti-rail bias, illustrated in a self-congratulatory review by the official principally responsible for public transport policy in South Australia for three decades. The paper, *On the Right Track*, chronicles 'reforms' to rail services consisting of deregulation, cuts and privatisation, including closure of the entire country rail passenger network. The author of the paper notes the closure of half-a-dozen rail lines in Adelaide, but adds a comment that illustrates the relentless bureaucratic pressure on governments:

Despite the analytical work undertaken by the Transport Policy Unit and other agencies, and the low level of patronage where the heavy rail network in essence carries but bus loads of passengers, the State Government remains committed to a continuation of the existing urban passenger rail services. At present there does not appear to be the same driving forces for change that has seen the major reforms in the non-urban network. (Scrafton & Skene 1998, p. 271)

A final illustration is the way the transport bureaucracy talked the incoming Victorian Labor government out of a Toronto-style expansion of suburban bus services, and their integration with rail. The bureaucracy's paper (Ministry of Transport 1982) 'proved' that providing an improved bus network would increase the public subsidy by 350 per cent.

urban transport, pollution and equality 153

This proof relied on the assumption that the 'elasticity of demand' was 0.5, meaning that a 100 per cent increase in service would only produce a 50 per cent increase in patronage, leading to a kind of law of diminishing returns. But, as explained in Mees (1996), this need not be the case if the additional services are added in a way that makes isolated routes into a high-quality network. That is why the Toronto bus service in Table 1 carries twelve times as many passengers as its Melbourne counterpart, while offering only five times as many services, giving an 'elasticity' of 2.4, not 0.5.

The passivity of the planners

Why does the public transport bureaucracy behave this way? The likely explanation is not malice, but lack of expertise. For historical reasons, public transport planners in Australian cities have had neither the qualifications nor the experience that would permit them to plan integrated, high-quality service networks. Lacking the necessary skills, they tend to fall into either the 'economic rationalist' mode of cuts and closures, or revert to the traditional engineer's recipe of new infrastructure and technology. Examples of the former have been illustrated above; an excellent example of the latter is the report on public transport prepared for the previous Federal Government's Urban and Regional Development Review (Glazebrook & Johnson 1995).

Another distracting influence has been an excessive focus on issues of urban form, particularly population density. Architects have directed contempt at the single-family home since Le Corbusier proposed his high-rise 'Radiant City' in the 1920s. Robin Boyd, influential author of *The Australian Ugliness*, excoriated the 'flat puritanical nothing-land' of suburbia, adding his name to a long list of Australian intellectuals who have expressed a 'generalised hostility' to suburbia (see Gilbert 1988). Urban planners have followed suit, and easily make the leap that explains car dominance and poor public transport as (yet another) outcome of the perverse refusal of most urban Australians to live in flats. This explanation has been taken up eagerly by both road and public-transport planners, since it offers the former a justification for continued road-building, and the latter an excuse for their failure to create public transport networks that attract passengers. But density is a rationalisation for car dominance, not an explanation: the densities of Australian cities are higher than their US counterparts and comparable to successful Canadian cities (Mees 1999).

Towards new policies

The '80s and '90s largely count as wasted decades in Australian urban transport policy, but there are positive signs. One is a growing realisation, particularly in places like Sydney and Brisbane, that it is not possible to solve urban traffic problems by simply building more roads. Another is a growing body of evidence, sadly almost entirely from overseas, that there are economically responsible, socially equitable and environmentally friendly alternatives to current urban transport policies.

The alternative to the traditional US-style approach is not some mythical notion of 'balanced transport', a popular catchcry of the 1960s that is often still heard. (The introduction to Melbourne's 1969 freeway plan proclaims 'balanced transport is our only hope'!) The approach of investing heavily in both public transport and road infrastructure is self-defeating: at best it leads to increased travel by all modes, at worst the road improvements draw patrons away from public transport, making the public-transport investment non-viable. It evades the notion that there is a fundamental conflict between catering for the car and building cities that are sustainable and equitable.

Rather, the time has come to adopt policies that give preference to less environmentally damaging forms of transport. This does not mean giving up cars; merely reducing their current near-complete dominance of urban travel. It does mean making some tough choices, including abandoning the fantasy that traffic congestion can be made to disappear in cities with millions of residents. A package of policies across a range of urban planning areas is needed to move cities in the right direction. The main ingredients would be:

- a high-quality, multi-modal public transport system, with an emphasis on comprehensive, integrated services providing 'go anywhere, anytime' convenience;

- management policies for car travel that provide an incentive to use alternative modes; and
- urban planning policies designed to reduce the need to travel and make it easier to travel by modes other than the car.

The direct responsibility for implementing these policies lies with State governments, but federal involvement is also critical. Currently, the federal influence on transport policy distorts outcomes in precisely the wrong direction: the National Highway system makes funds available for outer-suburban roads but not public transport; federal tax breaks for infrastructure projects encourage the construction of facilities that increase the demand for travel when we should be reducing it; national competition policy discourages the necessary transition to planned, integrated urban public transport; and federally funded research bodies such as the Productivity/Industry Commission and the National Road Transport Commission are core components of the road–public tansport competition cheer squad. Removing these distortions, making funding available for sustainable State transport strategies and sponsoring research that widens, rather than narrows, the transport debate are all important Commonwealth roles.

The adoption of a package of policies like these offers the opportunity to advance social equity by making the car an option, not a necessity, while at the same time contributing to ecological sustainability and more livable cities. Such a policy is likely to be fairer and more effective at reducing environmental damage than the 'road pricing' and other increased charges recommended by 'economic rationalists'. And surely that would be a worthy way of carrying on Don Dunstan's legacy.

Section III: Postmodernism and Identity Politics

chapter 10

Break-out from the giggle palace: social democracy, the postmodern economy and the prospects for political renewal

by Guy Rundle

Throughout the 1990s the first-world consensus was that the battle between the free market and socialism had been absolutely won by the former, and that even the most moderate forms of non-market economic organisation were discredited (Fukuyama 1992). The United States abolished the welfare state, throwing millions into utter poverty; in Britain the 'New' Labour opposition refashioned itself as a social-market party; in Germany the centre-right continued to dominate and to push European integration towards a minimalist fiscal program. A mood of confidence suffused the right, summed up by Fukuyama's now notorious 'end of history' thesis. Then, in 1996, the Thai economy collapsed, starting off a chain reaction which devastated all the debt-ridden economies of Asia, sparked off a default and devaluation in Russia, and a fiscal crisis in Brazil, and toppled a series of highly speculative US hedge funds, leading to fears of deflation in the United States and Europe in 1999 (Krugman 1997). The move reversed the ideological flow, and the free-market mantras of the early '90s began to be seen around the world — save for a few redoubts such as the *Economist* and the *Wall Street Journal* — as hollow jokes.

Simultaneously a major political transformation began occurring in Western Europe, with the new left-leaning governments of the Britain and France joined by Germany, and the election of a former communist to the premiership of Italy. Eleven of the thirteen EU governments are now dominated by social democratic parties, and they have not hesitated to use their new-found power to assert changes in the political order that the conservative regimes of the early '90s had been attempting to implement. The disarray of the global financial system has given them a great deal of tactical advantage, and made two key battles easier to win. In September, France scuttled the MAI treaty — which would have allowed a free flow of foreign direct investment to override local labour or environmental laws — and Germany's (now departed) Oskar Lafontaine mounted a campaign against the 'depoliticised' autonomy of the new European Central Bank, which manages the new 'euro' common currency. The French and German governments made no secret of the fact that they were attempting to roll in a wave of new social legislation guaranteeing a 35-hour week, and sundry other benefits, and even the Britain's centre-right New Labour introduced a host of new measures in its 'Fairness At Work' Bill. While everyone made noises about the need to give the market elbow room, the capacity of the government to intervene in order to correct its excesses was reaffirmed (Anderson & Mann 1997). The prospect for a reinvention of social democracy seemed bright, a reignition of the light on the hill.

It will be my contention here that the new light on the hill is less a beacon to the future and more St Elmo's Fire — a glow generated by static friction in high places. Quite aside from the demoralising impact of the election of governments such as John Howard's, and the reminder that any social democratic program, no matter how anodyne, is a convenient target for the most craven sort of reaction — as witnessed by Howard's attack on the dockers, his slashing of ATSIC funds, and his refusal to continue the process of reconciliation — hopes for a revival of a genuinely social democratic/democratic socialist tradition in anything resembling its prior forms are hopelessly misplaced. There have been fundamental changes to the world in the last 50 years —

changes as epochal and far-reaching as the agricultural and industrial revolutions — which have completely transformed the political dimension of social life. Worse, the active pursuit of such a program would lead us away from, rather than towards a liberating political project. Such changed circumstances — which go under the general term of 'postmodernity' — offer unique possibilities and perils. Sketching out the new political frameworks and orientations postmodernity demands requires a rather long detour through contemporary history.

Postmodern labour

A genuinely material and self-critical analysis of the recent world changes must begin by looking at the way in which the relationship between manual and intellectual labour has changed since the end of World War II, and how the latter has come to occupy the centre of the economy. The economy of modernity, of classical capitalism, was organised around manual and manual-machine labour, which thus determined the form of its value creation. Intellectual and cultural production was confined to entrepreneur-inventors, the relatively small spheres of the universities, the media as reproducers of ideology and/or as intellectual representatives of the working class, and the subgroup of artistic creators. The postmodern economy reconstructs the modern economy in such a way that scientific/intellectual production comes to the very centre of life, and subverts old class relationships. The ability of nuclear physics, chemistry and molecular biology to repeatedly revolutionise productive capacity takes the value of manual labour-power towards zero, and creates a world in which the hitherto taken-for-granted structures of physical reality are reconstructed (Toffler 1991; Drucker 1993; Castells 1996).[1] In this era the robot factory, the supercomputer, the PC, the global satellite began to come into their own. This revolution in production creates new social categories, based on clashing social ontologies. In modernity, the classical bourgeoisie and proletariat may have varied in their economic interests and social psychological structures, but they shared a common view of the world as transformable only to a certain degree, but no further. The battle over the social question rested on a bedrock of unquestioned nature, governed by visible, mechanical physical processes, assumptions about essential, fixed characteristics of the genders, races and sexualities, and about 'natural' social forms such as the nuclear family. Modernity thought itself to be the revolution against all received ideas about traditional authority and non-evidentiary truth. It did not know that its own limits were dictated by the technical limits to the manipulation of physical reality and biological reproduction. The advent of nuclear fission, quantum mechanics, knowledge of DNA, and their adoption as standard tools of production in metallurgy, telecoms, medicine, biotechnology and other fields, creates a framework of understanding in which the world is endlessly transformable, manipulable, atomisable, in which no given level of reality — no nature — is final. As such intellectual production increases, the group of intellectual producers swell in numbers and power. Negligible in modernity, they now become a significant social category, whose take on reality is at variance with that of the old classes. The penumbra of this core group — the vast army of people in communications and the media — share a capacity, a necessity to automatically regard phenomena as transformable until proven otherwise. They cannot not think of the world as less fixed and given — to varying degrees — than their parents did.[2]

The spread of media technologies and the transformation of the subject

As such an economy starts to develop, several key factors come into play — the spread of media technologies changes the amount of time, and degree of importance that 'instant presence' media play — TV, radio, the Internet — in everyday life, and gives these media a fundamental role in the ontological development of the child, while the spread of the consumer economy and culture increases the individuation of the subject, and the degree to which meaning is found to be related to the satisfaction of individual desire, rather than to the fulfilment of fixed social roles and obligations. The education system is reconstructed to prioritise scientific mathematical training and language competence, as well as to create subjects who are more flexible, more adaptable than those of a prior generation. The use of a consumer economy as a necessary mode of keeping economic growth running, and the increased flexibility of the subject, resulting from a media-dominated culture and a transformed education system, create a type of subject whose mode of self-formation is not bound by the psychological formation modes of the classical modernist classes. The new type of person is increasingly oriented to creation from a wide variety of sources, frameworks, value systems. This is the underlying structural transformation which made the '60s possible — a questioning of all forms of received authority, an attempt to fuse libertarian personal values with a socialist agenda, combined with a re-sensualisation of the world via the rediscovery of nature, different types of music, drugs, and the sexual revolution. Such themes and modes of life had been a part of small bohemian subcultures since the 1830s; their spread to a more general social group occurred because economic changes had given a new generation of people the cultural-psychological structure of the bohemians — malleable, self-creating, etc. The '60s was a site of struggle about the way in which this process of world transformation would go. The classics of social criticism of the time — Fromm, Marcuse, Illich, etc. — emphasised a critical relationship to the expansion of productive forces (Fromm 1998; Illich 1989; Marcuse 1992). The failure of the cultural revolution inspired by such works, burning out in punk and euro-terrorism in the late '70s, was an inevitable result of the contradictions it carried within itself, but it has left a vacuum — a widespread pessimism about the capacity of people to transform their lives — into which have flooded gung-ho visions of a one-dimensional high-tech world (Gates 1996). In the post-'60s ideology all forms of life — sense of place, embodiment, family, life activity — are held to be improved by increasing automation and cyberisation. The town becomes the exurban no-space, work becomes the hot-desked telecommute, the body becomes the technically modified cyborg, agriculture becomes genetic engineering, the bar becomes the Internet chat 'room', and visions that life could be radically otherwise are consigned to the back of the cupboard, with the kaftans and Jefferson Airplane LPs.

The collapse of the first socialist project

The advent of a postmodern framework — postmodern in that what, in the modern period, were assumed to be limits to the process of social transformation have now broken down — created insoluble problems for both revolutionary socialism and social democracy. Marx's communism had been a pastoral world of 'hunting in the morning, fishing in the afternoon, and theorising in the evening', yet the postmodern person has real psychological needs anchored in a mediatised world — movies in the morning, Net-surfing in the afternoon and then Gameboy till bedtime. Contrary to the enthusiasms of the 'carnivalesque' school of cultural studies, such consumption actually bolsters a commodified production system, no matter how much rhetoric is directed against it (Hebdige 1989). For social democrats, the capacity of the market, momentarily, to satisfy immediate demands of workers through increased consumption removes the imperative that made common ownership a great popular cause. The increasing speed of the economy makes effective central planning impossible. The inevitable failure of countercultural movements which sought to find a sort of mystic utopian libertarian communism in which total individual freedom was not in contradiction with communal life, and in which it was assumed that one could unbecome postmodern, soured people to the possibility of alternative ways of life, and pointed them back towards consumption as the only path to a meaningful existence. Into the vacuum created by such a collapse, moved the political complex known as the 'new right', whose diagnosis of the dilemmas of social life is a camera obscura image of social reality. The fraying of traditional forms of life (marriage, religious authority, etc.), for good or ill, has been made possible by the transformation of psychological subjectivity brought about by new economic forces — by people becoming the type of person for whom 'forsaking all others, till death do us part' becomes, given their psychological mobility and fluidity, a literally impossible demand. Yet the new right saw only a culturalist process whereby secular-humanist intellectuals had white-anted traditional life. Despite the capacity of consumer capitalism to pull the rug out from under whole societies, and ways of life, the new right saw no contradiction between a program of deregulation and celebration of 'traditional' — usually invented and sentimentalised pictures of nineteenth-century middle class — modes of life (Bloom 1988). Under their neo-liberal political regimes, the economy could move to a new stage. The ratio of financial capital to investment capital jumps markedly in the early '80s, as funds become globally mobile; the biotech industry moves ahead in leaps and bounds. Simultaneously, the first effects of a generation of image/commodity culture becomes apparent. Postmodernism, a cultural form emphasising pastiche and autonomous processes, comes to the fore and high cultural and low cultural divisions break down. 'Poststructuralism' — the notion that no system of thought can make absolute truth claims by which it could definitely interpret all other systems of thought — becomes the key ideology of humanities intellectuals who had hitherto been part of the coalition known as the 'new left' and had subscribed to various forms of increasingly complexified neo-Marxism. Cultural studies, which find subversive practices in mainstream popular culture, comes to the fore, displacing the late-Frankfurt-school/Marcuse position hostile to the culture industry. The USSR and its satellites collapse, their economies unable to make a transition to network structures. Politics moves from structural concerns — as the polity recedes into the ideological distance — and becomes increasingly about cultural identities. An absence of fixed meanings — as were hitherto guaranteed by kinship, neighbourhood and obligational structures — begins to erode people's capacity to live a meaningful existence. Clinical depression, chronic fatigue syndrome and other postmodern disorders which go beyond the body–mind division become the key health problems of the age (WHO 1999; Showalter 1998).[3] The artefacts and practices of cultures with concrete frames of meaning — new age regalia, tarot cards, herbal medicine — become used in attempts to regain meaning. Popular culture becomes increasingly niche-produced with pre-programmed genres as guaranteed emotion delivery systems — à la the 'feel good' movie.

The meaning of life for the contemporary person is so bound up in the consumption of images and commodities as a necessary part of psychological self-reproduction that any alternative way of life remains — at the moment — literally unimaginable. If the framework is thus regarded as given, then the market is the only efficient way of organising a society which produces at such levels of surplus, and the political economic question, in the way it has been defined since the 1790s, is over, decided in its favour. Social democracy, in the sense of a mass movement which tied a class to a party which represented it, is over, and in its place are social-market parties, bound to seek funding from business, and increasingly run by a small cultural group of self-selecting political professionals.

As social norms break down in a population that has become increasingly hyper-individuated, state repressive measures — closed-circuit cameras, privatised prisons, electronic tagging, detention of those with 'dangerous personality disorders', teenage curfews — become increasingly employed. Biotechnology joins nuclear technology in having a potentially catastrophic power — the capacity to wipe out all or a large part of humanity — via lethal viruses arising from a commercially transformed biosphere, or via nuclear or bio-terrorism, and as the collapse of cultural meaning becomes a central fact in many lives, the politics of existence, a struggle about the fundamental ways in which we shall live, comes to the fore and outflanks existing political formations. At the height of modernity, working-class and liberal middle-class people would flock in the tens of thousands to debates — about guild socialism versus distributism, about welfare statism versus cooperatives — whose topics strike most today as out of the category of public participation. 'Who gets what when how' politics has been so instrumentalised that most people would no more think of participating in debates around it than they would in a discussion between two chemical engineers about alternative methods of dye separation. People are not merely alienated from such politics; it has been re-categorised out of their lives altogether. But this has not been done by sleight of hand, or by a brainwashing tabloid press, or by a carnivalised public culture; it has occurred because; within the framework that the mass of political parties take as given — a society based on increasingly commodified, specialised, automated and maximally instrumentally abstracted production and consumption —

prospects for political renewal 167

there is very little alternative. The mode of production and life dictates the political form, which can only vary across the narrow spectrum band between a free-market quasi-police state — like the United States — or a social-market economy such as Germany, where the once anti-systemic Green Party now finds itself in a government which endorses the continuation of nuclear power well into the next century, and the bombing of cities for foreign policy purposes.

In such a context, traditional politics is a matter for those whose interests or ambitions turn them toward the minutiae of administration and systems management. What most people still (self-)labelled socialists are offering are systems that are either hopelessly unworkable — self-managed workplaces attempting to steer global production allocation through wider feedback mechanisms — or a masked bid for power by the intellectually related groupings, in a totally managed society. Many have taken hope from the persistence of social movement politics across the '80s and '90s, and the rise of so-called 'DIY' culture — the sustained and strategically creative campaigns conducted by animal liberationists and environmental protesters, as well as the increase in 'ethical' investment and consumer schemes. Yet the very subcultural nature of such campaigns should alert one to their limitations. Based largely around a category of young people who combine a radical non-speciesist morality with a neo-primitive personal style — with an emphasis on personal expression in manner such as body-piercing, tattooing, etc. — the lifestyle is all of a piece. This gives it a great deal of solidarity and one should not diminish its achievements in attacking environmental damage or wanton cruelty to animals, still less the dedication and courage of its participants, yet it is not the same thing as a mass political movement of the old working-class type which could draw upon a core mass social group, and numerous adjuncts — bohemians, intellectuals, scientists — whose participation was despite the absence of a shared culture, rather than due to the binding effects of a common one. In other words, contemporary social movements are a subculture, a mode of expression with a politics, rather than a politics proper. While a core of people maintain their allegiance to such cultures throughout their lives, most pass through as part of the extended process of postmodern identity formation which currently extends forms of psychological adolescence until well into the late twenties. In the 'political economic' era, the major parties could count on mass membership from the young of the social classes they represented. With the exception of the National Party, this is no longer the case, and membership of the organic institutions of one's vestigial class — party, trade union, fraternity (Masons, Rotary) — is seen as a voluntaristic, rather than automatic, act of a person attaining their maturity. As we move into a 'post political economic' period of grand coalitions and regimes that are one-party by default, this process will be exacerbated, political participation streamlined as either a career choice or a lifestyle one, until exterior events (large-scale land war, environmental collapse, or biotech disaster) or the rise of anti-systemic forces (arising from a socio-cultural crisis) supervene.

Political renewal

Where politics does come alive is where a mass of people begin to think outside the system, and to situate its lineaments and assumptions within a broader conception of the good and the true in human life. The recent struggle over genetically modified foods in Britain is a case in point. Largely due to the BSE crisis, the British public has a more heightened awareness of the dangers of making fundamental alterations to the food chain — such as feeding cows bits of other cows — and so the attempt by large biotech groups to introduce GM foods more belatedly than in the United States met with a wall of resistance, and direct action — digging up GM crops, clearing supermarket shelves of GM products — that recalled a whole history of British radicalism right back to the original Diggers themselves. Yet such campaigns are not motivated by demands for more consultation, for public panels, and the like — they are first and foremost an absolute 'no' to such a fundamental alteration of reality (McKay 1998). Such a position should not be taken as an endorsement of the idea that social movement politics should be celebrated in preference to the politics of the socio-economic framework. Quite the contrary. The object must be to reconnect the latter to a politics that talks about the way in which social production is managed. But this can only occur when the system itself can be made visible — in the same way that Marxism made the capitalist system visible — and demarcated from life. This quickly catches us in a vicious circle. For life to be otherwise, the way of life must be different. The current round of life is one in which labour and production occur within contexts that are maximally abstracted (i.e. geared to the production of commodities for a global market, increasingly of a text- or information-based nature) and instrumentalised (the process is steered by an undebated commitment to technological development and capital accumulation whose primary purpose is the reproduction of the system itself). Consumption and personal formation occurs in a context of maximally abstracted spectacle. Mass-produced high-tech images and texts — movies, TV, computer games, the culture of celebrity — become the substitute for prior frames of meaning such as religion or nationalism. Of course people still have grounded areas of life, such as families, free life-activity, and so on. Indeed one way of seeing postmodern life is as a continual struggle to reclaim and preserve a sphere of grounded meaning — the parts of one's life that one holds to be inviolable, unexchangeable and unsubstitutable. A contemporary person will move from their birthplace if they prefer another location, but they will not exchange a child of theirs for another merely because the child is brunette and they prefer blondes.[4] Yet a pre-modern person would find changing homes as bizarre — as much of a category error — as the idea that one could exchange children and preserve the meaningful nature of the relationship. As the processes of postmodern life extend into every sphere of a person's life, the spheres of such inviolability recede until they are virtually nil, as is the meaningful content of the person's life.

Where this sphere once extended to one's whole kinship group, home, and world, it has now shrunk to the immediate nuclear family, and even this is attenuated. Friendships, romantic relationships, social groups are another relatively less abstracted part of life, but they are often undermined by the atomising and fluidising effect of a maximally abstracting society to undermine the capacity for grounded mutual obligation and reciprocity. In life-activity areas — say gardening or DIY — people do labour that they could pay for more efficiently and cheaply because they value the self-recreating and densely meaningful nature of the activity itself. More to the point, such activities become a part of necessary psychological self-repair given the lacerating effects of life in the office and the website.

There is no reason to believe that this post political economic process will occur in a significantly different way in Australia than elsewhere in the West. The ALP has failed to put forward any radically alternative policy to the process of social marketisation as it is practised elsewhere, yet it is impossible to suggest policies that it could advance, if it is presenting itself as a party of government in a globalised world.[5] Nor is there any point in looking for regional specificities or variations, since the process of a world of maximally abstracted instrumental life abolishes the specificity of particular traditions and histories in favour of a uniform administrative process. While there may be some minor advantages to be gained from the time lag that still occurs in our adoption of current political fads — we may be able to avoid the worst of the new law and order fads which attract the authoritarian personality types to be found in the higher echelons of social democratic parties — in the last instance we are another carriage on the same monorail. Nor is there any hope to be seen in the notion of a 'third way' or a 'radical centre' which has reached a level of vacuity in the recent work of Anthony Giddens that is only exceeded by the rhetoric of Tony Blair and Gerhard Schroder. The bulk of such proposals are merely social-market proposals to intermesh private funding with public projects.

To imagine the possibility of a democratic socialist society is to realise that change will only occur when people have begun to have enough of this sort of life. At the moment, cultural dissatisfaction with the grim giggle palace of postmodern culture is largely expressed through individual and psychological dysfunction — the depression 'epidemic', chronic fatigue syndrome, the therapy and self-help industry, and so on. In the space of the next generation, extrapolating current trends, these disorders will be of such magnitude that they will have moved to the centre of cultural life, and begun to disrupt social reproduction. At that point these atomised cultural concerns will become a political movement which produces alternative forms of social and economic organisation, largely through fundamental social reorganisation on the ground, but with a political and even revolutionary flow-on. This is not a process that can be jump-started by a sort of postmodern Leninism, because postmodernity is not a form of false consciousness, but an ontological bind, a real structure that is self-contradictory at its root. If there is a key political task of the moment, it is to make the lineaments of this deep structure as clear as possible to as many people as possible, and to demonstrate the obsolescence of political forms and processes that are now outdated. We are at a historical point akin to that of 1849 — one in which the level of understanding and theoretical framing of the forms of oppression and alienation is so far behind actual historical developments that effective strategic and tactical planning of alternatives is impossible.

Looking ahead

The task of those whose practice it is to provide interpretative frameworks and do theoretical work (i.e. the people reading this book) is first and foremost a self-critical analysis of their own positions and the bases thereof, in the light of the abject failure of existing frameworks to provide anything less than a 'slightly less worse' form of contemporary society. Much of what passes for current political argument is no more than a forlorn clinging to theoretical positions that are as relevant to the contemporary world as, say, Swedenborgianism or theosophy.

That does not give any easy answer to those with an inclination to be involved in systemic politics in the current period, aside from saying that putting any faith in the capacity for significant political change at the level of the political is foolish and misplaced. There is obviously a need for people who are willing to hold the line against the real barbarity that an uncontested free market can create — a sort of mix of the worst of the contemporary United States, Brazil and Russia, a world where the surplus population is locked up in the millions, electronically tagged and used as a bank for spare organs for a rich elite revolving in a hyper-culture of super-prozacked excess. Such a statement is usually rejected as hopelessly hyperbolic — a dystopian vision as ludicrous as the idea, for example, that a civilised nation might melt down 6 million people into soap and lampshades. Yet ultimately, if we are to renew the broad vision of socialists and radicals as diverse as Marx, Proudhon, William Morris, Emma Goldman, John MacMurray, Bernard Shaw and countless others, then we must first transcend the limits of a political framework that is no longer appropriate to the forces against which we must contend.

(With thanks to Geoff Sharp and Dennis Glover.)

chapter 11

Mediating democracy: politics and the media in the postmodern public sphere
by Catharine Lumby

In his 1996 book, *Breaking the News*, eminent US journalist James Fallows outlines a thesis which passes for commonsense in middle-class discussions of contemporary democracy. Americans, he argues, have become radically alienated from public life (Fallows 1996). The great problem for American democracy in the 1990s is that people barely trust elected leaders or the entire legislative system to accomplish anything of value. The politicians seem untrustworthy while they're running for office, and they disappoint even their supporters soon after they take office. Then by the time they leave office they're making excuses for what they couldn't do (Fallows 1996, p. 7). Despite a perfunctory acknowledgment that deep structural forces are at play in this disenchantment, Fallows goes on to lay a large portion of the blame at the door of the mass media. He writes:

> By choosing to present public life as a contest among scheming political leaders, all of whom the public should view with suspicion, the news media help bring about that very result ... They increasingly present public life mainly as a depressing spectacle, rather than a vital activity in which citizens can and should be engaged. The implied message of this approach is that people will pay attention to public affairs only if politics can be made as

> *interesting as the other entertainment options available to them, from celebrity scandals to the human melodramas featured on daytime talk programs.* (Fallows 1996, pp. 7–8)

In an era when media coverage of the White House has become synonymous with coverage of the President's sex life, Fallows' jeremiad for the public sphere holds an obvious appeal. Certainly his lament has been echoed by hundreds of public commentators over the past decade. Public life, we're told by both liberal and conservative scholars and media commentators, is in decline. Citizenship, cultural literacy, political engagement, civic pride, community spirit ... all these hallmarks of a healthy democracy are being effaced. In their place, we've erected the false gods of consumerism, mass entertainment and the cult of personality, gods whose shadows are conjured in the theatre of the mass media.

Yet just how inclusive is the definition of 'public life' which underscores these eulogies for democracy? What counts as 'political engagement'? And how should we go about drawing the boundaries of 'community' in a mass-media age? Questions like these highlight the assumptions which have grounded liberal conceptions of how democracy and civic consensus should work — assumptions which equally ground critiques of the media's role in democracy from both the conventional right and the left. In this essay I'll examine these premises and argue that they are not only incapable of accounting for the media's impact on the public sphere (in popular terms, the imaginary and real places where we come together as citizens), but they also fail to grasp resultant and fundamental changes in the shape and scope of contemporary democracy.

This essay will challenge both traditional and radical liberal assumptions about the role of the media in contemporary democracy with a view to rethinking the political boundaries of the public sphere. In doing so I address three themes: firstly, I look at how the media has influenced the shape and scope of politics in Western democracy; secondly, I examine the way the boundaries of public life have been broadened by both the media and alternative political movements such as feminism; and thirdly, I explore the diverse voices and languages which make up public debate today and ask how we can have a meaningful collective dialogue. I draw on both Australian and US examples to sustain my argument for a number of reasons. Firstly, the globalisation of media flows means that domestic political scandals in the United States are now consumed and debated across the Western world — the Clinton–Lewinsky saga is a case in point. More importantly, I believe that the media's role in US politics offers Australians a window onto current and impending developments in the Australian political landscape. North Americans have been living with a highly competitive multi-channel media environment since the late '70s — an environment which Australians are just beginning to experience with the advent of pay television and the growing importance of the Internet as a source of news and current affairs.

It's an environment which will only intensify the collapses between politics and entertainment and between the private and public spheres, which I detail below, and one which I believe will rapidly change the face of Australian political life.

Publicising the public

When Ivy Lee advised the Pennsylvania Railroad Company to help reporters cover a train accident, rather than simply cover it up, he laid the foundation for one of this century's most successful industries: public relations. The first decade of the twentieth century saw the professionalisation of media relations, with politicians and private business hiring spin doctors to craft press releases and conferences. Following Woodrow Wilson's largely successful campaign to enlist the cultural and intellectual elites in a campaign to build support for World War I, Walter Lippman published a book titled *Public Opinion*. In it he argued that Western societies were no longer amenable to rule by mass democracy (or 'public opinion') because of the specialisation of knowledge, the diversity of public institutions and events, and the likelihood that information would be manipulated by the media or political parties. In the place of active government by the masses, Lippman proposed a body of experts who would shape public opinion and good governance via the media (Lippman 1922). It's a model which captures many of the enduring assumptions about the media's 'proper' role in democracy: quality journalists should translate complex issues into accessible language for their audiences, they should disentangle facts from spin-doctored accounts and they should provide the general public with access to expert analysis. Public relations practitioners (along with entertainment-oriented or tabloid journalists), according to this model, actively hinder the public interest by distorting events and issues, distracting citizens with trivia and spectacle, and inflaming populist prejudices.

The separation of information from entertainment, facts from bias, and material of public interest from material which appeals to the basest interests of the public are central to enduring liberal conceptions of the media's role in democracy — and they're values which continue to be held up as ideals in debates about the quality of contemporary journalism. Yet they're equally abstract goals which evade the reality of the contemporary media sphere and are unable to account for its complex implication in political and public life.

Today's political journalists and politicians operate under very different conditions from their counterparts in the era before the advent of television and the growth of the public relations industry, which now acts as an intermediary between the two groups. Contemporary politicians and media producers are, in one sense, captive to similar forces — both groups are in the business of competing for public attention and both rely heavily on market research as a guide to what their public wants. It's perhaps not surprising, then, to learn that the public is equally disenchanted with politicians and the media. Indeed, despite the fact that public opinion has its temperature taken every other minute, the patient seems close to dying on the operating table. In both the United States and Australia, voters have deserted the major parties and expressed strong support for independent candidates like Ross Perot and Pauline Hanson. And the public is equally sceptical of journalists, who, like politicians, are now frequently portrayed as self-promoting, venal and out of touch with ordinary people.

In his book, *The Politics of Pictures,* John Hartley argues that the mass media is now at the heart of 'representative' democracy. He writes:

> *In classical Greece and Rome, assuming you were a free man — rather than a woman, slave or foreigner — you could walk into the agora or forum and participate in public life directly, as a voter, a jurist, a consumer, or as an audience of oratory in the service of public affairs. ... But nowadays there is no physical public domain, and politics is not 'of the populace'. Contemporary politics is 'representative' in both senses of the term; citizens are represented by a chosen few, and politics is represented to the public via the various media of communication. Representative political space is literally made up of pictures — they constitute the public domain.* (Hartley 1992, p. 35)

In such an era, attempting to separate politicians from their images is futile. Political campaigns are now structured entirely around media events and key debates are inevitably broadcast on television, ensuring that appearance, tone of voice, demeanour and the ability to speak in short, witty grabs are at least as important as the substance of what is said or argued.

Televising democracy

The mediation of politics can be traced back to the Kennedy era. Media analysts Donovan and Scherer argue that the real dividing line lies between 'what politics was before 1948 when US television was born' and 'what politics has been since'. They write that:

> *[T]he day after his dramatic victory over Dewey in 1948, Truman articulated the essence of the 'old politics' when he said 'Labor did it'. A mere twelve years later, after defeating Nixon in 1960, Kennedy's comment went to the heart of the 'new politics'. 'It was TV more than anything else,' he said, 'that turned the tide.' While not the only determinacy of a candidate's popularity, television has become an unavoidable threshold to political power.* (Donovan & Scherer 1992, p. 239)

By the late 1990s, television was no longer simply influencing election campaigns across the Western world; in many cases it had become identical with the campaign itself. The policies politicians presented to voters were almost entirely encapsulated in nightly news grabs and newspaper photo opportunities, which left little time for reporters to get behind the issues. In Australia, this collapse between media performance and politics was graphically illustrated by a 1993 television debate in which the Liberal leader, John Hewson, squared off against the Prime Minister, Paul Keating. Channel 9 augmented the debate with a device known as 'the worm' — a wiggly white line moving up and down an approval graph rating and manipulated by the studio audience. The worm is an extremely graphic illustration of how politicians' speeches and performances have become received and analysed as a series of media grabs.

But if politicians are becoming increasingly expert in using television to stage media events and perform for the public, the continued growth of the mass media and the blurring of the lines between information and entertainment is also bringing new kinds of stories about politicians into the public eye: stories which are harder to control or spin-doctor.

The first months of 1998 were dominated by detailed international media coverage of Bill Clinton's alleged relationship with young White House intern, Monica Lewinsky. The story originated in allegations published in *The Drudge Report*, a gossipy Internet site run by a 30-year-old out of his Los Angeles home. US *Newsweek* was the first major news organisation to investigate the story, but ultimately decided not to publish it. *The Drudge Report* then reported both the story and the fact that *Newsweek* had decided not to run with it. As a result, news of the Lewinsky scandal spread and ultimately surfaced in the *Washington Post* and the *LA Times*.

Renowned US journalist and editor of the on-line journal, *Slate*, Michael Kinsley (1998) commented: 'The Internet made this story. And the story made the Internet. Clinterngate, or whatever we are going to call it, is to the Internet what the Kennedy assassination was to TV news: its coming of age as a media force.' Or some might say media *farce*. The only reason Drudge beat television or newspapers to the story, according to Kinsley, was 'lower standards'. Drudge's scoops, he wrote, 'are generally the stuff the grownups either have declined to publish or are about to publish' (Kinsley 1998).

The same criticism has often been levelled at the traditional tabloid news programs or magazines, but, like *The Drudge Report*, these sources of news and gossip now have an increasing impact on which stories make it into the mainstream media, because once a story is in the public sphere in some form, the increased competition between news outlets makes it almost inevitable that a respectable organisation will pick it up.

It's often unfairly assumed that tabloid news sources are always less accurate than mainstream outlets. Yet during the O.J. Simpson trial, the *National Enquirer* was publicly acknowledged as a key news-breaking source by authorities as reputable as the *New York Times*. What's more, the treatment traditional news sources give political scandals is increasingly harder to distinguish from tabloid coverage.

In the case of the Lewinsky scandal, mainstream media outlets, such as CNN, *Newsweek* and *Time* magazine, unhesitatingly devoted intense coverage to the allegations — including speculation about whether Clinton defines oral sex as infidelity, whether the President's penis had strange identifying characteristics and whether Lewinsky owned a dress stained with the President's semen.

Perhaps the strangest thing about the mainstream media coverage of the Lewinsky scandal was that the revelations appeared to have no adverse impact on the President's approval rating. Quite the reverse, in fact. Clinton's approval rating actually increased at the height of the crisis from 56 per cent in December 1997 to 59 per cent on 25 January 1998, according to a CNN–USA Today Gallup poll. Yet only 35 per cent of the same people polled answered 'yes' to the question 'Is Clinton honest and trustworthy?', compared with 49 per cent in 1997.

One plausible reason for this disparity is that Americans are reluctant to convict a president of wrongdoing until all the evidence is in. Another is that Clinton is simply an expert political performer who exploits the fact that tomorrow's TV image is far more important than yesterday's newsprint. Political ratings, in this sense, may have something in common with television ratings. People can hate what a program depicts but still enjoy watching it for its entertainment or shock value. As US journalist Kurt Andersen speculates:

> *For modern Americans, politics happens on television. And the titillating new story line that gooses the ratings of an old hit*

> show (Paul and Jamie having a baby on 'Mad About You', say) is now an established TV gimmick. Before the Monica Lewinsky subplot, the audience was beginning to get bored with the Clinton administration. Now they're interested again. (Andersen 1998)

The notion that US politics has been reduced to a long-running sitcom may seem, at first glance, a ludicrously cynical claim. Yet, for the majority of Americans, politics has become entirely synonymous with media coverage of politics. And media coverage of politics is, in turn, increasingly driven by the desire to entertain the public and hold their attention in a highly competitive market. The result is a vicious circle.

Publicising the private domain

Sex scandals undoubtedly rate well, but they also heighten the growing confusion over where the private begins and the public stops. The story about President Clinton's alleged dalliance with Monica Lewinsky was legitimated by allegations that Clinton had lied about the affair in sworn testimony presented to prosecutor Kenneth Starr. But much of the speculation surrounding the affair, and related incidents allegedly involving other women, had little to do with the question of perjury. The revelation that Bill Clinton was accused of an extramarital dalliance was hardly news. Clinton all but confessed to a long-standing affair with Gennifer Flowers in his first Presidential election campaign and his womanising tendencies were given a thorough airing in the wake of Paula Jones's allegations that he sexually harassed her while he was Governor of Arkansas. Two responses were common among the liberal commentators who held forth on both CNN and the major US news channels (which were available to Australian viewers via pay television), when Kenneth Starr announced his intention to interview Monica Lewinsky: the whole thing was a political vendetta by right-wing moralists and the President's sexual behaviour was a private not a public matter.

The contradictions in this line of argument quickly became clear. After decades of campaigning for laws which recognised that sexual advances by superiors to inferiors in the workplace were not a purely private matter, US feminists were suddenly tripping over themselves to distinguish Clinton's conduct. Writing in the *New York Times* (and reprinted in the *Sydney Morning Herald*), Gloria Steinem claimed that the guide to divining what is and what is not sexual harassment is simple — you've just got to remember that 'no means no; yes means yes' (Steinem 1998). Paula Jones was a government employee who claims Clinton invited her to a hotel room when he was governor and asked her for oral sex. Kathleen Willey (who came forward during Starr's investigation) was asking Clinton for a job when she claims he touched her breast and placed her hand on his erect penis. Clinton was in a quasi-employer relationship to both these women when he made his advances. But Steinem argues that this is irrelevant: what matters is that he accepted rejection and didn't press his suit. In Monica Lewinsky's case, she claims that 'Welcome sexual behaviour is about as relevant to sexual harassment as borrowing a car is to stealing one' (Steinem 1998).

Steinem's attempt to neatly separate abuse of public power from private sexual intentions has a hollow ring, since it was the recognition that you cannot easily separate the two which gave birth to sexual harassment laws in the first place. Further, as Christopher Hitchens notes, the accusations against Clinton went much further than allegations of sexual impropriety or possible harassment. He writes:

> *Plainly put, a man who has often been accused of humping the help, or hitting on the help, was asked — under ordinary penalties of perjury, and also under a law he had initiated — if he was getting any action while on the White House payroll. He lied ... there was a clear 'controlling legal authority', and Clinton knew it.* (Hitchens 1998, p. 54)

The general liberal evasion of the fact that Clinton lied in a deposition and, later, to a grand jury is symptomatic of a broader failure on the part of the left to come to terms with the way leftist politicisation of private behaviours (such as sexual harassment and domestic violence) is implicated in far larger shifts in the shape of the public sphere itself. The dismissal of Kenneth Starr's 'grubby details' as mere tabloid fodder was at best wishful thinking, at worst political opportunism of the most transparent kind.

Since the late '60s, a host of progressive political movements have politicised issues once seen as purely personal or apolitical. Feminism, gay rights, the environmental movement and numerous struggles to combat racial inequality have all highlighted the way personal attitudes and actions have profoundly political consequences and are therefore worthy of public scrutiny and sanction. This expansion of the boundaries of public interest would have been impossible, however, without the concomitant expansion of the mass media. The political movements mentioned above didn't flourish in a counter-public sphere vacuum — their claims to political legitimacy were brought to public attention by an increasingly pervasive media, particularly by television. From the Vietnam War protests to the latest feminist celebrity, television has been instrumental in forging a connection between the public sphere and the private space of the home.

Indeed, the relationship between the media and alternative or progressive political movements might best be figured as a *Möbius* strip on which it is impossible to locate origins or end points. The politicisation of issues legitimated an expansion of media attention into the private sphere, yet media attention equally broadened the scope of issues and events which have become available for political debate. The two shifts, then, have to be seen as intertwined — a fact which makes it increasingly difficult to argue that media coverage of a sexual relationship between a politician and a subordinate, in one instance, is clearly a matter of public interest and, in another context, is clearly a tabloid intrusion into the private sexual affairs of an individual. Where you draw the line between matters of public interest and invasion of privacy today depends, in other words, very much on how you construe vexed areas such as sexual harassment in the first place. As the fierce debates over the propriety of Clinton's advances to a host of women make clear, such areas remain sites of intense political conflict.

Finding the public in the media marketplace

In *The Politics of Pictures* and *Popular Reality*, John Hartley sketches a new model for understanding the public in the age of mass media (Hartley 1992, 1996). He analyses audiences for popular media (or 'readerships', as he dubs them) as political assemblages which intersect and interact in a virtual public domain. In *The Politics of Pictures* he writes that 'the media are simultaneously creative and participatory. They create a picture of the public, but it goes live, as it were, only when people participate in its creation, not least by turning themselves into the audience' (Hartley 1992, p. 4).

Hartley elaborates this claim in his later book, *Popular Reality*:

> *[This chapter] is concerned with the knowledges that pertain to the development of what can be called the 'postmodern public sphere'; not so much knowledge of public affairs as traditionally defined, but new modes of knowledge which bespeak new ways of forming the public, in communities whose major public functions — the classical public functions of teaching, dramatizing and participating in the public sphere — are increasingly functions of popular media, and whose members are political animals not in the urban forum but on the suburban couch; citizen readers, citizens of media.* (Hartley 1996, p. 155)

An important extension of this argument lies in Hartley's claim that as participation in the traditional public sphere declines in democratic societies, we need to rethink our formulation of what counts as political in both form, content and deed. He writes that:

> *Such a rethinking would suggest that the traditional idea of the public domain has faded in significance in the twentieth century, to be superseded by a privatized, feminized, suburban, consumerist and international domain of popular media entertainment; a domain constructed in the three-way space between texts, politics and popular readerships.* (Hartley 1996, p. 58)

Hartley's recognition that political meaning is not exclusively attached to the institutional and economic structure of media production or to the content of media products but is, rather, made in the interaction between such producers, texts and consumers is critical. It's a dynamic portrait of the interaction between media consumers and products which cuts across the grain of the traditional leftist construction of the commercial media as, in crude terms, a kind of propaganda machine which keeps the passive masses in their proper place. The left has tended to cherish the notion that the public sector automatically provides a more just and democratic mechanism than the market, and that publicly funded media are more likely to present diverse and alternative political views which challenge the claims and interests of the rich and powerful. But while there are certainly remarkable examples of publicly funded media around the world (Australia's versatile SBS is just one), it's not true that organisations such as Australia's ABC, Britain's BBC or the United States' PBS reflect the interests and values of all the citizens who pay for their services. The programming of all three networks is skewed to cater to educated and/or middle-class audiences.

While publicly funded media undoubtedly provide a critical alternative to the commercial media, it is important to recognise that the latter is not simply an amorphous banal lump. Dividing the media into public and commercial camps ignores the very real diversity of the commercial media. Worse, dismissing the commercial media and their vast audiences risks reducing the public interest to a narrow group of elites.

In his introduction to *The Phantom Public*, Bruce Robbins argues that rather than appealing to 'the universalising ideal of a single public', we should pay attention instead to 'the actual multiplicity of distinct and overlapping public discourses, public spheres and scenes of evaluation that already exist' (Robbins 1993, p. xii).

To argue that the contemporary public is actually composed of a diverse array of intersecting publics isn't to argue that all claims are equal or that everyone has equal access to having their say. My point, rather, is that while dominant groups or ideologies may continue to shape much of our media, media consumers do not simply passively absorb media messages, but rather negotiate and sometimes resist them. The best example of this is the widespread cynicism about mainstream politicians and their attempts to seduce the public through polished media performances. Regardless of the level of conventional education they've received, contemporary media audiences demonstrate a high level of media literacy in a variety of ways. They consistently express scepticism about the ethics of current affairs programs and their reporters in vox pops and surveys and they avidly consume the numerous comedy programs on commercial radio and television which base their humour in poking fun at politicians and the media.

Beyond the unified public: re-evaluating the meaning of difference

A common concern on the part of both liberals and conservatives is that the fragmenting of the media is dividing the public sphere into diverse interests and audiences and that public conversation will consequently become impossible because everyone will be speaking a different language. In an essay on the contemporary public sphere, Nancy Fraser rejects the idea that the growth of diverse interest groups over the past few decades has necessarily weakened democracy. She points out that most interest groups (which she dubs 'counterpublics') have one thing in common: they want to disseminate their ideas and aims widely. Counterpublics, she says, have a dual character: 'On one hand, they function as spaces of withdrawal and regroupment; on the other hand, they also function as bases and training grounds for agitational activities directed toward wider publics' (Fraser 1990, p. 15).

The connection between the formation of publics and publicity that Fraser makes here is a crucial one. In the contemporary world, the mainstream mass media has effectively become a global village hall, a place where diverse public interests collide. And while it's true that the Western media is itself a hydra-headed beast, it is equally the case that there are particular events, personalities and stories which cut across its diverse formats and consumers, and forge national and even global audiences.

The stories and spectacles which arrest us often do so for complex, symbolic reasons. The O.J. Simpson trial which captured the attention of the international media for well over a year was frequently attacked by highbrow commentators for distracting public attentions from genuine political issues. What these criticisms miss is that the saturation coverage of the trial brought debates on domestic violence and racism to the fore in American society in a way which more 'worthy' reporting of these issues often fails to do. Media coverage of the Simpson trial may have been personality-driven, but it was equally a multi-layered story about contemporary race and gender relations in the United States, as well as a focus for debates about the jury system and the media. Like all public debates, debate about the trial was characterised by dissenting voices. It is true that some of the media coverage of the trial was underwritten by racist and/or sexist stereotypes, but it was also a focal point for debating these stereotypes.

Contemporary popular culture may seem irrational, contradictory, prurient and spectacular when compared with the sober, rational and discursive public sphere ideal. But it has a multitude of virtues which weren't in the original Athenian blueprint for democracy. In the late twentieth century, Western public spheres have become a forum for voices and interests which were largely excluded from public debate even 30 years ago.

This eruption of new voices and groups, identified by race, ethnicity, gender, sexuality, and allegiance to new political movements, has necessarily caused concern, not just to social conservatives but to liberals who believe that community consensus, not fragmentation, lies at the heart of democracy. But is this the case?

In his book *The Ethos of Pluralization*, US political scientist William Connolly argues that it is in fact the drive towards consensus which is so often responsible for social disharmony. He writes:

> *The stronger the drive to the unified nation, the integrated community, and/or the normal individual, the more powerful becomes the drive to convert differences into modes of otherness ... The biggest impetus to fragmentation, violence, and anarchy today does not emerge from political engagement with the paradox of difference. It emerges from doctrines and movements that suppress it.* (Connolly 1995, p. xxi)

Connolly uses the term 'difference' in a particular way here. He argues that identity — the sense of who we are and who we belong to — is always bound up with a recognition that others are different from us. Calls for solidarity and to affirm a community consensus about who 'we' really are, he argues, are often equally calls to suppress differences among us. The resulting 'consensus' is not, then, a true or natural reflection of the community, but the imposition of the views and interests of dominant groups. Yet if the majority (or the powerful minority) doesn't rule democracy, who does?

Connolly offers a different proposition for managing the diversity which defines contemporary culture. Rather than thinking in grand categories like the nation-state to understand political action, he suggests, we should look at politics as it happens on the micro level and pay attention to the way different groups constantly interact, form and reform. In Connolly's view, modern society isn't made up of fixed groups, political alliances or identities, it is a constantly shifting and already diverse community of interests. Harnessing this pluralism, then, requires a constant awareness of difference, not an assertion of sameness or identity.

In concrete terms, awareness of difference means being aware that who any of us think we are as individuals or groups can appear as 'hostile others' to other individuals and groups. An excellent illustration of this was the shock many urban lefties felt when they discovered that rural Hanson supporters regarded them as a powerful elite. Urban lefties tend to identify powerful elites with the Kerry Packers of the world, and see economically disadvantaged groups like Hanson supporters as being in need of their protection. The rise of One Nation forced the left elite to question their own identity and their claim to the political moral high ground. Conflict, like collaboration, with groups who see themselves differently can be enormously productive, then, because it reminds us that who we think we are is never stable or universal.

The media sphere is a kind of virtual map of the diversity which defines contemporary democracies. From right-wing talkback radio, through highbrow current affairs shows which appeal to urban elites, through daytime talk shows which deal with the disasters of everyday life, to the most amateur website, the media is a vast collage of diverse viewpoints, audiences and forms of speech. It's a sphere saturated with politics, but not simply the politics of dominant groups. Politics bubbles up from below as much as it trickles down from above. It's there in the heated exchanges of talkback callers with their host and with each other, it's there in impromptu accolades or denunciations of the studio audience on daytime talk TV, it's there in the disgust viewers have for televised political stunts, it's there in workplace debates about the latest media scandal and it's there in the millions of newsgroups which make up the Internet.

The media is the foundation of our public conversation today. And, like democracy itself, it can sometimes seem like a Tower of Babel. But it also offers moments of unexpected convergence, media events which draw us as a local, national or global community and give us a forum for thinking about our differences and our claims to identity. Negotiating these differences does not require us to reach agreement, but it does entail a recognition that there are always other ways of speaking and looking around.

chapter 12

A capitalist faggot at the end of the millennium: musings on the disappointments of politics
by Christos Tsiolkas

In October 1998 I received an email asking me to send condolences to the parents of Matthew Shephard, a young man brutally beaten and murdered in the United States allegedly because of his homosexuality. That same month I also received an email asking me to protest the anti-feminist and anti-homosexual laws of the Taliban in Afghanistan.

I posted a reply to the Shephard family — I did so immediately. Their grief and distress were visible; their images were in magazines, on the television news, splashed across the pages of *Time*, and on the Internet. My response was empathic: I was appalled by the slaughter. I also wished to pledge a commitment to a very American understanding of civil rights, an encompassing of sexual identity and sexual freedom as integral to the notion of human society.

The second request proved to be much more difficult for me. It is not that I am not disturbed — more than that, I am disgusted — at the policies of the Taliban towards sexual heretics, but I can't articulate a consistent politics through which to express my anger. Whereas in the context of the Shephard murder I found myself sharing a communality with the politics of gay activists and civil libertarians, this was not possible when it came to expressing something about the seismic events in Afghanistan. I found myself at the keyboard and was unable to type, unable to speak. I massaged the keyboard and the words on the screen that were reflected back to me lacked integrity and seemed only to speak from a position of privilege and ignorance, a combination that fuelled only guilt at my position as a Westerner. I sent nothing.

It is this reconciliation between two spheres of politics and political understanding that I find most difficult to navigate. It is as if there is one pole of politics that I still identify as dealing with the 'macro' politics of economics and international relations. Then there is the other pole, that of 'micro' identity politics, which encompasses my concerns to do with sexuality, gender and culture. It is possible that my separation is false, that rather than being opposite, these spheres of politics continually come into conflict and tension with one another. Possible, but ultimately a separation is always there, even if within my own consciousness. What else can explain the hesitation I experience in addressing the violence of the Afghanistan state? The collapse of the communist project assisted in exacerbating the polarisation of my own politics, in the sense that my commitment to a radical socialism gave way to a much more hesitant and exploratory politics which laid less stress on grand commitments to mobilisation. Instead it gave way to a more strategic and finally contingent political involvement. Within the sphere of identity politics, I sometimes articulate myself as a democratic humanist; sometimes I advocate social democracy, sometimes anarchism. Within the complex matrix of gender and sexual politics, I firmly espouse a politics that agitates for minority rights and which argues against censorship and moralist conclusions. When it comes to economics and international distribution of wealth and power, I find myself still speaking from within socialist ideology:

> *Now the naturalist liberation of desire has failed. The more the theory, the more the work of social criticism, the more the sieve of that experience, which tended to limit obligation to certain precise functions in the social order, have raised in us the hope of relativising the imperative, the contrary, or, in a word, conflictual character of moral experience, the more we have, in fact, wit-*

> nessed a growth in the incidence of genuine pathologies. The naturalist liberation of desire has failed historically. We do not find ourselves in the presence of a man less weighed down with laws and duties than before the great critical experience of so-called libertine thought. (Lacan 1992, p. 3)

Early in the '80s, after Thatcher's arrival but before the fall of the Berlin Wall, a friend described a sexual encounter in a sauna in Melbourne. He said it was the best sex he ever had. But afterwards, as the man slipped into his tie and business suit and as my friend put on his op-shop shirt, they started to argue. The man he had fucked worked for a mining company and complained loudly of greenies and lazy Aborigines. My friend called him a fascist and the man slammed the locker shut. They left without talking, just glaring at each other.

I remember my friend telling me this, over a drink at a pub. It serves me as a reminder of an innocent time, when something called a sexual or ethnic or gendered or racial or even subcultural identity offered a promise; a promise of unified commitment or at least belief. This was the historic moment of the utopian political statement. We used words like 'we' inclusively, believing, for example, that it was possible to speak something for all homosexuals. The rude post-coital conversation in the locker room was a warning and I think we even saw it that way, back in 1983. That homosexuality in itself was not necessarily indicative of an egalitarian or socialist ethics. It would still take some time, many years, the collapse of a wall, before I came to understand that this was not only true for fags, but also true for women, true for all social collectivities. True for something called a working class.

I think back to this conversation with my friend because it makes me reflect on a possibility I wanted for gay politics — that it would be a politics of allegiance to a broad social transformation promised by the utopia of revolution; that gay and lesbian people would themselves be part of a massive restructuring of the social, a truly egalitarian economy. That dream is sometimes still seductive, but I no longer have a commitment to it. I have come to understand that sexual politics will be encompassing of a range of beliefs and activisms, which will range the spectrum from conservative to reformist to radical politics. And that is true for all political positions centring on the specificity of identity — feminism, queer politics, multiculturalism. My involvement in these political spheres remains distant. I will involve myself in a specific campaign, go to a particular demonstration, but there is no allegiance to a movement or to a party, or even really to a collectivity of individuals. Not because I don't believe politics is possible to enact from within 'identity', but rather because I understand that identity always remains elusive and malleable.

Nevertheless, though I no longer espouse terms such as 'gay' or 'homosexual' as being able to speak for a politics of communality, I still believe in a politics centred on empowerment and for an equality of rights and means: I still believe in the possibility of social and economic egalitarianism. It is for these reasons I am ambivalent about the images and texts I see circulated on the Internet and in much of commercial gay media. Though there are attempts to counter the commodification of the body and to counter the stereotypical gendered assertions of the masculine body, increasingly the images presented to us and sold to us are such that they only intensify the alienation from our own bodies: the homoerotic body sold to us is masculine, unblemished, young. And if it is not so, it seems only allegiance to particular fetishes allows an access to communal participation. I can identify as 'gay' as a consumer or as a practitioner of a particular sex rite but if I am interested in a politics beyond consumption, beyond the body, then I find myself increasingly alienated from 'gay'.

Ya know you shouldn't pick them up
Ya know they'll probably rip you off
Ya know they are probably very high
Ya know they'll talk trash for hours on end
Ya know they probably haven't washed for a while
Ya know they'll steal your credit cards, your stereo, tv and pc
But you pick 'em up guys, don't you???

The above is a poem that appears on the first web page of a site called 'Street Trash', a collection of galleries featuring pictures of nude men, men that are identified as 'amateur' (i.e. non-professional) models. That isn't completely true —

among the dozens of scans in the galleries I noticed a few actors who have appeared in professional pornos. At the same time the site obviously contains many images of nude men snapped while in suburban lounges and bare motel rooms. The shots are admittedly arousing, equivalent to the harshly lit amateur photographs sent in to the soft-core magazines such as *People* and *Pix*. They are a suburban and a rural erotica of women and men caught by the straightforward, unadorned lens of the family camera. Malcolm from Esperance, WA — a truckie with the Madonna tattooed on his belly. Jeanette from Liverpool, NSW — blonde, sunglasses and a conspicuous and attractive belly. Unlike the faces and bodies of Hollywood actors, the bodies in amateur pornography are tantalisingly close — they might live next door. This is, I would argue, one of the attractions of amateur pornography, that it brings oneself into a visceral relationship with a sexual community. But something else as well is occurring within the boundaries of amateur pornography — whether on the Net, on video or on the page. Another possibility opens: to insert one's own body and fantasies into a public realm and within that realm to exchange the body and the sex act for monetary gain. You can buy the photos on the screen, you can organise a session with a prostitute. Many of these sites I discover as I type the word 'gay' into one of the search engines on the Internet. The list of websites comes up, and the majority of sites are simply advertisements for sexual product. The scale of commercial sex exchange on the Net makes visible the intensification in the commodification of sex and sexuality that has been escalating over the last couple of decades. What the Internet offers, at this point of 'infancy' as a technology, is the possibility of examining the changes and movements that sexual identity and sexual commerce are undergoing in an increasingly global and highly technological economy.

The 'Street Trash' site seems to me to be instructive of some of the current meanings and assumptions attached to the subject of the 'gay consumer'. The client of sex product is assumed to be different from the object that he is interested in attaining.[1] On entering 'Street Trash' we are made aware that the object to be 'viewed' (after we first pay a membership fee) is a very different construction from the assumed 'viewer' or 'member': the body on display is constructed as *not* gay. The various pornographic images are filed under titles such as 'Straight', 'Military', 'Rough Trade'. This distinction between the bourgeois gay subject and the non-gay object of desire is a continuous, disturbing thematic of homosexual life, continuous since the modern period. The term 'rough trade' itself signifies that the body attractive to the homosexual subject is itself heterosexual, desirable for the very fact of its heterosexuality. Whereas the bodies on display in 'professional' gay pornography are hyper-stylised bodies — excessive muscles, movie-star looks, healthy — the bodies that can be immediately understood as 'straight' prove attractive no matter how variable the looks and health of the model. The pornography utilising the attraction of rough trade will also make obvious the commercial transactions involved between the gay and straight subjects. (For example, the images of military men on 'Street Trash' are introduced as marines hoping to make a quick buck from a horny fag — who of course never oversteps the boundaries of the sexual exchange, i.e. he is never pleasured). Though a related lesbian mythology centres on the importance of the butch–femme relationship to modern lesbian identity there are crucial differences, the most salient being that the female subjects within this relationship are *both* inhabiting identities that are traditionally working class. The other important difference is that the butch–femme relationship is not necessarily one involving prostitution. A site such as 'Street Trash' indicates that class distinctions still structure the commodification of sex within the metropolitan gay worlds and that the metaphor of prostitution is instructive for understanding this process. Instead of resisting what appears to be the fraught political conclusions of this metaphor — gay equals bourgeois — I think it is worth shifting our gaze away from identity and concentrating instead on the politics of prostitution and pornography. In that shift, what ceases to be of importance is the sexuality of the participants involved in the exchange and instead what becomes imperative is working out how sex and bodies come to function as commodities.

This is not to deny the importance of identity politics nor the importance of sexual politics that speak out on behalf of the varied issues and questions that are seen as relevant to contemporary gay life. However, whether these issues are concerning the right to legalised marriage or the need for a greater representation of lesbian and homosexual characters on TV, I see them largely as concerns that are part of a continuum of liberal and democratic politics. When it comes to something called 'socialism', I am faced with a very different set of questions. Whereas the end of the twentieth century has seen a consensus emerging on the validity of democratic freedoms, the questions regarding the creation of more equitable and more egalitarian economic social conditions are still to be answered. It is precisely here at this point that I believe Marxist and post-Marxist politics still have an important part to play, though undoubtedly any left-wing politics has to take into account the central importance of democratic ethics in countering the totalitarian history that has created the current crisis for socialism. But by shifting the focus of socialist and feminist sexual politics away from identity to the fields of sex work, sex exchange and the commodification of the body, I believe that it is possible to begin one possible resurrection of the socialist project. Of course, this will have the effect of challenging much of the commercial exchange current in many gay and lesbian communities, including challenging some of the more individualistic and libertarian assumptions underlying gay conceptions of democratic freedom and civil rights. Some of these challenges will include resisting and countering the exploitative effects of the sex industries, most importantly countering the movement of these industries into Eastern Europe and into Southeast Asia, where the traffic in human bodies is currently resulting in widespread human misery. This is no return to moralism. What I am arguing for instead is activist work that needs to concentrate on the conditions and possibilities for people engaged in sex work, activism that seeks to struggle for the rights and conditions of these people. Prostitution and pornography in this model of politics are no longer relegated to the unconscious of sexual politics but become integral to understanding the functioning of sex in our society and in our world. Instead of sexual identity being the central marker of an engagement with sexual politics, our relationship to sex work and to the sexual economy becomes the strategic point around which our socialist sexual politics finds its expression.

In one sense I am arguing that the politics of sexual identity are best deployed through the current categories of democratic rights. This is in part what makes it difficult for me to answer the request to counter the violence of the Taliban. The understanding of the modern citizen as having rights centred on their gender, sexuality and cultural history emerges from very specific capitalist, secular and Western locations.[2] All the terms of contemporary sexual politics can be isolated, given specific histories and genealogies — gender, feminism, sexuality, gay, libertarianism — but my interest is increasingly in how these terms cannot be spoken of *politically* without reference to one another. Prostitution, pornography, sexuality and sexual freedom are bound together morally, culturally and economically. The pursuit of the truth *or* the lie of these affiliations is what gives much of contemporary feminism and queer politics their contradictions and tensions. I want it to be clear that these contradictions are not only resident in something called 'identity politics' or only make sense in a Eurocentric Anglophone context. Whether it is visible in the arguments between pro- and anti-pornography feminists in the United States and Australia or in the collisions between gay tourists and those working to 'end' the traffic in sex in colonised and former colonised regions, the associations between pornography, prostitution and sexuality refuse to be silenced, to go away.

The mass circulation of pornographic material on the Internet speaks of two at times contradictory shifts in the exchange of sexual commodities. On one level there is an acute increase in the amount of pornographic material available to the consumer. Type the words 'sex' or 'gay' or 'porn' into a search engine and there are literally hundreds of thousands of sites that will come up. To trace the origin of the images and the products is to reveal a vast economy based around the selling of sex. At the same time, while a large number of these images are increasingly distributed and produced by agencies and corporations involved in the sex industries of the Americas, Europe and Asia, there is also a proliferation of images and sites which are self-produced sexual product emanating from people's own homes and studios. Type in the words 'amateur sex' to be subjected to this. What becomes clear searching through and examining these sites is that though the main objective of the commercially produced pornography is to make money — through membership to sites and through the on-line selling of sex product — there is also a relationship between libertarian anti-censorship rhetoric and the production of porn. Blue ribbons signifying support for anti-censorship are pasted on the web pages. There are often short paragraphs supportive of free speech and personal freedoms. Even if the site being utilised is largely selling and distributing images of heterosexual sex, the site will be supportive of homosexual pornography and often offer links to 'gay' material.

There is something going on here that is more complex than simply the defining of the homosexual subject as a hyper-idealised consumer. It is, I think, a matter of accepting the historical links between capitalism and sexual freedom. There are arguments to be made that there existed pre-capitalist social forms which allowed a tolerance of sexual minorities — but these are highly romantic and speculative histories and none that I know of include communities which did not valorise marriage and the reproduction of the heterosexual citizen or member. To accept the historic link between capitalism and sexual freedom (a link also applicable to ethnic and gender freedoms) is not to assert the primacy of capitalism but simply to acknowledge the necessity of speaking our politics through this knowledge. If more and more I find myself moving away from any interest in sexual identity per se, I find myself intrigued by the possibilities of sex and sexual behaviour to illuminate questions of political economy, rather than being interested in the civil and democratic quests of the contemporary queer movements.[3] I am fascinated by the ways in which the pursuit of democratic inclusiveness within capitalism generates a massive investment in, distribution and exchange of sexual labour and sexual artefacts. There is no denying the historic reality that an increase in tolerance to sexual difference in itself creates the opening up of pornographic enterprises and sites for prostitution and sex exchange. The traditionalist panic against sexual minority rights (be they articulated in religious or political rhetoric) — that they will result in an increasingly 'immoral' society is not foolish or 'conservative'. It is, in fact, true. A liberalised sexual culture will accelerate the opportunities and sites for the exchange of sexual labour, and for the traffic in sex.

The Taliban are not pre-modern at all in this sense. Their legal and philosophical commitment to sexual repression is crucial if they are undertaking an administering of a national culture which requires that sexual exchange be firmly maintained only within marriage. Just as crucially, radical feminist opposition to pornography and prostitution also makes sense if one of the agendas for radical feminism is the elimination of the traffic in women's bodies. The collapse of traditional socialism, however, has made it difficult to give expression to alternative understandings of how this sexual economy can be administered or organised to alleviate the more exploitative effects of such an economy. If I have a disappointment with sexual politics it is that there has been an abandonment of a politics that argues beyond sexual identity and is able to encompass an inclusive politics that allows for alignments, not merely on an existential level of 'identity' but around affiliations of sex work. For me, 'rough trade' is not simply a term of the past but speaks to the continuing presence of heterosexual activity in a field defined as 'gay' or as 'queer'. This is not in itself simply a defence of a polymorphous bisexuality. Bisexuality, again, merely refers to a sexual identity, and I am arguing for a socialist politics centred on sex labour and work rather than around 'choice'. Whatever the sexual identity of the 'trade' in getting 50 bucks for a blow-job is, the political imperative is not whether he comes to a definition of himself as gay, bi, queer or straight, but rather that he is able to undertake the transaction in safety and that the sex work he is involved in is not being marginalised as 'dirty' or 'perverse' or 'illegal': that it be argued for as legitimate. Within this understanding of sexual exchange, both feminist and/or queer politics that still rely on moral categories to define sexual behaviour are highly problematic. That isn't to say that ethical understandings of human relationships are unimportant — they are — but moral divisions of sexual activity and labour into categories of 'good', 'bad', 'sound', etc., only reinforce the marginalisation of people who work within the sex industries. Obviously this is not only of relevance to feminists and/or queers; I would argue that all socialist and social democratic activism requires cognisance of the limits and dangers of sexual moralising. Historically, however, it has been feminism and gay politics which have largely defined the agenda of sexual politics, at least in the postmodern era. It is therefore of strategic importance that it is feminist and gay activists and intellectuals who assist in bypassing the traditional moral categories surrounding sex work and sexual exchange.

Any engagement with something termed 'gay politics' at the end of the twentieth century must come to terms with a disappointment, an *acute* disillusionment, with the experience of 'gay'. It is prominent in the active academic pursuit of a politics of queer over a politics of gay, it is there in the abundance of books, movies, videos and websites that argue for a critical distance to be maintained against the visibility of commercial gay worlds and which critically distance themselves from the active pursuits of Anglophone gay politics: same-sex marriage, equal opportunity law, the rights of non-heterosexual men and women in the military. In part this is a reaction against the dominance of a North American dominance of sexual politics, but it is also speaks of a reflective acknowledgment of the limits of identity politics as such.

On my computer I have saved a file, a photographic image. I typed two words on the search engine — 'Russia' and 'Gay' — hoping to come across information on the contemporary gay movement in Russia. I was led to a website which promised naked images of Russian soldiers. There, in colour, was a badly lit image of a supposedly young Russian man, nude except for his military cap, flying the old Soviet communist flag. This image comes from a website called 'Russian Barracks'. Cheap amateur photographs, a procession of Russian youth smiling at the camera. The erotics of the photograph rely completely on the fiction that these young men have posed for money. The fiction might well be true. The point is that on looking at this photo I cannot help undergo a sadness and a disappointment. The disappointment has to do with saying farewell to a socialist and feminist politics that was once utopian, that said that it was possible to conceive of a society free of exploitation. The young man is smiling. Though my disappointment is real, so is my awareness that what underlined my utopian fantasies was a crushing will to resist the ambiguities and contradictions of life. The Taliban are right to see any concession to feminism and to homosexual freedom as destructive of tradition and of monogamous marriage. Sexual freedom does inevitably lead to a proliferation of sites for sexual expression (be that expression pornographic or aesthetic) and the increased acceptance of sexual minorities will inevitably give voice and empowerment to those subjects involved in sex work. Rather than turning away from these realities, I think it imperative to accept the necessity for struggling to enable the human beings involved within the sex industries to demand that their labour is not exploited and that neither they nor their clients be punished for engaging in those industries.

There is a disappointment with 'gay'. The promise of a non-exploitative sexual economy is unrealised and the image of the Russian man only reconfirms my nostalgic despair. But despair does not lead to effective politics; only to the retrograde inefficacy of the spent radical gesture. If something called left-wing politics is to have an effect, it must be able to speak to a range of political and economic subjects about possible ways of extricating oneself and one's community from the most damaging effects of exploitation. The Taliban offer a return to a Mosaic and Mohammedan code. American gay activists argue for the centrality of civil rights. Both, finally, are political strategies that can only have meaningful results within the boundaries of national culture. But within an increasingly international field of sexual exchange — sex tourism, pornography from Thailand and Eastern Europe, the Internet — if socialist politics can have any meaning and any urgency when it comes to sexual politics, it seems imperative to me that we concentrate on the economics of the sex industries and on the value and rights of the human beings involved in those industries. For gay and lesbian activists, their activity may well be defined by equal opportunity legislation, by working for gay marriages and for the rights of gay men and women in the military. For the socialist activist — whatever the sexuality — the work is in sex work.

(Thanks to Angela Savage.)

chapter 13

Charting democracy and Aboriginal rights in Australia's psychological *terra nullius*
by Larissa Behrendt

Gough Whitlam once observed: 'Australia's treatment of her Aboriginal people will be the thing upon which the rest of the world will judge Australia and Australians — not just now, but in the greater perspective of history' (Reynolds 1992, p. 183). As Whitlam recognised, Australia's unreconciled relationship with her indigenous people continues to haunt her.

Aboriginal Australians pose a specific challenge to Australia's democratic institutions. As the most socio-economically disadvantaged group within Australian society,[1] they are also a numerical minority, comprising just 2 per cent of the population.[2] Health, education, poverty and legal indices are evidence that democratic institutions in Australia are failing indigenous people. These socio-economic disparities under supposed equal laws betray an institutional discrimination producing disparate living standards and conditions. Equal laws for all are not producing equality. Indigenous peoples, as a community, fail to enjoy the same standards of living and the same level of rights enjoyment as the rest of Australian society, and any system of laws and government which fails to protect the most disadvantaged minority is failing to produce substantively democratic results. In 1967, 90 per cent of Australians voted in favour of constitutional changes that would permit the Federal Parliament to make laws with respect to indigenous peoples and to include their numbers in the census. Many Australians believed that these changes, embracing a formal recognition and a formal equality, would allow Aboriginal people equal recognition and access in Australian society. The 30 years plus since the Referendum, which produced a formal equality, did not lead to an equality in result, that is, substantive equality. Aboriginal people are still living in Third World conditions in their 'first world' country. In order to counter these inequalities there needs to be an understanding of how discrimination is institutionalised in Australia. One example of how apparently neutral laws and institutions operate to produce inequalities can be found in Australia's property law regime. A comparison between protections offered to indigenous property rights and those of all other Australians will highlight an institutionalised discrimination. It will also reveal the way in which legal and political institutions embody the (sometimes prejudiced) perceptions and ideologies of the community.

Entrenched institutional discrimination: Australia's *psychological* terra nullius

The courts

Property rights are central to the English legal system. They were imported with this status into Australian law, and are today protected tenaciously. Australian law has an expansive interpretation of the notion of a property right. Property rights have been deemed to 'extend to every species of valuable right and interest including real and personal property, incorporeal hereditaments such as rents and services, rights of way, rights of profit or use in land of another, and choses in action', and to include 'any tangible or intangible thing which the law protects under the name of property' (*Minister of State for the Army v. Dalziel* (1944) 68 CLR 261, 290, 295 (Starke J; McTiernan J)).

What property is and how it should be protected have been judicially considered in relation to section 51(xxxi) of the Australian Constitution. That section states:

The Parliament shall, subject to this Constitution, have power to make laws for the peace, order, and good government of the Commonwealth with respect to ...

(xxxi) The acquisition of property on just terms from any State or person for any purpose in respect of which the Parliament has the power to make laws.

In *WSGAL Pty Ltd v. Trade Practices Commission* (1994) the court held that the words 'for any purpose in respect of which the Parliament has the power to make laws' are not to be read as an exclusive or exhaustive statement of the parliament's powers to deal with, or provide for, the involuntary disposition of or transfer of title to an interest in property. For there to be an acquisition of property by the Commonwealth, there must be an acquisition of an interest in property; this was given a broad definition to include 'slight or insubstantial' interests (*WSGAL Pty Ltd v. Trade Practices Commission* (1994) ATPR 41–314, 42, 175–7, 585, 678).

Property has been given a broad definition that extends to many valuable interests. Extinguishment of these rights is not taken lightly; indeed, they enjoy constitutional protection. The protection given to indigenous property rights provides a stark contrast to these fundamental principles.

Australia was claimed by the British on the basis that it was *terra nullius* — vacant land and/or a land without a sovereign.[3] The British used this doctrine to perpetuate a myth that the land was 'settled'. This myth was institutionalised in the legal system but it was also the basis of a historical fiction, well suited to the aims of a colony that sought to expand its frontiers and establish a lucrative pastoral industry. From the earliest days of the colony, the British saw themselves as being in competition with indigenous peoples for land. Through massacres, dispossession and removal, large tracts of land were lost to traditional owners (Goodall 1996; Reynolds 1982, 1987). The loss of traditional land was crippling to Aboriginal communities. Not only were Aboriginal communities less capable of surviving in unfamiliar territory, but religious and cultural life was seriously impaired or lost.

Although land did become claimable under land rights legislation passed in the 1970s and 1980s in certain Australian States and Territories, these legislative acts were framed in benevolent terms and did not recognise a title by right.[4] The historical perceptions that Australia was *terra nullius*, an uninhabited country, supported this conception that any property given to indigenous peoples was a charitable act. By removing historical context and ignoring Aboriginal presence, Aboriginal occupation and Aboriginal title, the land returned to Aboriginal communities under land rights legislation was perceived as a gift.

The legal fiction of *terra nullius* was finally destroyed in 1992 by the *Mabo v. Queensland (No. 2)* case. The High Court defined native title as a right that exists when an indigenous community can show that there is a continuing association with the land (shown by the Aboriginal community); and that no explicit Act of the government, federal or State, has extinguished that title (extinguishment is to be shown by the government).[5] The majority of the court found that compensation was not payable under common law for extinguishment, although there existed a statutory right after the enactment of the *Racial Discrimination Act 1975* (Cth).[6] The narrow interpretation of native title meant that, for many indigenous groups, the High Court decision was a declaration that their property interests had been extinguished. Since there was no common law right to compensation, those groups who lost their rights before 1975 were left without redress. There were also several grey areas in the decision that left aspects of native title interests uncertain.

The recognition of native title in Mabo was the identification of a legitimate property right in the Australian system that had been ignored, and left unprotected, for over 200 years. These property rights were not created by Mabo; they were only finally recognised by the decision in that case.

Even though legal recognition of native title interests had taken so long, the decision to finally afford them legal protection was controversial. Modern Australia is a country that is built on the land of its indigenous people, land that made the country rich through pastoral and mining industries. Advocates for mining and pastoral interests have resorted to scare tactics that have maliciously misled and unnecessarily frightened Australians. By implying that Aboriginal statehood was the real goal of Aboriginal communities and that the High Court's decision made freehold land vulnerable to claims,[7] lobbyists and mining companies contributed to and exploited this ignorance by warning that the decision in Mabo could lead to the confiscation of private property (freehold title). This was an underhanded untruth, easily dismissed by a cursory reading of the law. Self-interested groups have characterised the recognition of native title as giving the indigenous people an interest in land for free. This racist characterisation feeds on the prejudices of sectors of the Australian population who remain ignorant of the barbarities of their own history and conveniently fail to recall the enormous theft of land that their country, even their own homes, is built on.

This public backlash was just as virulent in the aftermath of another native title case, *Wik Peoples v. Queensland; Thayorre Peoples v. Queensland* (1996). The Wik and Thayorre peoples made a native title claim on the Cape York Peninsula, which was subject to a pastoral lease. The issue in the High Court was whether the grant of a pastoral lease extinguished native title rights. The High Court declared that native title can only be extinguished by a written law or an Act of the government that shows a clear and plain intention to extinguish. Pastoral leases did not give exclusive possession to the pastoralists, which is to say that the grant of a pastoral lease did not extinguish native title interests. Native title could therefore coexist with a pastoral lease, but if the interests of the landholders conflicted, the native title interests would be subordinate. In other words, the nature of native title rights (for example, the performance of a ceremony) must in no way conflict with the purposes of a lease (for example, farming or grazing).[8] Whenever there is a conflict between the use under the lease by the pastoralist and the indigenous people's native title interest, the interest of the lessee farmer or miner will prevail.

The legal interests of farmers remain unchanged. There is no impact on the value of the pastoral lease as a result of the High Court decision. Financial institutions base their loans on the property's ability to generate income, the equipment owned by the pastoralists and improvements to the land. These matters were unaffected by the decision in Wik. It was only the pastoralists' perception of their property rights that changed.[9]

As with the result in Mabo, the decision in Wik ignited public hysteria, which was further fuelled by the deceitful misrepresentations of industry and government.

The legislature

From the beginning Prime Minister John Howard's government made it clear where their loyalties lay on the issue of native title: they had no interest in preserving the property interests of a vulnerable minority. The Howard Government's response to Wik was laid out in their proposal to implement a 'Ten-Point Plan'. This plan sought to extinguish native title interests by converting the leasehold interest into freehold interests — a windfall to the farmers since they would gain freehold title of land they currently hold as leasehold. The cost of conversion and any compensation that would become payable due to an extinguishment of native title was to be covered by the public purse. Indigenous peoples would lose, even if compensation was payable. If the native title interest was the right to enter the land and perform a ceremony, the monetary amount payable for the extinguishment of that right would fail to compensate for the substance of the right being extinguished. Such compensation would be a percentage of the property value and would thus only account nominally for the loss of cultural and religious practices. Aboriginal people, in most instances, would prefer to keep their property interests.

The Federal Government tried to gain popular support for its Ten-Point Plan by portraying pastoral leases as small, family-run farms. The Prime Minister continued to push an approach informed by the ideologies of white Australian nationalism and a psychological *terra nullius*, playing into 'settlement' myths of Australia's land being tamed by brave men who struggled to make a living off the land. In a speech reported in the *Age* on 1 December 1997, Howard stated:

> *Australia's farmers, of course, have always occupied a very special place in our heart ... They often endure the heartbreak of drought, the disappointment of bad international prices after a hard-worked season and quite frankly I find it impossible to imagine the Australia I love without a strong and vibrant farming sector.* (Savva 1997, p. 2)

This is an emotive response which in no way mirrors the way Mr Howard feels about Aboriginal Australians. They fill up no such romanticised, nationalistic place in his heart, consciousness or hisimage of Australia. In reality, the pastoral industry is dominated by big individual and corporate farmers. Foreign-controlled corporations also have rural landholdings of millions of hectares (Jopson, Verrender & Vass 1997; Ramsay 1997). With this windfall at stake, mining and pastoral industries pushed the Liberal Government to take an inflexible line with the proposed Bill.

The government's approach ignored the fact that what Mabo and Wik found was that a legitimate property right was vested in indigenous peoples; it brushed over the historical context in which dispossession took place. Howard used the rhetoric of equal laws for all Australians to justify his political stance, claiming that there should not be special laws for one section of the Australian public: '[W]e have clung tenaciously to the principle that no group in the Australian community should have rights that are not enjoyed by another group' (Kingston 1998). This rhetoric ignored the fact that property laws in Australia had not been applied equally to all Australians; this 'equal law' had facilitated the dispossession of indigenous Australians, something that Mabo and Wik were seeking to rectify. In fact, Howard attempted to block any objection to his decontextualised reasoning by raising the alarm that talk of the historical context is only the 'politics of guilt': 'Australians of this generation should not be required to accept the guilt and blame for the past actions and policies over which they had no control' (Woodford 1997).

Howard's rhetorical approach to indigenous property rights in Australia shows how institutional discrimination is married to a psychological *terra nullius* rooted in a particular, romanticised version of history. His lack of historical context — massacres, dispossession, government policies of assimilation and removal of children — allow him to view the recognition of native title in a vacuum. It is not that he is without any appreciation of history. In fact, conversely, while unlocking native title from the historic events that have failed to recognise and respect those rights, Howard claims that any historic wrongs are historic; they should not affect our contemporary thinking and policy-making. This ignores the legacy of those historic actions, the fact that failure to recognise indigenous native title only ended in 1992 and that dispossession still continues today (facilitated by the likes of the Ten-Point Plan).[10]

Howard's rhetoric highlights three contemporary perceptions in the public consciousness:

- That when Aboriginal people lose a property right it does not have a human aspect to it. Farmers can evoke an emotive response; Aborigines cannot.

- Aboriginal people, in getting recognition of a property right, are seen as gaining something rather than having something that already exists and should be protected recognised. Aboriginal property interests are seen as a 'special right'.

- Aboriginal property interests are seen as threatening the interests of white property owners. The two cannot coexist.

Understanding the way Australians perceive Aboriginal land rights reveals much about their perception of their own history and their sense of self. For most Australians, the right to own property and to have property interests protected is a central and essential part of their legal system; Australia's property laws reflect this priority. For Aborigines, Australian law has operated to deny property rights or to acknowledge them sparingly, only to extinguish them again; it has been a tool of oppression and colonisation. For a society in which all members are supposed to be equal under the law, an analysis of the way in which property rights have been valued according to a discriminatory double standard reveals the dual legal system that has operated in Australia since 1788: one for white Australia, the other for indigenous Australians.

These recent developments concerning Aboriginal property rights in Australia have been frustrating for the Aboriginal community and the advocates and supporters working to protect those rights. Each incremental and piecemeal gain made within the judicial system has been truncated or extinguished by a legislature with a conflicting ideology and agenda. For Australia's indigenous peoples, the legacy of *terra nullius* may have been overturned by Mabo, but another ideological enemy remains: while Australia has a dominant group who embraces a psychological *terra nullius*, any legal advances are vulnerable to legislative extinguishment. This psychological *terra nullius* allows Australians like John Howard to separate the property rights of indigenous Australians from those of all other Australians. It is a distinction which devalues indigenous property rights. Until this *terra nullius* mindset is overturned, Aboriginal property rights will remain vulnerable.

This mindset is encapsulated in the notion of a 'psychological *terra nullius*'. This concept captures the notion that, whilst formal equality may have been seen to be accorded through Australia's democratic institutions, parts of the Australian community are still under the spell of the myth of *terra nullius* to the extent that they are not yet capable of affording the property rights of indigenous Australians equal protection. Democratic institutions and sectors of the Australian community still embrace a version of history that ignores indigenous presence, that continues the myth that Australia was unoccupied or without sovereignty before white settlement. Australian courts may have overturned the legal fiction but, through the political system, indigenous property rights remain vulnerable to extinguishment. Coexistence will not be achieved until all Australians and Australian institutions come to terms with the historical realities.

The Constitution

Piecemeal gains in the court are vulnerable to political legislative actions. If court victories offer only sporadic and episodic protections, which are limited or overturned by the legislature's political will, the Commonwealth Constitution remains the last bastion for rights protection. This area offers very few guarantees. Australia has no Bill of Rights and minimal rights are recognised in the Constitution; more have been implied. The issue of whether the race power, which allows the Federal Government to make laws with regard to indigenous people, could be used to deprive indigenous people of their rights was raised by the plaintiff in *Kartinyeri v. Commonwealth* (1998). In that case, brought in a dispute over a development site that the plaintiff had claimed was sacred to her, the government sought to settle the matter by passing an Act, the *Hindmarsh Island Bridge Act 1997* (Cth). The Act was designed to repeal the application of heritage protection laws to the plaintiff. The plaintiff argued, inter alia, that when Australians voted in the 1967 Referendum to extend the federal race power in the Constitution (s 51(xxvi)) to include the power to make laws concerning Aboriginal people, it was with the understanding that the power would be used to benefit indigenous peoples. The court did not directly answer this issue, finding that the *Hindmarsh Island Bridge Act* merely repealed legislation. The majority held that the power to make laws also contains the power to repeal or amend them. Only Kirby J dissented, making reference to international standards and Australia's international obligations. Gaudron, Gummow and Hayne JJ implied the possible existence of a supervisory jurisdiction of the court to protect 'manifest abuse' of the race power. Kirby J in dissent held that the race power could not support discriminatory legislation. This decision was seen as a victory by the Howard Government, which saw constitutional challenges to amending legislation that extinguished native title rights as much harder to mount.

Equal protection

Even when indigenous rights are recognised under the law, they are valued less than the property rights that vest in other Australians. Indigenous property needs to be valued in the same way as non-indigenous property and native title needs to be conceptualised as a valuable property right, like all other property rights. Constitutional protection is uncertain. When it is remembered that there is a large body of case law that supports a broad definition of property and its protection, this lack of protection of indigenous rights is an anomaly in Australian law. If there is a guarantee of equal protection, all property rights need to be protected in a way that values the right held by the individual, whether that protection is in the form of recognition of the right or in the form of just terms compensation.

If these broad interpretations and protections were applied to native title, they would work to protect native title against extinguishment, pay just compensation when extinguishment has occurred, recognise fishing rights where the elements needed to establish native title can be shown (Behrendt 1995), and recognise native title where mining and pastoral leases have not substantially disrupted the attachment to land.

Central to the recognition of indigenous property rights is the need to recognise past injustices and past discrimination. Though this may seem tokenistic, such recognition has four consequences that could have profound effects on the relationship that Aboriginal people have with the rest of Australia:

1. It restores dignity to Aboriginal people, which is fundamental to self-respect and a feeling of acceptance.
2. It understands that recognition of the treatment of Aboriginal people and the true story of how Australia was invaded will have a profound effect on Australia's national identity.
3. It acknowledges that recognition of prior ownership by Aboriginal people could have legal implications.
4. It also counters the psychological *terra nullius* which allows arbitrary lines to be drawn between the rights of indigenous Australians and the rights of others. This seeks to place Aboriginal claims in a rights-based framework rather than base them on the notion that such rights are derived from a special status held by the minority group. The argument shifts from: 'As the indigenous people of this country we deserve our land rights' to: 'Every individual is entitled to have his/her property rights protected. Since native title interests are legitimate property rights they should enjoy the same status and protection as other property rights.'

Democratic principles: substantive equality and effective participation

Due to their numerical minority, indigenous Australians are largely dependent on (politicised) legal victories and public sympathy — such as the groundswell of public support in 1967 — to bring attention to their situation and to seek reform. Rights protection needs to be institutionalised so that basic rights are not vulnerable to political whim and ideology.

If weaknesses in Australia's democratic institutions can be identified, institutional change that will produce different results from the inequities which currently exist can be developed. Such changes need to be made with Aboriginal political aspirations in mind to ensure responsiveness to those aspirations and to avoid paternalism. Australia's property rights regime points to two democratic principles which can give guidance to this much-needed institutional change: substantive equality and effective participation.

Substantive equality

Australia's apparently neutral property laws operate in such a way as to produce a result where the rights of one group of Australians are valued less than the rights of all others. It is not enough that laws be equal on their face; their application must generate equality.

Equality needs to be measured not by the mere existence of a rights framework, but by assessing the end results of that framework. The focus needs to be on what happens after the institutions and ideals are placed on society, not on how it looks in the abstract; equality needs to be substantive and must be judged on its results. Every society owes its members an environment in which basic rights (equality, participation, association, protection of property, etc.) can proliferate. Rights conferred on members of a community should be applied to all segments of that society equally.

Effective participation

Perhaps the biggest condemnation of Australia's institutions is revealed in the fact that many of the rights that indigenous people are seeking are ones that other Australians unquestioningly enjoy; rights to medical treatment, education and food and protection of property all feature prominently in the claims of indigenous rights.

As a democratic government, Australia embraces the notion of a representative government. Members of the community are represented by the elected members of political parties. Given the small numbers of the Aboriginal community, it is hard for representative government to be effective. If Aboriginal people are 2 per cent of the total population, their voice is not going to be strong. In some areas, like the Northern Territory, numbers can be higher, making political representation much more responsive to community needs, but in urban areas Aboriginal people might make up less than 0.5 per cent of the population in an electoral district, even if they are living in an enclave where their community makes up almost 100 per cent of the four or so blocks that they live in.

Universal suffrage has been ineffective in providing equality and participation for indigenous peoples. Aboriginal people were given full citizenship rights but as a numerical minority it has been difficult for them to create the political pressure necessary to initiate changes in their socio-economic position or to change school curricula or national sentiment to create a more tolerant and diverse environment.

Any group within society which is alienated from political processes is subject to discrimination, and its socio-economic disadvantage presents a challenge to any society which holds democratic principles as ideals. Inclusion in society needs to be given content through effective participation. The right to participate in the political structures of society is central; it is recognised in the right of self-determination. This right is vested in every person, regardless of his or her relationship with the state. Even if Aboriginal peoples are not recognised as 'peoples' for the purpose of international law, their right to self-determination is guaranteed through the international human rights regime, as Australians, and this gives rise to the right to be involved in the political institutions which govern their lives.

Applying the principles

This situation of disempowerment could begin to be rectified by:

- empowering Aboriginal people at a grassroots level through the decentralisation of decision-making (this means allowing communities to take more control over the policies and programs implemented within their local areas); and

- promoting a fluid political climate which encourages alliance building between different interest groups so that Aboriginal people can join with other political minority groups to form a majority on certain issues.

It is this broader vision of democracy which should be a starting point when seeking to accommodate disadvantaged and poverty-stricken groups within society. These two democratic principles of effective participation and substantive equality are important goals in a program of institutional transformation which would empower Aboriginal communities and break down socio-economic disparities. Working towards these democratic goals will create institutions that include all members of society; the most vulnerable and disadvantaged providing a litmus test to measure how effectively those goals are being met.

Even though the Australian legal system has overturned the legal fiction of *terra nullius*, the next challenge for those working to ensure the recognition and protection of indigenous rights is to counter the permutations of the psychological *terra nullius*, still prevalent in some sectors of Australian society. This would include considering measures such as:

- symbolic recognition to counter expressions of a psychological *terra nullius* — for example, recognition of prior ownership, custodianship and/or guardianship of Australia by Aboriginal and Torres Strait Islander people; formal apologies from governments for the removal of indigenous children from their families and other practices of genocide and assimilation; inclusion of indigenous experiences and perspectives in school curricula;

- the delegation of decision-making powers to Aboriginal and Torres Strait Island communities to facilitate self-government at a grassroots, local level; and

- the development of a rights-based framework that rejects notions of formal equality in favour of a model that embraces substantive equality and looks at the effects of policies and laws on indigenous populations.

Until Australia takes an honest look at the situation of Aboriginal people and their continued exclusion from a system of supposedly representative government and reassesses its notions of national identity to recognise the honest and broad experience of all Australians, true representative democracy will be elusive. The current situation of indigenous Australians demands that all Australians come to terms with their history and their ideals. It requires a critical questioning of what democracy means in Australia. Indigenous people can be agents to facilitate the energised politics necessary to begin the path towards the transformation of institutions as part of the democratic process. Felix Cohen stated:

> *The Indian plays the same role in our American society that the Jews played in Germany. Like the miner's canary, the Indian marks the shift from fresh air to poison gas in our political atmosphere; and our treatment of Indians, even more than our treatment of other minorities, reflects the rise and fall of democratic faith.* (Cohen 1960, p. 202)

Aboriginal people, as Gough Whitlam observed, are Australia's 'miner's canary'. They are the measure of substantive equality and effective political participation, the true test of Australia's democratic institutions and the standard by which history will judge Australia.

chapter 14

To praise youth or to bury it?
by Tony Moore

A burning question confronting teenagers and young adults today is how as a democratic society we are to move from an industrial to a post-industrial society without sacrificing yet another generation (Eckersley 1989). While the governments of Hawke and Keating managed necessary change during the 1980s and '90s, Labor pushed its reform agenda without fully appreciating how economic restructuring was overturning the career paths of young Australians. In place of a job — the passport to adult citizenship — many have endured a no-man's-land of unemployment, casual dead-end work, mean-spirited welfare and warehousing in schools and training courses. Now, under the Coalition, the Federal Government is abandoning even its training and welfare commitments, stripping young people of the last vestiges of labour market protection while demanding conformity to an anachronistic 1950s' work ethic. The centrepiece of John Howard's youth policy, the punitive work-for-the-dole scheme, wantonly disregards the skill demands of the contemporary economy and blames the young victims for their own unemployment at a time when the real causes are well known.

Hardest hit by unemployment and its attendant woes of poverty and cultural dispossession have been kids from working-class communities. Yet Labor's 'youth policy' ignored cries from its heartland and was insensitive to differences of class among young Australians. At both the federal and State levels Labor and Coalition governments in the '80s and '90s adopted a crude, monolithic concept of 'youth' — shorn of social diversity, difference and citizenship rights. The Labor Party's continuing failure to move beyond the platitudes of youth rights and come to terms with the messy reality of post-industrial youth subcultures threatens the loss of a new generation, to both the nation and social democratic politics. In this chapter I examine the failure of both major parties on *the* key youth issue of their times in government, and suggest a sharper analysis for today.

Roots of the 'youth problem'

Labor is often touted as the party with youth appeal. Certainly since the Whitlam 'It's Time' campaign the party has tended to poll well with younger voters. But have Labor governments returned the favour?

When Labor swept into office in early 1983 unemployment was at 10 per cent and the new government embarked on an ambitious expenditure program to create jobs in the private and public sectors. The Hawke Government's admirable ambitions to get the unemployed, and particularly young people, back to work were to run aground against its wider agenda to integrate Australia into the global economy and the Treasury's adherence to the new orthodoxy of neo-liberal market policy.

The problem of youth unemployment refused to go away, despite the creation of a million new jobs and impressive economic growth (Polk & Tait 1989, p. 18). As teenagers became more visible on the streets, politicians, media, police, clergy and youth workers began to talk about a 'youth problem' associated with an escalation in disobedience at school, joblessness, homelessness, substance abuse, delinquency and crime (Irving, Maunders & Sherrington 1995, pp. 226–31). Paradoxically, the elevation of 'young people' to Hawke's 'Priority One' in 1985 set them up for new reversals. Youth unemployment remained entrenched at a level between 15 and 20 per cent, yet the young suffered heavily under subsequent federal cutbacks to services and benefits and endured declining incomes and job opportunities throughout the '90s (Polk & Tait 1989, p. 21).

Labor did not come to terms with the fundamentals, eschewing job creation in 1986 for increased retention in schools and short-term programs designed to teach job-search skills and provide basic vocational qualifications (Sherrington & Irving 1989, p. 19). Good intentions, patronising politics and professionally administered programs filled glossy government reports but failed to address what ABC Television saw as the 'crime of the decade', as school leavers from working-class backgrounds encountered a restructuring labour market that did not need many full-time teenage workers.

Many long-term unemployed drifted into aberrant behaviour, delinquency, substance abuse, ill-health and, increasingly, suicide (Eckersley 1989, p. 3; Polk & Tait 1989, p. 22). Others just became passive welfare recipients or underemployed, never quite living up to their potential — a lost generation. (Polk & Tait 1989, p. 18). A 1989 ABC television documentary[1] and the Human Rights and Equal Opportunity Commission's report *Our Homeless Children* both warned that Australia risked creating a permanent youth underclass extending into the next generation if urgent action was not taken. Sadly this appears to have happened. On the latest evidence, one-fifth 20–25-year-olds are at risk of falling into long-term unemployment *despite* improved economic conditions. A recent report, *Australia's Young Adults: The Deepening Divide*, concluded that over the last two decades young adults up to the age of 24 have actually slipped backwards in job prospects and income levels, stuck in work that is low skilled, part time and casual, largely in small companies offering little training or security (Dusseldorp Skills Forum 1999, pp. 2–5).

The Howard Government blames high youth wages, inadequate skills and a poor work ethic, but most commentators now see the 'radical transformation of work' as the prime cause of a structural unemployment among teenagers and young adults (Eckersley 1988; Freeland 1986; Polk & Tait 1989). These changes have eliminated not just the entry-level occupations, but also the career pathways within industries. Unemployment has hit some regions and types of work much harder than others (Polk & Tait 1989, p. 19). Skilled and semi-skilled blue-collar employment in manufacturing has declined while the information and service sectors have greatly expanded, offering the extremes of high-skilled, well-paid jobs for some and low-skilled, poorly paid under-employment for others. Well-resourced children from privileged and educated families, together with the smart and the lucky, went to university and had a chance, but the children from Labor's heartland were the casualties of change.

Looking back, the approach of governments to the 'youth problem' was to quarter the redundant in education, training and labour market programs (such as EPYU, Participation and Equity Program, Job Start, New Start, Skill Share), while demonising the troublemakers through moral panics about dole bludgers, graffiti, street kids, Asian crime, drugs and gangs (Davis 1997, pp. 232–54; National Inquiry into Racist Violence 1991).[2] Campaigns by politicians on both sides have maligned the cultures and curtailed the actual liberty of teenagers and young adults. The rhetoric of the Howard Government suggests that 'youth' is now synonymous with an undeserving welfare category that is resented by taxpayers (including workers under 25), who want the young unemployed to work for their meagre unemployment benefit.

The best and brightest youngsters, patronised as 'Australia's future' for going on two decades now, complain about another 'gangland', a middle-aged power elite who squat comfortably at the centre of political and cultural life (Davis 1997). Today the limbo of 'youth' is extending de facto into the early thirties of a so-called 'generation X'. In conferences, seminars, roundtables and stand-alone chapters we are witnessing the ghettoisation of a generation, an afterthought tacked on the end of the 'real' debates about trade, industry policy, taxation, immigration and constitutional reform.

Corporatism and the youth discourse

Today, with the ALP in opposition after ruling for thirteen years, it is important to consider how Labor governed and what aspects of its administrative style undid the best intentions of the party and its leaders. In the lead-up to International Youth Year in 1985, Australian governments followed the UN's lead and defined citizens aged fifteen to 25 as 'young people', a group with unique and urgent needs (Irving, Maunders & Sherrington 1995, p. 235). Under federal Labor, 'youth' became a special interest group with its due slice of the disadvantaged orange, along with ethnics, the disabled, Aborigines and women. In a bid to neutralise dissatisfaction with entrenched teenage unemployment and to woo a new generation of voters, bureaucracies were established in a flurry of platitudinous rhetoric. With the best intentions, public servants, in tandem with youth workers, educators and trainers, went about constructing a new age-based segregation that legitimated the 'warehousing' of under-employed citizens until well into adulthood. Younger Australians were cleaved from other citizens as an essentialised 'other'. This crude categorisation was suited to a corporatist style that identified social groups, co-opted favoured leaders into the bureaucracy and traded reforms for electoral mileage.

The idea of 'youth' is a conceptual and public relations disaster, homogenising social reality, blunting policy formulation, absolving attacks from the right, and masking economic redundancy. Artificially divorced from other elements in society — especially class — youth policy during the Labor years did little to shepherd young Australians through the period of accelerated changes to family life, women's roles, education, work, technology, ethnic diversity and the role of the state (Eckersley 1989, p. 3). Many in the community sector, the broad left, the social movements, the ALP, the Democrats and the ABC, remembering the student radicalism of the '60s, uncritically applaud 'youth politics' as progressive when in fact three conservative themes dominate the construct: elitism, dependence and homogeneity.

Since the discovery of 'adolescence' in the nineteenth century, Western society has seen the elongation of 'youth' and postponement of adulthood in tandem with the removal of children and younger teens from the workforce (Sherrington & Irving 1989, p. 12). Legislation protecting children from industrial exploitation went hand in glove with the new idea that the next generation should be educated and trained for citizenship and work in modern industry.

The establishment of compulsory primary education in the late nineteenth century was followed this century by vocational continuation schools, technical colleges, apprenticeships and selective high schools for the academically orientated minority.

A generational discourse has attained the status of commonsense over the past four decades, in the wake of the commercial discovery of the teenager in the 1950s, the student ferment post-1968, and the growth in unemployment since the late 1970s. The language used by the youth activists of the Labor years was lifted from 1960s generational rhetoric and tended to universalise the idealistic, articulate, middle-class university student. Thanks to the eloquence of some vocal 'spokespeople of a generation', the ideas of generational homogeneity and prolonged youth were entrenched in the media (Gerstner & Bassett 1991, pp. 1–36). By the early 1970s, the popular consciousness was saddled with the notion of a new generational class that was changing the world (Alomes 1983, pp. 35–42). The catchy theme of the American TV show *The Monkees* said it all: 'We're the young generation, and we've got something to say.'

Homogeneity

'Youth' is an artificial construct because it denies the incredible diversity of class, ethnicity, education, geography and interest within any age group. 'Youth' politics ignores the messy reality that younger people, like their parents, are different from each other and take these differences into adulthood. The growing diversity within Australia is especially marked among younger Australians, where the impacts of immigration, economic restructuring, family dysfunction and new media are manifested. Policies informed by the modernist categorisation of human beings into mass groupings looked good on paper but struggled to keep up with cultural change since the '80s, such as the emergence of identity politics, the widening of social division and the fragmentation of teenagers into a dizzying array of subcultural tribes.

This is not to discount the shared experiences that bond a particular age cohort and make people growing up in a particular time and place distinct from older people who preceded them, and from younger people who will come later.

This is the unique cultural disposition of a generation that Raymond Williams called the 'structure of feeling' (Williams 1961, p. 47). But whether the experience confronting the young is war, economic boom, unemployment or the Internet, such experiences are mediated through the socio-economic and ethnic background of the family, neighbourhood culture, and by the education and the type of media the child absorbs.

As personified by Ari, the troubled young man living between worlds in the novel *Loaded* (Tsiolkas 1995) and the film *Head On*, boys and girls assemble multi-identities from the material surrounding them as they grow up — the immigration experience, family, religion and politics, global TV and music culture, neighbourhood norms and opportunities — which are expressed through gendered bodies and personalities still trying to sort out their sexuality. In their protean, constantly morphing lifestyles, young people of the last two decades have explicitly rejected the 'generational' roles and labels that have typified twentieth-century marketing and social management.

Elitism

During the '80s the idea of 'youth' as a special interest was elevated to giddy heights, nursed at the bosom of youth workers, promoted by Hawke corporatism and revered as gospel by a new generation of fashionably left-of-centre 'youth' leaders and bureaucrats. Labor politicians thought they were being radical, tapping the 'voice of youth', but it is important to see how comfortably 'youth participation' dovetailed with the elitism of traditional youth leadership movements, such as the Boy Scouts and Girl Guides. The all-purpose solution to the problems of youth was a fuzzy concept of consultation and participation called 'empowerment', which passed from the United States via the community youth sector into Commonwealth and State governments' Offices of Youth Affairs during International Youth Year (Irving, Maunders & Sherrington 1995, p. 312). Occurring within a classless framework, this principle degenerated into the selection and promotion of teenagers sufficiently articulate and confident to negotiate the new youth bureaucracies (Irving, Maunders & Sherrington

1995, p. 340). Youth was empowered by putting a handful of well-meaning high-flyers on committees, a practice that continues today with the Howard Government's Youth Roundtable and numerous State-based equivalents. Unfortunately, though, it is doubtful whether young workers or the unemployed are even aware that they have acquired a voice.

Less than adult

In order to work for International Youth Year (IYY) it was preferred that you scraped under the magic age of 25. I was lucky enough to land a job as policy officer for IYY in New South Wales and confess that prior to taking the job had never thought of myself as a 'youth'. Growing up in Wollongong I was accustomed to the blue-collar idea that once in work you were an adult who paid board to the family household. My friends at university had also seen themselves as men and women going places, and were eager to take leadership roles in society. Looking back, I still recall the feeling of *dis*empowerment that accompanied the metamorphosis from adult man of 24 to a patronised, token 'young person'.

Australians between eighteen and 25 forfeited citizenship for 'youth rights' and forfeited the sort of real power past generations had enjoyed in times of full employment. Youth is a dubious basis from which to argue for rights, as it conjures associations less-than-adult, such as 'dependency', 'inexperience', 'apprenticeship' — people not quite up to making a proper contribution to society.

It seems that for politicians, 'youth' sets in motion a chain of conservative values that underpin policy prescriptions: young people are vulnerable and belong at home with the family; they are the responsibility of their parents; they are unskilled; they should be supported financially by their parents; they have fewer commitments, lower living costs and require less income; their parents subsidise them anyway; if young people have higher unemployment it is because they have few skills, poor attitudes and expect too much; youth wages should be lowered to make them more competitive; young people should earn their dole; anyway, kids should be in school or tech and not making a nuisance of themselves in public places ...

Dependency

The income support policies of Labor and Coalition governments share the assumption that young people up to the age of 25 are the responsibility of parents and have lower living costs. The Hawke Government's 'reform of income support', with its age-based tiers, and family means tests (tightened and zealously policed since the Coalition came to power), failed to grasp that unemployment is concentrated in the multi-disadvantaged families least able to support children over 16 (Howe 1989; Polk & Tait 1989, p. 18; Van Ryke 1986; Trethewey & Burston 1989, pp. 47–9). Universalising the experience of better-off youth subsidised by parents, governments incorrectly assume that parents of the unemployed are able and willing to support them. But research shows that many parents of early school leavers not only cannot support them, but regard children over 16 as independent adults who should pay board (Mass 1990, pp. 24–9; Trethewey & Burston 1989; Moore 1988). Since 1982 the number of 15–24-year-olds dependent on their parents has increased by 12 per cent, reaching 58 per cent in 1996 (Dusseldorp Skills Forum 1999, p. 4). The result is increasing family tension (Eckersley 1989, p. 4).

The push to dependency flies in the face of reality. Out in the suburbs, over-18s confront the burdens and responsibilities of adult citizenship: paying tax and rents, buying clothes and food at the same price as everyone else. Less than a fifth are students. Some are in unions or are eligible to join. If they commit a crime they go to adult prison. They can join the army and serve overseas. Over-18s can vote. Many young people are married, in de facto relationships and are parents of young children themselves (Dusseldorp Skills Forum 1999, p. 4). Many are struggling to buy a home. But you seldom hear about these young adults and their concerns from the professional, tertiary-educated 'youths' anointed by governments, arts bureaucrats and the media.

By defining this age group as less than adult we weaken their access to citizens' rights, such as the right to a living income when working or when searching for work. The ideology of youth legitimates a drive by both Coalition and Labor governments to prolong far into adulthood the juvenile period of dependency and quasi-citizenship. The economically redundant are warehoused well into their midtwenties within education and training programs, often at their parents' expense. Welfare is privatised within the family.

Policy without class

The issue of class was missing from Labor's youth policy, the ghost at the IYY banquet. Working in the youth sector alongside government officials in the mid '80s I was astonished that the term 'class' was never used, indeed never occurred to technocrats, who spoke about the 'disadvantaged', a condescending code for non-middle-class people who needed correction.

This omission is surprising given that some of the Labor ministers erecting this mandarin-slice view of society were socialists. It came about due to the collusion between Hawke's right-wing consensus view of Australian society and the broad left's naive internationalisation of '60s generational rhetoric.

Yet the best minds of the intellectual new left, including sociologist Bob Connell, educationalist John Freeland and political economist Frank Stilwell, had produced ample evidence of the persistence of class division in Australia (Connell et al. 1982; Freeland 1986, 1987; Stilwell 1986). Study after study shows that the disadvantage endured by many teenagers in welfare, wages, education, health, transport and recreation stem from where they live and from the position their families occupy in the economy. Indeed an articulate case for a class perspective based on thorough research emerged from within the youth affairs sector itself in the mid '80s, but was largely ignored by government policy-makers (Van Ryke 1986, pp. 42–5; Pisarski 1987). The fuzzy idea of 'disadvantage' that was built into some programs identified indicators that impede 'middle-class' expectations, such as coming from a non-English speaking background or being 'rural and isolated', but never came to terms with the unravelling of the working-class way of life.

'Youth unemployment' is a misnomer, obscuring the reality that it is unskilled and semi-skilled jobs traditionally undertaken by early school leavers that have disappeared. Those who are culturally predisposed and who can afford to remain in education until their early twenties are unaffected by the retraction in working-class jobs, taking the lion's share of part-time and casual work in the service sector while studying and moving into new areas of the expanding information economy after graduating (Dusseldorp Skills Forum 1999, p. 5). What we now have is working-class and rural unemployment that lasts well into adulthood and often into the next generation.

This class blindness marred Labor's ambitions for a 'clever country' with increased participation in higher education. Between 1981 and 1987, Year 12 retention rates rose from 34.8 to 53.1 per cent — still low by OECD standards but a revolution for Australia. Persuaded that education, rather than the labour market, was the place for older teenagers, the Hawke Government restricted access to unemployment benefit for 16–18-year-olds, in comparison to a more generous Austudy. However, teenagers from Labor's heartland continued to leave education early and endure unemployment on less money. The stick-and-carrot policy ignores the studies showing the difficulties working-class kids have with the competitive academic curriculum of the senior years of high school (Connell et al. 1982; Dwyer, Wilson & Woock 1984, pp. 47–68; Walker 1988). Senior school participation remains lowest in Anglo-Celtic areas where the traditional working-class culture is proud of manual work and the wages it used to command and can be culturally hostile to the abstract way schools teach knowledge and credential ability.

Schools impart and assess upper-middle-class culture, not the commonsense of working life or popular culture and neighbourhood peer groups. Once, working-class kids who did not perform well academically left after they turned fifteen, like Paul Keating, to get a full-time job. They were not drop-outs; they were simply on a different career path. Now that these career paths are gone, those kids compelled to stay at school are learning about failure. But teenagers remaining in school perform the valuable service of being absent from the unemployment statistics.

Cultural gangland

If things have been awful for the young unemployed, what of the young people who swelled John Dawkins' expanding universities in the 1980s and '90s? Students who matriculated into universities got saddled with fees, then graduated to face loan repayments and an uncertain labour market.

In *Gangland*, Mark Davis documents a network of old boys and girls from the '60s, rusted into positions of control in gatekeeper institutions they helped create, censoring new ideas while jealously excluding the best and brightest of the younger generations. The boomers' new motto — don't trust anyone *under* 30. In this sense the term 'youth' is used to keep competitors in the margins, to exclude and disempower competition, to hoard resources. That's why Lindsay Tanner and Mark Latham are called 'Young Turks'. Younger academics, artists, media workers and politicians complain with some justification of a cultural myopia, a nation entering the next century with its eyes keenly on the 1960s. Recently, however, Australia has witnessed a spontaneous creative outburst from much younger film-makers, comedians, musicians, web-page designers, publishers, journalists, politicians and agents provocateurs such as Jon Safran. A breath of fresh air, these new cultural and political guerillas have little respect for their elders and are too busy creating their own public spaces to be concerned with traditional institutions like Aunty ABC or the *Sydney Morning Herald*.

Davis is impressive in documenting the growth of a left–right conservative anti-youth rhetoric by middle-aged commentators pledged to defend civilisation. Just as in the 1960s, today's moral panics target both delinquents (usually working class or 'ethnic') and the 'ratbags' involved in fringe politics, alternative lifestyles and outrageous ideas. While rap music, 'homeboys' and Asian gangs threatened law and order on the street, greenies, postmodernists, deconstructers, cyber-pornographers and 'political correctness' white-ant our universities, schools and the Internet.

All parties and governments need to reconsider their censorious attitude to culture and their paternalistic attitude to young people. In the name of protecting youth, the Coalition seems hell-bent on returning to the censorship regime that operated during the Menzies years. We are seeing an alarming tightening of censorship of media culture under the Coalition Government, an offensive that targets young people as both innocents to shield and perpetrators to fear. But the Hawke and Keating governments, on the other hand, were far too fond of ham-fisted social engineering crudely applied by toady bureaucrats.

The problem with Labor's penchant for policing culture is that working-class people, the young, Aborigines and newly arrived migrants are less able or inclined to police their language or jettison long-held customs in favour of the latest version of middle-class manners. Cultural policing assumes that signs have fixed meanings shared by everyone, that can be measured and seen to have an effect, which is never the case in the real world where young people, especially, experiment with identities and negotiate their differences.

The future

As a no-man's-land between childhood and adulthood, 'youth' is an easy target for law and order campaigns, employers bent on lower wages, and governments looking to cut spending. I advocate a new approach to young people based on citizens' rights. A social democratic government should acknowledge that all Australians 16 years and over share the same human rights as citizens, and cannot be discriminated against on the basis of age, especially with regard to wages and income support. Australia should bite the bullet and lower the voting age to 16. The advocacy of youth rights is bad politics. Instead, argue for the rights of citizens or for universal human rights. Unfortunately, the federal opposition's populist capitulation to the Coalition's entrenchment of junior wage rates suggests Labor still believes adult rights begin at 21.

It is essential to dismantle the barrier that divides the unemployed from workers and youth from adults. It is not helpful for the up-and-coming generations to be corralled in a youth ghetto, whether in training and welfare or TV programming and arts grants. Good communities are made up of people from all ages, helping and learning from each other. Mark Davis is right — Australia has a bad dose of cultural constipation, caused less by boomer intransigence than by the structural and ideological lockout of a generation. Cross-generational dialogue makes for a healthy, open-minded society and will enhance empathy and cultural renewal.

That goes for politics as well. In the present hostile climate, youth advocates should be building bridges with other progressive bodies, not constructing a single-issue fortress. The community 'youth' sector that represents young people to government has long internalised the stereotypes of 'youth' as students or welfare recipients. The corollary is that unions have often ignored workers under 25, especially when they are unemployed. The union movement's spirited determination to abolish junior wage rates, despite swinging voter opposition and Labor's cave-in, shows real policy strength and points the way forward. Younger workers will only join up if unions are seen to be delivering the material benefits and protection they so badly need. Unions will become irrelevant unless they get their heads out of the blue-collar past and make a *militant* effort to organise young people working in the information and service industries of the private sector.

The Howard Government blames the young unemployed for their fate, and pretends that lower youth wages and a bit of industrial discipline via the electorally popular work-for-the-dole scheme will actually remedy the situation. The Dusseldorp Skills Forum argues that neither market deregulation, lower youth wages and less protection from dismissal, nor training and skills acquisition has eased an unemployment level among young adults, which is stuck at around 10 per cent — with a further 8.7 per cent in neither the labour force nor education (Dusseldorp Skills Forum 1999, p. 4). Future governments should treat this figure as a *class* problem. Economic growth has created jobs, but not too many for unqualified early school leavers (Polk & Tait 1989, p. 18). The big challenge for social democrats is to help young people from working-class backgrounds find work in the new expanding areas of the information and service economy.

School reform — the key

A cultural predisposition to manual work instilled in families over generations disadvantages these kids at school, and makes it difficult for boys in particular to find a place in the new working world of service and communication. The fundamental reform of public secondary schooling is a priority, so that education can truly be a bridge from the old society to the new for those least able to make the crossing. State governments embarked on a similar project at the beginning of the twentieth century to shepherd potential workers into the industrial age, and future governments should have the vision to erect an education system for the new age (Sherrington & Irving 1989, p. 11).

Unfortunately, our schools remain organised like factories in an age when there are few factories to go to, imposing industrial-age discipline on young adults who live in a post-industrial age, and a tertiary-orientated curriculum on kids who will not go to university. Hence the 'crisis in public schools' prevails, as working-class kids 'act out' against this babysitting, and middle-class parents desert the local comprehensive for private and boutique selective schools. Governments and employers harp on about schools teaching vocational skills, but specialised workskills will be obsolete in no time, narrowing an employee's options when what is needed is flexibility. The key goal today should be cultural literacy, by which I mean the acquisition of creativity, knowledge, self-discipline and the skills necessary to prosper in a fluid work environment, develop individual potential, encourage lifelong learning and participate in a democracy. Teachers should be more valued and value-added, which means better educated, frequently re-educated, better paid and encouraged to move in and out of the profession to get a grip on the changing world outside the school.

Career paths

The market has not delivered lifelong careers in the post-industrial economy that take a teenager from, say, burger-making at McDonald's to restaurant management. This is a problem that starts when people leave education but reverberates throughout a person's life. Government must intervene to create career paths between the mish-mash of temporary, part-time and casual jobs that dominate the lower rungs of the information and service sectors (Dusseldorp Skills Forum 1999, p. 7). Labor's introduction of traineeships in fragmented industries was a good idea, poorly marketed, as opposed to Howard's careful use of the blue-collar-friendly term 'apprenticeships'. The Dusseldorp Skills Forum suggests public incentives for employers to convert casual jobs into traineeships. Any government-created employment opportunities must be enmeshed into the growing areas of the new economy. Offering public subsidy to employers to take on the young unemployed in real jobs in private businesses, the government sector and community organisations is preferable to the dead-end work-for-the dole scheme.

Optimism

There is cause for optimism. The passing of the industrial era has caused great dislocation, but it is an opportunity for a true liberation of human potential as younger people respond to the increase in information, the loosening of Fordist discipline, the end of fixed lifelong roles and the sharding of mass culture. In the absence of steady careers, more and more young people are finding identity in what they *do* rather than in what they are *paid* to do. What was so good about hierarchical, boring industrial jobs anyway? Why have social democrats become the nostalgic defenders of a postwar Keynesian settlement that the new left originally believed to be pretty dehumanising? Socialism was always a means to an end — an unleashing of our full humanity.

In an information-saturated post-industrial economy where we produce value-added information rather than manufactured objects, cultural production will occur in small self-managed units which cater for a diversity of groups that make up the market, with a reduced emphasis on assembly lines, mass markets and vertical control by hierarchies of management. The times favour younger producers open to new ideas and flexible ways of working. The young have never been more skilled. Evidence suggests a growth in creative recreation and hobbies among the young, a move from passive consumption to active cultural production. From web-page design to short films to comedy to TV, younger people are taking a leaf out of the old punk adage and doing it themselves.[3]

In cultural policy, social democrats need to move away from outmoded ideas that progressive culture lies with 'community' or 'avant-garde' practitioners, and engage with the creativity and vitality of popular culture. Today the immersion of young people in digital technology, the Internet, music and identity subcultures suggests a way forward for a postmodern assertion of identity beyond the market. Significantly, unwaged cultural practices that contribute to a community often lead to careers in the new economy. Kids are building incomes and careers out of their cultural pursuits. Social democratic government should encourage, through community infrastructure, the *actual* creative, productive activities of the young.

There is no going back. At the century's end Australia's middle-aged leaders are locked in a battle for competing nostalgias. Howard's Liberals yearn for a mythical white-bread, picket-fenced 1950s without today's noisy minorities, while too many on the left cling to 1960s radicalism and the Whitlam renaissance as the measure of all progress. But young Australians are creating the future regardless of government plans, and it behoves all parties to embrace their cultural reality. Social democrats need to move beyond generationalism left over from the 1960s, acknowledge the persistence of class, and embrace a politics based on diversity, difference, autonomy and identity.

chapter 15

Evolutionary multiculturalism and cultural diversity
by Jason Yat-Sen Li and James Cockayne

I was born in Paddington Women's Hospital in Sydney. I grew up playing touch football with my mates on the grassy playgrounds of Kingsgrove and Hurstville public schools. I grew up with the understanding of freedom which the treasure of space in Australia gives to young children. I grew up with the sea by my side.

I had been in The Hague, the Netherlands, for over a year. My heart was low that night and I had returned to the sea at Schevengingen to walk. Closing my eyes, I could hear the gulls' squawks and the sounds of the waves and I could feel the presence of that immense body of water in front of me. And for that moment I felt grounded, secured, because it reminded me of Australia.

Soon after, I entered a bar, and as one does, struck up a conversation with a Dutchman. 'Where are you from?' he asked. I told him I was Australian. His brow furrowed. 'You know, you don't look very Australian. Are you sure you're not Japanese?'

Introduction

Since 1945, more than 5.5 million immigrants have come to this country. Twenty-five per cent of all Australians now come from a non-English speaking background (NESB);

40 per cent of us are migrants or the children of migrants. In the last half-century, Australia has — by design or accident — undertaken one of the greatest experiments in pluralistic immigration, culture and citizenship in the world. Only Israel has had a greater rate of immigrant intake.

Yet immigration must not be understood as a modern or postwar phenomenon. In truth, Australia is, and has always been, the land of the immigrant. Putting aside the history of the arrival of indigenous Australians to the continent, the modern history of Australian immigration begins in 1788. Then, Australia was already a multicultural, multilingual continent (Ruddock 1996, p. 1). Since 1788, immigration has built our Australian population and, together with cultural diversity, underpins our modern Australian heritage.

The attitudes of Australians to immigration and cultural diversity remain complex. Between 1901 and 1945, the Federal Government pursued policies of monoculturalism, excluding some people from Australian citizenship and even residence on the basis that their culture, ethnicity or race was different. Difference precluded equality. After World War II, monoculturalist policies were continued as Australia attempted to assimilate new European citizens, forcing them to abandon their cultural and ethnic difference.

This assimilationist immigration policy failed. Cultural difference could not, as was hoped, be simply absorbed by the Anglo-Celtic mainstream and immigrants could not humanly peel off a lifetime of learned attitudes and experiences. Australia was becoming a divided nation. To reflect the reality of difference and to harness it, broad support emerged for a policy of multiculturalism. This policy accepted the reality of cultural and ethnic difference, bestowing equal rights and obligations on all Australian citizens despite difference. This policy was a policy of static multiculturalism. It saw culture and ethnicity as static and unalterable characteristics of individual identity.

In the late 1980s and the 1990s, many Australians began to question the basis of a policy that appeared to confer unequal rights and opportunities on the basis of difference. That seemed to run against the egalitarian rhetoric of Australian life. It seemed to smack of the same discrimination for which the racist monocultural policies of prewar Australia were condemned.

It is, in part, the failure of the policies and rhetoric of static multiculturalism upon which Pauline Hanson's One Nation Party builds some of its many shonky populist platforms. Rather than advocate a progressive step forward from static multiculturalism, One Nation instead hankers for a return to the past, for a return to monoculturalism and access to equality which is predicated upon sameness.

Today Australia stands at a crossroads. We move together soon into the new millennium, our third century of modern citizenship. It is perhaps no surprise that we have been confronting and will continue to confront issues of our identity: reconciliation, as the struggle to understand our past with honesty and courage, and to build upon it; the republic, as a natural and progressive step into our future; and multiculturalism, as a description of our social reality on the one hand, and policies to reconcile equality and difference in a population of increasing diversity on the other. These are intangible issues of a nation coming to terms with its own maturity and looking inwards at itself. Who are we as Australians? What does an Australian look like? What are the things that bind us together as a people and a nation? These are questions at the heart of our national self-consciousness. They are, as Lindsay Tanner names them, 'issues of Australia's soul'. Honest answers to these questions require an honest understanding of the role of immigration and cultural diversity in our society. Honest answers to these questions will lead us along a path to an inclusive Australian identity and a reinvigorated notion of citizenship rather than a citizenship based on what language one speaks or how one looks. To achieve this inclusivity, it is necessary to develop an evolutionary conception of multiculturalism, one which takes into account the way cultures change when introduced to the Australian context as well as the way Australia changes over time due to this process. Seen in this light, it becomes clear that real equality can only be realised through difference.

Monoculturalism: inequality and indifference

Geoff Wong was a school mate. He was a heavily built Chinese-Australian, whose family had migrated to Australia in the 1920s. He played in the First XV rugby team and treated other Asian pupils with disdain. A common taunt would be 'Bloody Asians ... why don't you all go back to Hong Kong?' I have little doubt how Geoff came to have developed that peculiar schizophrenia of identity. I myself have struggled with my identity as an Australian of Chinese heritage my entire life. Feeling and sounding Australian, but looking different, we did all we could to fit into the traditional images of Australian identity. But it was never of any use. In the prevailing social climate, you could never escape the way you look. We still had 'Go home, Asians' shouted at us.

From 1788 until 1972, most of our modern history, Australia pursued a policy of monoculturalism. At its core, monoculturalism ties equality to sameness. It demands that individuals look, feel and sound the same as the dominant group if they are to receive the same rights, benefits and treatment as members of society. It is a fundamentally exclusionary dogma, a doctrine of homogeneity. It has excluded outsiders from entering and engaging with Australia. It has also excluded those 'outsiders' who lived in Australia from entering our national self-consciousness. It is a doctrine which tells a story of Australia that does not match reality. It leaves immigration and cultural diversity out of the picture.

Progress into the future must proceed from an honest understanding of the past. Rather than acknowledging that white colonials were immigrants to a continent inhabited by over 200 Aboriginal nations, the monocultural story depicts Australia as a vast, empty continent. Literally 'a country of no one' (*terra nullius*), waiting patiently for the arrival of whites.

Monoculturalism misleads. It suggests Australia was not always multicultural. It writes richness, diversity and difference out of our history. Australian histories mention only cursorily the presence of Chinese communities from the earliest days of white 'settlement'. They do not mention that the first ferryman in Australia was Jamaican. They exclude the contributions of non-whites from Australian myths and legends. They exclude almost all of the details which expose the reality of Australia: always culturally diverse, always, in one form or another, multicultural. By doing so, such histories create the impression that the Australian population before postwar immigration was all white. This ignores the massive inflows of non-white immigrants throughout the nineteenth century — 14 000 in 1855 alone.

Monoculturalism reflects a profound and xenophobic rejection of difference. David Malouf has posited that Australia's geography as an isolated island is reflected in an aspect of the Australian psyche that believes Australia's uniqueness can only be preserved by keeping Australia separate from the rest of the world, free from contamination (Malouf 1998, pp. 10–11).

One of the first Acts passed by the newly formed Commonwealth Government after Federation was the *Immigration Restriction Act 1901*. This was the Act which enshrined monoculturalism in law, legitimising the exclusionary social practices of the colonies, preventing all non-British immigration into Australia.

Speaking in support of the Bill that became the *Immigration Restriction Act* in the Commonwealth Parliament, Alfred Deakin, the Federal Attorney-General and one of Australia's 'Founding Fathers', made the exclusionary and racist core of the White Australia policy perfectly clear. He proclaimed: 'We here find ourselves touching the profoundest instinct of individual or nation — the instinct of self-preservation — for it is nothing less than the national manhood, the national character, the national future, that are at stake.' What was it that imperilled that 'manhood'? '[T]he admixture of our people with other races.'

This statement reflected the prevailing attitudes of the day. It was the highest duty of Australian citizenship to preserve the racial purity of Australians. Australia was to be one nation: one people. One race. Other people were to be excluded. Access to citizenship,[1] political suffrage and the mechanisms of the state were formally prohibited for 'natives' of Asia, Africa or the Pacific Islands (except New Zealand) in the *Naturalization Act 1903*. From this starting point, Australia has already come a long way. Australia has become precisely the sort of the nation that the Founding Fathers would have deplored.

Policies of exclusion wrote a false story of Australia. They prevented the reality of cultural diversity within Australia from entering our national self-consciousness, psyche and identity. They wrote a British history of Australia, with Australian myths and icons dangling from the apron-strings of the 'mother country'.

These icons are an integral part of who we now are. They are the truth, but they are not the whole truth. To achieve inclusiveness, we must embrace national symbols and icons that reflect the multicultural reality of Australia's history: that the Diggers to whom we owe our national security included indigenous Australians and Asian-Australians; that pioneering frontiermen and -women included families of NESB. We must embrace those symbols and icons as also ours. We must recognise that opposition to Asian immigration has formed the anvil on which we have hammered out an exclusionary identity (Yarwood & Knowling 1982).

Exclusion does not just mean keeping difference out. It also means eradicating the difference within. Monoculturalism has for too long shaped the relations of indigenous and non-indigenous Australians. It was the norm that justified the kidnapping of indigenous infants for their 'assimilation' into Western society. It is the norm which has eroded and eradicated not simply Aboriginality, but Aboriginals. In that, it is a norm which generates policies of genocide (see HREOC 1997).

Assimilation

Until the end of World War II, monoculturalism was the backbone of Australian identity. It was what united us — 'the greatest thing we have achieved,' said Prime Minister Billy Hughes in 1919 (DILGEA 1998, p. 19). It ensured that 'this country shall remain forever the home of the descendants of those people who came here in peace in order to establish in the South Seas an outpost of the British race,' said Prime Minister Curtin (DILGEA 1998, pp. 19–20).

At the end of the war, Australia faced a massive labour shortage. Attempts to encourage British immigration to increase labour supply failed because of Britain's own labour shortage at that time. As a result, the Federal Government was forced to relax immigration restrictions. The White Australia policy remained in place — only the 'white' was now extended to all Caucasian Europeans.

The relaxation of the White Australia policy was justified by reference to monocultural norms. Arthur Calwell, the Minister for Immigration, suggested that Australia must 'populate or perish'. Australia's very existence as a nation, a people, was under threat. From whom? The Asian 'hordes' to the north. The 'one nation, one people' policy was not threatened: the new arrivals would be 'assimilated' into mainstream Australia. Australia would become a 'melting pot' which boiled their ethnic and cultural difference away, turning them into model (Anglo-) Australians.

Assimilation did not work. It could not have worked. Human beings, though flexible, could not be expected or forced to shed their cultures and instantly love the game of cricket, let alone understand it. Between 1947 and 1960 more than 2.6 million immigrants arrived in Australia. Of these, more than 50 per cent were non-British. Rather than maintaining the integrity of Anglo-Australia, saving it from 'perishing', this surge in immigration reinforced and extended the reality of Australia's cultural diversity.

Whilst assimilation indirectly fostered difference by providing a false sense of security to the government sentinels of Australian cultural purity, it was a policy that intrinsically bred inequality. It dehumanised migrants, it proceeded from an assumption of British superiority. Its fundamental implication was that migrant cultures were at best inferior and undesirable and at worst, positively dangerous and threatening. The new migrants of the late 1940s and the 1950s were segmented (perhaps even segregated) from Anglo-Australian society. They were given different, often harder and more dangerous work. They were housed differently, paid differently and treated differently (Lack & Templeton 1995, p. 10). Immigrants were treated as second-class citizens despite their valuable but largely unsung contributions to 'mainstream' Australia. The Snowy Mountains Hydro-Electric Scheme, for instance, was achieved through immigrant labour. Immigrants also contributed generally to GDP and increased consumption (Castles et al. 1992, p. 13). Rates of depression and emigration in migrant communities rose steadily (Martin 1978; Kerkyasharian 1991, p. 8).

Inevitably, the Federal Government realised that its policy was backfiring. From assimilation, which assisted migrants 'to become just like other Australians', a subtle shift was made in the late 1950s and 1960s to a rhetoric of 'integration'. Integration represented the first cracks in the policy of monoculturalism. It suggested that cultural difference did not matter, as long as it was compatible with the dominant norms of 'mainstream' Australia. Where difference in culture generated conflict, migrants and ethnic groups were expected to jettison their offending cultural baggage.

Federal Governments began to recognise cultural diversity in the Australian community. Increased efforts were made to help 'new Australians' integrate into existing structures, including the introduction of funded places in full-time English courses for migrants in 1969. Cultural diversity, however, remained a 'problem' to be overcome. In 1972, on the grounds of the need for 'social cohesion', the Federal Government restricted foreign-language programs to 2.5 per cent of a commercial radio station's weekly hours of transmission. Linguistic difference was under attack. It was seen as a threat. The government continued to discourage an Australian identity that embraced cultural diversity. Citizenship and Australian identity remained tied to a monocultural norm.

That was set to change.

Multiculturalism: equality despite difference

'I think it's disgraceful how migrants are granted residency and citizenship, but can't speak English,' proclaimed the father of a friend over dinner. Here was a man I respected profoundly, highly educated and successful, well read, politically sophisticated. 'We must all be treated equally. It's the "multicultural industry" I have a problem with,' he added. With those terms, I knew at once he had read Sheehan.

In 1972 and 1973, the Whitlam Government abandoned the White Australia policy and with it, the model of monocultural citizenship. A new social norm, multiculturalism, soon gained bipartisan support. In one sense, multiculturalism simply expresses a social reality: it is what you see in the Australian streetscape, the whirling myriad of human colour that has become a defining characteristic of Australian society, at least in the larger cities. To deny multiculturalism in this respect would be nonsensical. In another sense, multiculturalism is a precept underpinning policies governing the relative rights, responsibilities and interactions between different ethnic and cultural groups in society.

It is at this juncture that one of the principal vexations of Australian politics in the latter half of the 1990s may be stated: how is it that so morally irrefutable a principle as multiculturalism, a precept entirely consistent with the much lauded Australian virtue of a 'fair go', should come under significant assault? How is it that a prime minister should deliberately avoid using the term 'multiculturalism' for years?

The history of multiculturalism in the 1970s, 1980s and 1990s has been rewritten — perhaps most notably by Paul Sheehan in *Among the Barbarians* in 1998 — to suggest that multiculturalism never became a generally accepted social norm; that it was always a politician's policy, foisted on a disgruntled public. This is the story told by One Nation and by other forces alienated from government and decision-making processes, forces opposing immigration, forces driven by the politics of hard times, rapid overwhelming change and economic instability.

Having said this, we need to recognise the inherent problems in the notion of multiculturalism that have underpinned policy in the past twenty years. It is these problems that have given rise to the monoculturalist reactionary voices shouting down sensible political discourse about diversity in the late 1990s.

The multiculturalism of the last twenty years is a static multiculturalism. It sees culture as static, as baggage that an individual retains or jettisons. Baggage that cannot be altered. What distinguishes static multiculturalism from monoculturalism is that where monoculturalism seeks to force individuals to jettison this difference if they want to access equality, static multiculturalism countenances the retention of the baggage. It suggests equality despite difference.

This attitude has been evident in the policies of successive federal governments from 1972 until the present day. The gradual introduction of ethnic broadcasting services, especially the Special Broadcasting Service, recognised that cultural difference was here to stay as part of the Australian landscape. It acknowledged that if Australia is to function as an inclusive political community, we must open up different channels for different groups to access that political community. The establishment of the Australian Ethnic Affairs Council and the National Ethnic Broadcasting Advisory Council in 1977 demonstrated real attempts to create channels for communication between ethnic groups and overarching political structures. The creation of Migrant Resource Centres at the same time, and later of Adult Migrant Education Programs, the Migrant Project Subsidy Schemes, the Migrant Workers' Rights Scheme and the Grant-in-Aid scheme extended this attitude beyond the political sphere to the grassroots community. Migrants were provided with resources to better engage with civil society, to find employment, security and equality despite the 'problems' their difference generated (Foster & Stockley 1988; Lack & Templeton 1995, p. 188).

Immigration policy was also transformed over this period. In 1986, Asia was for the first time the source of the greatest number of migrants in the total intake for the year. Immigration policy began to reflect a greater tolerance of difference within the Australian community.

Static multiculturalism fostered an understanding of culture and ethnicity as inherently immutable (Zubrzycki 1977; Smolicz 1985). The idea became entrenched that ethnicity and cultural difference create segmentation and division. Seen in that light, static multiculturalism is a half-hearted attempt to embrace cultural and ethnic difference. It suggests that difference should be tolerated — but only up to a point. Which point? The point of 'social cohesion'. It is the cry of 'social cohesion' which has been used over and over again, not only by John Howard in 1988 but also by the Labor Government in 1986, to suggest that difference presents a threat. If difference presents a threat under the rubric of monoculturalism, we should exclude it. Under the rubric of static multiculturalism, we should tolerate it.

The failure of static multiculturalism lies in its flawed understanding of cultural and ethnic difference. It presents a simplistic and reductive view of culture and ethnicity, superficially reducing these notions to lifestyle and nothing more. It encourages Australians to see culture as something static and immutable. The value of culture and ethnicity has never been properly embraced because it has never been properly championed by government — with courage, honesty and leadership. This lack of understanding of the value of diversity was evident throughout the 1980s. It was evident in the Labor cuts to immigration in 1983, which suggested that immigration was a threat to Australian stability. It was evident in the temporary abolition of the Australian Institute for Multicultural Affairs, the Multicultural Education Program and cuts to funding for English as a Second Language (ESL) courses in 1986. It was evident in John Howard's call in 1988 for a reduction in Asian immigration, again characterised as a threat to 'social cohesion'. It was evident in his call in 1989 for a concept of 'One Australia': an identity characterised by the 'core norms' of the dominant group (Jayasuriya 1996, p. 221).

Extraordinarily, immigration and multiculturalism are today again under threat. The measures established (with not only bipartisan but broad community support) in the 1970s and 1980s which allowed ethnic groups to better interact with the rest of the Australian community are now described as a 'multicultural industry' (Sheehan 1998). It is static multiculturalism that is responsible — by presenting an idea of culture as static and encouraging the private fulfilment of unchanging cultural needs, it created institutions that appeared to give special benefits to different groups. The tolerance of difference seemed to be a cover for inequality.

As a result, many Australians now ask 'Why should we tolerate difference at all? It produces inequality.' And it was this attitude that spawned a new political party: Pauline Hanson's One Nation.

Research has revealed that One Nation supporters view immigration, racial and Aboriginal issues as far more important (relative to other issues) than do supporters of other parties (Goot 1998, pp. 51–74). Hanson's support stems largely from a rhetoric suggesting that we should 'start looking at equality not colour'.[2] In other words, we should ignore difference. This is the politics of monoculturalism reborn. It suggests we exclude difference — from our stories, our thinking, our 'One Nation'. Though starting in relation to immigration, ethnic and indigenous issues, Hanson's central policy of excluding difference has been extended to other policy areas. The economic policies of the One Nation Party aim at excluding foreign investment in Australia, even when that capital seems to have tangible benefits to Australians. The 2 per cent flat 'easy' tax idea flagged at the 1998 Federal Election sought to ignore difference by abolishing marginal taxation and treating everyone 'equally'.

One Nation is a political manifestation of disillusionment with the multicultural ideal in Australia. It offers a return to monoculturalism. That is an offer that many Australians find attractive. It has undoubtedly profoundly influenced the political agenda in this country. It has made politicians again contemplate the exclusion of difference. Even the renaming of the New South Wales Department of Ethnic Affairs as the 'Community Relations Commission' could be interpreted as suggesting that difference is out.

What we need is a new path. A path that does not treat difference as an obstacle to equality.

Beyond static multiculturalism: equality through difference

Sydney's Central Railway Station teems with cultural difference. At peak hour, you are pressed up against the flesh of diversity. If you open your eyes and ears, you will hear the myriad languages that break up the sameness of ubiquitous English: Arabic, Cantonese, Greek, Italian, Vietnamese, Mandarin, Spanish, to name a few. You will notice that many younger Australians, visibly NESB, are talking to each other in Australian English with accents of the broadest vernacular. If you keep listening carefully, you will hear those young Australians lapse out of English into another language, and then effortlessly back again to English.

One evening, a group of young Australians speaking to each other in smatterings of Greek and English were joined in the train carriage by a group of young Australians talking Mandarin Chinese. They ignored each other the entire journey, except when one of the Greek speakers turned to one of those speaking Mandarin and said: 'I'm learning Chinese at school. It's good for business, eh?'

To understand how difference and equality may be reconciled, we need to understand what actually happens to immigrants when they come to Australia, and what happens to Australia when immigrants come here. We need to rewrite the wrongs of the stories told by monoculturalism and static multiculturalism.

What we find is that static multiculturalism presents a false image of reality. Culture evolves; it does not stay the same forever. Culture is carried by individuals. As they interact and evolve, so does the culture they carry, produce and reproduce. Asian immigrants are Australianised, not because they are forced to, but as a natural process over time. Language changes incrementally. Culture grows. Individual identities alter culture, which shapes individual identities. The reality of multicultural and multifaceted life is a reality of constant change, dynamism and organic growth. To understand it and work with it, we need a model of evolutionary multiculturalism.

Evolutionary multiculturalism is not theory. It is how our nation works. To understand this we have to debunk the myths of monoculturalism and static multiculturalism. We have to embrace diversity as an opportunity, rather than fear difference as a threat.

We can begin with the obvious factual inaccuracies. Pauline Hanson's claim in her maiden speech to parliament that we are being 'swamped' by Asian immigrants (Grattan 1998, p. 80) is simply false. If Asian immigration (including immigration from 'West Asia' or the Middle East) continues at its current rate for 25 years, roughly 7 per cent of the population will then be Asian-born, and only 13 per cent of Asian ethnicity (Castles et al. 1998, p. 41). Hardly a swamping. At present, Anglo-Celts still comprise roughly 85 per cent of our population by ethnicity (Jayasuriya 1996, p. 208).

Paul Sheehan's fallacious claims in *Among the Barbarians* are particularly dangerous because they are emotional and populist, but are presented with the apparent weight of authority beneath them. They tap into the powerful vein of cynicism about politicians and the political establishment. They are based on gross ethnically based generalisations. Sheehan claims that the 'multicultural industry' lines the pockets of immigrants and ethnic groups, privileging them over other Australians. Sheehan could not be further from the truth.

The reality of modern immigration is a life of extreme hardship (see Leser 1998, p. 16). When immigrants arrive in this country they are refused all income support for two years unless there is a 'substantial change in their circumstances' beyond that person's control. The effects of this policy are extreme, forcing many skilled, educated migrants into conditions of extreme poverty, depression and a battle to survive.

For most immigrants, coming to Australia means a daily struggle to build financial security and status in a new society where they could have inherited neither. The first overwhelming needs of immigrants are also the most human: physical needs such as shelter, food and clothing; and social and economic needs such as employment, friends and emotional support. It is not easy uprooting your existence and starting again in a foreign society. Continually you face the possibility and reality of discrimination. At best, it means never seeing role models in public life who 'look, fee and sound' like you. At worst, it means constant harassment and sometimes violence. The mundane reality, however, is that immigrants experience continual stereotyping and prejudice. They face a near-universal presumption that ethnic groups exhibit a higher rate of criminality and that they do not participate in the political life of the country. Not only are these prejudices oppressive, they are counterproductive, because they are wrong: non-Anglo-Celtic immigrants and ethnic groups display lower rates of criminality than the Anglo-Celtic population taken as a whole (Castles et al. 1992). Non-Anglo-Celtic immigrants are almost twice as fast and twice as likely to take up Australian citizenship as Anglo-Celtic immigrants (BIR 1991; Evans 1988; Kelley & McAllister 1982; Wearing 1985).

Immigrants to Australia do not, despite the propaganda, form ghettos. Even in such places as Cabramatta and Richmond, the predominant social trend is ethnic mixing. If there are ghettos in these places, they are not ethnic ghettos: they are concentrations of low-income, welfare-dependent groups of a variety of ethnicities and cultures, including a large proportion of Anglo-Celts (Castles et al. 1998, pp. 93–9).

Immigrants and ethnic groups do not have divided loyalties any more than non-immigrants (Kerkyasharian 1991,

p. 14). Inevitably, immigrant groups and their Australian-born children adopt English as their primary language (Clyne & Kipp 1997). Inevitably, ethnic groups are drawn into political affiliations and representation (Jennings & Niemi 1974; Castles et al. 1992). We see it clearly in the politicisation of the Greek, Italian and Polish communities. We are beginning to see it in the Vietnamese and Chinese communities.

A realistic picture of Australian cultural diversity is not one of assimilation or even straightforward static cultural pluralism. A realistic picture is one of evolution, dynamism, interaction and convergence. It understands that individuals affect each other's identities through their interactions. To move forward we must do more than simply right the wrongs of static multiculturalism and monoculturalism. We must understand why Australians feel the way they do today and how they might feel tomorrow. We must learn how to harness these natural forces of socialisation which draw Australians together, unifying them through their diversity.

Support for One Nation is much stronger amongst older voters. As Murray Goot has pointed out, many of these voters 'would have come to political maturity in a country where White Australia was still the official policy ... and where assimilationist ideals went largely unchallenged' (Goot 1998, p. 72). The mass demonstrations of Australian high-school students against One Nation foreshadow a future that is infinitely heartening. These new Australians experience diversity in their everyday lives as entirely normal and enjoyable. They feel none of the divisive hostilities One Nation claims exists. They reject the mad racist rhetoric,which is fundamentally at odds with the Australia they know and love.

This is the reality of contemporary Australia: immigration and cultural diversity provide strength to Australia. Immigration has improved and continues to improve Australia's economic performance and the standard of living of all Australians. It increases employment, expands aggregate output, increases per capita income (without reducing average real wages), improves the balance of payments in both the short and long term, and contributes more to public revenue than it costs (Wooden 1990; Withers 1990; Nevile 1990; CIE 1988; CAAIP 1988; Clarke et al. 1990; Junankar, Pope & Withers 1996; Castles et al. 1998). Immigration even seems to increase export output (Stanton & Lee 1995; Forsyth et al. 1993). NESB Australians run more than a quarter of our small businesses: the everyday infrastructure that underpins Australian community (Castles et al. 1998, p. 63).

Beyond economics, we need to recognise that cultural diversity gives us both social and political strength. Diversity means flexibility, opportunity for interaction and a depth of inputs. In evolutionary terms, diversity is strength. Australians speak over 240 languages at home (Clyne & Kipp 1997). Our cultural diversity is a source of richness; not simply richness of lifestyles, but richness in a deeper social and political sense. Diversity is the fuel of democracy. It is the differences of opinion, of outlook and attitude which force us, through discussion, negotiation and debate, to constantly evaluate opinions, including our own. Diversity provides the opportunity for self-awareness and understanding.

The Indonesian motto is 'Diversity in Unity'. It could be rephrased as 'Unity despite Diversity'. Australia could adopt a similarly worded, but radically different motto: 'Unity through Diversity'. Paradoxically, it is the difference we all share which makes us the same. If there is one thing that is the same for all Australians — especially young Australians — it is this: we have grown up among diversity. Diversity has been our environment. We have learnt to build ourselves from the plurality that surrounds us. Diversity is a broad notion. It embraces also sexual, racial, religious and physical diversity.

Understanding Australian identity as unified through diversity does not require a radical break with our current self-perceptions. As Bob Carr put it, it is just 'an acceptance of reality' (*Sydney Morning Herald* 1998).

It may be quite a simple task for us to recognise ourselves as a culturally diverse people. It may be straightforward for us to recognise that this should be a source of strength and unity. It may even be a relatively painless task to develop symbols and icons that match the reality of our organic, diverse history. Those icons surround us: the Snowy Mountains scheme, Mr Okimura (the bronzed Aussie lifesaver), the quintessentially Australian local Chinese takeaway restaurant and the North Indian diner, 'Wogs out of Work', Cathy Freeman ...

These tasks may be simple. What will not be simple, though, is putting policies of evolutionary multiculturalism into practice. Such policies recognise our diversity and seek to retain and foster it within a broad, stable, liberal democratic framework. They are policies that foster difference. Inevitably, those that fear difference will portray them as policies that foster inequality. We must overcome this fear.

We are not afraid to treat rural and urban Australians differently on the basis that their needs differ. We do not perceive this as inequality. We must find a similar attitude, similar policies, which extend this thinking to other axes of difference within Australian society.

Putting evolutionary multiculturalism into practice

What are the policies that will vindicate evolutionary multiculturalism?

First, they are policies that encourage us to recognise that we are all different. The politics we face is a politics of fluid, evolving individuals. It is a mixing pot, rather than a melting pot, where individuals are constantly evolving through their interactions with others.

Secondly, they are policies that recognise that we treat group membership as politico-economic resources (Jayasuriya 1996, p. 220). They must recognise that we all belong to more than one community, more than one group (Kerkyasharian 1991, p. 15), and that we use our group membership as a social and cultural 'marker' (Castles et al. 1992) to our individual advantage, adapting it as we see fit. We try to fit in. Individuals can alter their own culture, their own ethnicity, their own identity. As individuals evolve, the cultures they bear, manifest, produce and reproduce alter. Our policies need to recognise that culture is a political tool, a political resource, and use it accordingly. Culture and cultural difference should not be excluded from politics. They should be embraced by politics.

Evolutionary multiculturalism will recognise that democracy is more than simply majority rules, where the overwhelming voting power of the majority smothers legitimate minority voices crying out legitimate minority concerns. The kind of policies that emerge from evolutionary multiculturalism will embrace and foster difference and diversity, including diversity of political opinion. Unless the major parties can open up and reflect and vindicate diversity internally, they must expect to share power in the Australian political landscape of the future with an increasing number of minor parties. Such parties will germinate not primarily for the exploitation of a single issue, but in a deliberate attempt to retain and encourage the kind of dynamic plurality that drives liberal democracy forward.

In other words, Australia requires a cultural infrastructure that allows different cultural and ethnic groups a meaningful opportunity to participate in producing and reproducing Australia — an opportunity of citizenship. Evolutionary multiculturalism means policies that encourage our political parties to reshape themselves, wholly embracing diversity, not only in policy, but in their internal structures. In both their rhetoric and their procedures for preselection and promotion.

Policies vindicating evolutionary multiculturalism will recognise the value of non-English-language programs designed to ensure that community languages do not die within Australia. With time, minority languages die (Pan 1995; Clyne & Kipp 1997; Waas 1993; de Bot & Clyne 1994; see also Llinos 1992, p. 23). That is a loss to the Australian community as a whole.

Policies vindicating evolutionary multiculturalism will attempt to systematically cultivate the human capital provided by ethnic and cultural diversity, through appropriate labour market, social welfare and education strategies. That means encouraging migration into rural and regional areas. That means reforming the welfare and income support entitlements of newly arrived immigrants to ensure that they are able to fully engage with the economic and social aspects of the community. It means encouraging not merely multicultural but cross-cultural education. It means determining and justifying immigration levels on more than a simply economic or political basis; perhaps through reference to the capacity of the applicant to contribute meaningfully to Australian diversity, as well as the reproduction of our economic wellbeing, our social health and our political institutions (see Thompson 1993, p. 12).

What this calls for is a reconceptualisation of Australian citizenship. It demands a notion of citizenship de-linked from cultural identity or membership of any particular group, other than the group we call Australia.

To be Australian

What does it mean to be Australian? What do we require of migrants and different individuals to belong to the political community, the nation we call Australia?

For a very long time, the answer to these questions has rested on cultural identity. It is time to reshape Australian citizenship. We must create a society that judges individuals by the content of their character, not on their ethnicity or culture. Neither monoculturalists nor static multiculturalists have done this (Brunton 1998, p. 40).

We need a model of multicultural citizenship based on an idea of cultural evolution. This has strong implications for policy. Evolutionary multiculturalism encourages us to enable citizenship for all individuals through the fostering of our diversity 'as one of our most precious natural resources' (Castles et al. 1992, p. 199). We must recognise that we 'have gone a lot further than any other nation in developing and reinforcing the social skills requisite to managing cultural diversity and integrating diversity as part of our national distinctiveness' (Castles et al. 1992, p. 199).

But we still have a long way to go. This 'new citizenship' is the citizenship not of cultural identity — not what we are — but of participation — what we do (Castles et al. 1998, p. 118). One becomes part of the group we call Australia by contributing to the production and reproduction of Australia (see Davidson 1993, p. 28). We have a lot to do to truly adopt this model. It means allowing everyone a real opportunity to contribute to the reproduction of Australia. It means giving everyone an equal chance. It means making sure that people get to the starting line. It means providing immigrants with income support when they arrive to make sure that they have a 'fair go' at contributing to our political, economic, social and cultural life. It means putting in place the cultural infrastructure that will enable all individuals to express themselves through our common political institutions (Doyal & Gough 1989; Taylor 1996; Gould 1988; Walzer 1983). And most urgently, it means recognising that the hereditary and monocultural British monarch no longer has a legitimate place or relevance as Australia's head of state. It means creating our own, unifying head of state who can unite Australians under the powerful and inclusive symbolism of the office of 'Australian President'.

Evolutionary multiculturalism, in turn, means recognising different needs and dealing with them differently. It means taking difference on as an issue, so that we do not continue to make the same mistake that we have done for the last 30 years: by pandering to equality over difference, suggesting we could have equality despite difference, we have left a space in which difference has produced conflict. We must realise equality *through* difference.

Equality through difference means we stick with multiculturalism, rejecting the seductive but myopic answer of monoculturalism. It means recognising that, when all is said and done, One Nation offers us nothing. It shows no one the way ahead. It offers only a path back — back to a 'one nation, one people' reality that is no longer here. In fact, it never was.

So we stick with multiculturalism — but we change it. We understand that diversity is not a problem to be overcome; it is a source of strength, flexibility, richness and unity. The future is in our hands ...

Imagine this: It is 1996, federal election time, and Pauline Hanson has recently been dis-endorsed by the Queensland Liberal Party for her statements concerning Asian migrants and indigenous Australians. Support for her is growing in her electorate of Oxley. An enormous crowd is gathering in a park to listen to an address. But it is not an address by Pauline. A motorcade drifts down the main street, lined with more people, each clutching Australian flags, waving them at the procession of white Commonwealth cars that drive past. A woman of Asian ethnicity steps out. She is ushered by the guards to the stage where she prepares to speak, bracketed by Australian flags on either side. She is the Australian President. She tells the crowd:

> *I was an immigrant who came to Australia many years ago. I earnt my citizenship by contributing to Australia for the new life*

that Australia offered me and my family. We have always welcomed others to our shores. All of us, apart from our indigenous Australians, who were here thousands of years before, are immigrants. We are united by our diversity. It is what makes us uniquely Australian. It is what makes us strong and competitive. It has made us who and what we are, and we are proud of it. As I am proud to be your President.

Given this opportunity to experience such optimism, patriotism and honesty, I wonder whether the electorate of Oxley would ever have given birth to One Nation at all.

chapter **16**

Migration law and policy for the new millennium: building nation and community

by Dr Mary Crock

Self-interest has always played a dominant role in shaping migration law and policy in Australia. Although hardly remarkable in the scheme of international state practice, Australia has stood out for the rigidity and the effectiveness of the measures it has taken to control migration. As an island continent settled in a more or less systematic fashion, Australia has had both the ability and the will to control who enters and remains in the country. The desire to ensure a uniform approach to the control of immigration is said to be one of the factors that compelled the colonies towards Federation in 1901. The form of those early laws and of the Australian Constitution itself was influenced by the desire to create and protect a healthy, white, Anglo-Saxon community in the image of Britain. There was little succour for aspiring migrants who did not fit the cultural or ideological norms of the time (Crock 1998a, pp. 11–13; Cronin 1993; Rubenstein 1997). Immigration control has changed dramatically in the century since Federation: the colour bar has been lifted and the absolutist measures designed to protect local industries and workers have long since vanished (Quinlan & Lever-Tracy 1990; Layman 1996). Yet there are elements of the present system which are every bit as harsh in their operation as the country's earliest laws.

Present trends reflect the 'inculturation' of our politicians with the ideology of economic rationalism. Not only have the laws and policies governing immigration been given a sharper economic focus, but the changes have come at the expense of family and, I will argue, the humanity of the migration program. It will be my contention that the changes diminish Australia as a nation and that they represent a short-sighted, if not misconceived, notion of the national interest.

The Federal Coalition Government has had three years in which to put its stamp on the face of Australia's immigration program. In light of the zero immigration policies of minor parties such as the Australian Democrats and the increasingly influential One Nation, it may be cause enough to celebrate that there still is an immigration program. What the statistics collected by Robert Birrell and Virginia Rapson show is that the present government has changed the balance and focus of the program. It has reduced the overall intake by over 17 000 places and cut the Family Stream intake both in real terms and in proportion to the intake of skilled and business migrants (Birrell & Rapson 1998). For a time the humanitarian intake was also reduced: in 1999–2000 this program was set at 12 000 places, with an extra contingency figure to compensate for under-subscription of the 1998–99 targets.

The changed focus of the program is apparent in measures that have been introduced in the area of spousal migration; in proposals to restrict the sponsoring of parents; in various measures designed to improve aspects of the skilled migration program; and in the tightening of the laws governing enforcement and the 'review' end of immigration control. As the country faces a new millennium and the traditional bipartisan approach to immigration policy breaks down, it is timely to take a step back and examine these new trends and developments. It may well be that 'political correctness' has stifled debate about immigration and population policy in this country (O'Connor 1998). Views may differ on the solutions proposed by the anti-immigration environmentalists. Nevertheless, I concur with the assertion that this country has dabbled too long with the politics of popular opinion. In so doing we have eschewed a balanced assessment of the long-term needs of Australia as a country with a fragile ecology; but also as a community held together with the emotional bonds of kith and kin.

The economics of migration

The one aspect of the migration program that has retained political, if not popular, support is that involving the admission of business and skilled migrants. The dominant view of the economists is that skilled migration represents a Pareto improvement for the country; that is, no distinct group becomes worse off as a consequence of such immigration (Baker, Sloan & Robinson 1994, chap. 3; Crock 1998a, chap. 6.1). As successive governments have been keen to trumpet, business migration has resulted in the transfer to Australia of considerable amounts of capital and investment money. It has seen the establishment or growth of businesses that have generated a great number of jobs for Australian workers. When the recent history of the various business and skilled migration programs is surveyed, it is plain that the present program has a better economic focus and generates fewer (economic) anomalies than has been the case over the years (Crock 1998a: chap. 6.1). The question that remains, however, is whether it is in the country's best interests to allow immigration policy to become the preserve of economic rationalism.

Filling 'skill' gaps: the merits of temporary or 'guest' workers over permanent residents

In recent years the government has continued and accelerated changes initiated by the Keating Labor Government. These have included legislative amendments that have made it easier to bring in foreign workers on contract to fulfil particular labour needs. Special visa categories remain for the grant of permanent residence to skilled migrants, who must show, amongst other things, that there is no 'Australian' available to do the job they are nominated to fill. However, if numbers are any guide, it is the cohort of temporary-stay (contract) workers who have most impact on the labour market. As is the case with all the initiatives in the area of skilled migration, legislative change has been a bipartisan affair. In spite of the commissioning of various government reports (which have generally focused on the best way to accommodate business interests), there has been remarkably little public debate on the subject.

The globalisation of business and the proliferation of international treaties makes it impossible to conceive of the protectionism that characterised the early years of Australian nationhood. On the other hand, the ease of importing 'guest' workers today does raise questions about whether the interests of local workers are being properly looked after. While it is important to accommodate the employment needs of companies and individuals in business, more could be done to foster the selection of local workers to fill the positions of need. The present visa criteria allow for the fast-tracking of applications where a sponsor can demonstrate the need for an employee in a key area of her or his business. Provided the nominee is to perform a 'key activity' in a business, the sponsor is exempt from demonstrating that an appropriate person could be found in Australia by lodging advertisements and 'testing' the market through other means. While the regulations provide that nominees must be needed for skilled jobs only, the regime is weighted very heavily in favour of the sponsoring employer. It represents an abandonment of one aspect of the government's linkage of immigration control with labour market schemes. This is an unfortunate step to take while unemployment remains such an intractable problem.

The 'points tests' and the selection of skilled migrants: good sense or racial elitism?

The selection of permanent migrants on the basis of skills is a matter of some topical interest, with significant changes made in July 1999 to the long-established 'points tests' set out in schedule 6 of the Migration Regulations. These tests apply in two main visa classes: that relating to 'Independent' migrants and that concerning 'Skilled Australian Sponsored' migrants, known formerly as 'Concessional' migrants. The classes cover non-citizens seeking permanent residence on the basis of their employability alone and those assessed on employability and their relationship with an Australian citizen or permanent resident relative. The tests also apply to some extent to non-citizens who are willing to settle in designated regions of the country under new regional sponsored and skills-matching schemes.

The new points test regime will have a simpler operation than the present model. Most significantly, it will require the assessment of a person's skills to be undertaken before any application is made to the immigration authorities for a visa. This will have far-reaching ramifications for the present administration, as there will be large parts of the determination process that will no longer be the preserve of either the Immigration Department or the Migration Review Tribunal. The changes are attracting bipartisan support as they contain a number of attractive features. For example, the simplification of the migration process is a welcome development, as applicants will know more immediately than they do at present whether or not their prospects of migrating are realistic. The Labor opposition is likely to welcome the renewed involvement of the Department of Industrial Relations and Small Business in identifying (and awarding higher points in relation to) occupations in demand. Another useful feature of the new regime will be the extension of the period in which applications can be held in abeyance or 'pooled'. The computerisation of all aspects of the applications made will continue to be used to match the skills of migrants with the needs of regional employers under the regional sponsored program.

On the other side of the coin are the universal requirement of proficiency in the English language, increases in the cost of applying and the emphasis on quite rigid work categories. These are likely to further skew the ethnic composition of the skilled intake by favouring the nationals of first world English-speaking countries. The language requirement favours the nationals of either the traditional 'favoured' source countries such as England and the United States, or those of the richer Asian countries in our region, such as Hong Kong or Singapore. Applicants from these countries are doubly advantaged, as the qualifications conferred by the relevant educational institutions are more likely to be recognised. In spite of the correlation that has been shown between the speed of a migrant's settlement and English language proficiency, the move to mandate language as a requirement is disappointing. It is trite to acknowledge that some of the country's most interesting and successful migrants arrived here with no knowledge of the English language. In some ways it seems that we are no longer so prepared to take a chance with our migrants; we want them to come fully formed, already qualified, wealthy and sure of their place in the world. It is my view that this is a rather short-sighted approach to take. The danger is that we can end up with a system that works against the kind of people that Australia needs most. These are the people working in cutting-edge industries not described in any of the established policy documents; people who have few qualifications but who have the vision and imagination to make a real difference to the way we live and work. Conversely, the selection of the skilled and the affluent can leave the country with very 'mobile' migrants, people with little commitment to remain in the country should their new life not live up to expectations.

The role of government in selecting and settling migrants

The developments in the area of skilled migration reveal an interesting philosophical and methodological vacillation. On one side is the laissez-faire approach (where the labour market is left to itself to determine intake levels for skilled migrants). On the other is an approach based on close government involvement in delivering migrants that are needed to fit particular gaps in the workforce. The former approach is apparent in the laws and policies governing the importation of temporary workers. The regime governing permanent skilled migration, on the other hand, is closely tailored to the country's perceived needs. The discrepancy between the laws and policies governing the admission of temporary skilled migrants and those governing the grant of permanent residence may be a product of the higher political visibility of the permanent migrants. It is this group that has received the most attention from anti-immigration forces such as Pauline Hanson's One Nation Party. Interestingly, it is in the treatment of these permanent residents after arrival that the growing divide between the major political parties is most apparent.

Although the criteria for selecting skilled permanent migrants reflects a 'targeted' approach to selection, the present government has eschewed the notion that it should be involved in the settlement process. Those given visas as skilled migrants are expected to bring the capital needed to establish themselves. They are expected to find a job without government assistance. Like most permanent migrants, they are not eligible for social security payments until they have been lawful permanent residents for two years; the only exceptions made are for non-citizens granted visas as refugees or humanitarian entrants. There are other ways in which the present laws throw the emphasis on the migration applicant as supplicant for a privilege, as a person who has no right to expect any quarter from the government. To enforce the obligation to remain independent of government help, 'Assurances of Support' are now binding contracts that can be enforced against an assurer by drawing down on a pre-paid bond. The law permits no exception to be made where a family member of a skilled migrant fails the mandatory health test; if one fails, all must be rejected, irrespective of the value of the primary visa applicant.

This approach is consistent with the general move under the Howard Coalition Government towards free-market governance, where job placement has become the preserve of private entrepreneurs rather than State or federal administration. It stands in sharp contrast to the more 'partnered' approach taken in earlier times. There the dominant view seems to have been that migrants will settle faster and make a greater long-term contribution if they receive government assistance in the initial settlement process. In my view, this traditional approach has much to commend it. Settlement assistance conveys a notion of reciprocal obligation that is more likely to foster commitment on the part of the migrant. The present regime, in contrast, presents Australia as a country that is prepared to take but not to give; for better but not for worse.

The place of families in the migration intake: cutting family streams and testing family ties

Where the predominance of economic rationalism is most apparent, however, is in the growing divide between the skilled migration program and what is known as the 'Family Stream'. For skilled migrants, the ramifications of the change are that a new job and a new life in Australia will often mean the severing of important family ties in the person's country of origin. In recent years it has become increasingly difficult for people in Australia to sponsor any family member who does not fall into one of the skilled categories in their own right.

The importance of family migration has long been a point of contention and potential division. One of the platforms on which the Labor Party successfully campaigned for government in 1983 was the relaxation of the rules for the admission of family members (Crock 1998a, chap. 6.1.1; Parcell, Sparkes & Williams 1994). Under the present government, there has been a significant change in approach to the place of families in the migration intake. This is apparent in obvious ways — most notably in the cut in the number of family members given visas — but also in more subtle institutional ways, with campaigns to reduce alleged abuses and changes in the selection criteria.

Spousal migration

One of the defining features of migration policy under Minister Ruddock has been the push to protect the 'integrity' of the migration program so as to regain the 'public's trust' (Ruddock 1997, 1998). The Minister's rhetoric has been loudest in his attacks on failed asylum seekers who have dared to challenge adverse rulings in the courts.[1] Less strident, but persistent nonetheless, has been the Minister's insistence that the increase in the number of people applying to migrate on spouse grounds in the early 1990s was reflective of an increase in abusive marriages. Birrell and Rapson (1998, p. 31) note five changes to the law and policies affecting non-citizens wishing to migrate on spouse grounds made under Minister Ruddock's administration:

1. Spouses and fiancés must now wait for two years before becoming eligible for social security or Austudy payments.
2. All spouses and fiancés are now required to wait for two years before being eligible for permanent residence, whether they apply offshore or within Australia — the standard tests for genuineness and continuity applying.
3. Limits have been placed on the ability of Australian citizens or permanent residents to sponsor more than two spouses or fiancés, with a minimum of five years between the two sponsorships.
4. Similar constraints apply to persons who were themselves sponsored as a spouse or fiancé and who wish to subsequently sponsor a partner.
5. De facto spouses must demonstrate a pre-existing cohabitation relationship of at least one year.

In addition, the fees for applying for a spouse or fiancé visa have increased to $1055.

Just as important as these legislative changes are the concomitant processing initiatives designed to catch out those 'rorting' the program. The government is throwing more resources into the interviewing of spouse applicants overseas, targeting the overseas posts where the bulk of such applications originate: the major Asian posts, Athens, Beirut, Cairo, Belgrade, Moscow, Warsaw and Auckland. Interview rates have climbed from 25 per cent in 1995 to 96 per cent in 1998 (Birrell & Rapson 1998, p. 34). Anecdotal accounts suggest that officials are uncovering a much higher incidence of document fraud and misstatements than was previously the case. What is apparent on the face of the statistics is that many more people are having their applications rejected (21 per cent up from 7 per cent in 1995 offshore, and 9 per cent up from 3 per cent in 1995 onshore). There has also been a marked decline in the number of people seeking to migrate on spouse grounds, particularly from the People's Republic of China (PRC), an important source country in recent years. The government points to these figures as proof that the incidence of migration fraud has been high and that its reforms are getting the problem under control.

migration law and policy

Whether the statistics are evidence of large-scale fraud is debatable without detailed empirical research. What is apparent is that the purity drive has generated something of a climate change within the Department of Immigration, reflected both in the raw statistics and in the type of cases going on appeal. Interestingly, the zeal of the departmental officials does not appear to be shared always by the independent reviewers. When the spouse cases go on appeal to the Migration Review Tribunal (formerly the Immigration Review Tribunal — IRT) the department's rejections are being overturned at a rate of close to 70 per cent.

Parents

One of the harshest changes instituted by the Coalition Government has been the alteration in approach to the admission of migrant parents — both 'aged' and 'working-age'. This group has been depicted as a drain on the Australian taxpayer because of their high social security take-up rate and the inevitable costs associated with a group of aged or ageing individuals. The government instituted 'caps' on parent intakes in 1997, cutting the total numbers admitted from 7580 in 1995–96 to 1000 in 1997 (Birrell & Rapson 1998, p. 26). This was at a time when demand was increasing. In April 1998 the backlog of applications stood at 15 000. As well as placing a cap on the number of visas issued, the government introduced 'processing priorities' which have acted as a back-door way of achieving initiatives blocked by parliament in 1996. These were designed to allow only Australian citizens to bring out their parents as migrants. The processing priorities simply give preference to persons sponsored by an Australian citizen.

The government's strategy for reducing the number and nature of migrant parents was contained in regulations that came into force on 1 November 1998. It is a measure of the controversy engendered by these changes that the Statutory Rules were disallowed by the Senate on 31 March 1999. The short-lived regulations underscored the user-pays and economic rationalist philosophy of the government by eliminating altogether the visa subclass for working-age parents. Under (disallowed) subclause 113, only parents who had reached retirement age were eligible to migrate; and then, only from outside Australia. The 'balance of family' test continued to apply. This operates to ensure that visas are granted only to parents who have as many or more children in Australia as they have in any other country around the world. The test was introduced in 1989 (see Crock 1998a, p. 84).

In addition, pre-existing arrangements for Assurances of Support became more onerous. The Assurance of Support bond — a mechanism for ensuring that sponsors carry the burden of settling in a sponsored migrant — increased from $3500 for the main applicant plus $1500 for each additional adult to $4000 plus $2000. People who provided an assurance were subjected to greater scrutiny to ensure that they were financially capable of meeting their obligations. Assurers had to show that their taxable income is at least equal to the level for obtaining the Family Payment above the minimum rate (i.e. $23 400 plus $624 for each dependent child and $2000 for each adult). The visa applicants also had to pay a health service charge that rose from $940 to $5000. After 1 November 1998, processing priority was to be given to applicants who had paid these higher fees.

For working-age parents, the only options were to apply under one of the standard skilled migration visa classes; to seek admission as a visitor — provided a genuine visit was intended; or to pay their way as a self-supporting retiree under a retirement visa. Further changes allowed persons who had held a retirement visa for ten years to gain permanent residence, irrespective of age or whether they meet the balance of family test.

With the disallowance of SR 285, the pre-existing regime governing parents and aged dependent relatives revived (Crock 1998a, pp. 84–86). The Minister responded to the move by reducing the parent intake for 1999 to 500 places. In spite of paying fees of up to $17 000 for one of the new visas, all applicants under the disallowed regulations have been told they must stand in line with all other applicants for a parent visa. With the backlog of parent visa applications approaching 20 000, the 'queue' for parent visas could mean that some applicants face a wait of up to 40 years before the granting of a visa.

That the opposition and minor parties were prepared to disallow the parent visa regulations is an interesting reflection of the new divide that has opened between the major parties in the area of immigration policy. For the Labor Opposition, the decision to support disallowance marks something of a return to the family-oriented policies which were an important part of their election platform in the early 1980s.

The arguments against the admission of parents are plainly economic: parents find it harder to find employment and are more likely to require health care than younger migrants. The countervailing arguments cannot be reduced as easily to figures but are no less significant for this. Put simply, the immigration process is most successful and complete where the migrant is able to build a stable family base in their new country. The presence of grandparents can be invaluable to the physical and emotional development of young families. In the case of aged parents, one must add to the equation the almost universal cultural imperative that family members look after parents in their declining years. The inability to bring out parents in need of care in the longer term brings with it emotional and practical costs that can have a serious detrimental impact on a migrant's ability to settle, prosper and thus contribute to the life of the nation.

Other restrictive measures impacting on families

There are a raft of other changes instituted by the present government that have had a negative effect on families or interdependent couples. Once again, the changes are apparent both in new regulations and in the administration of the intake program.

'Health concern' non-citizens and the AIDS virus

The rationalist focus of the administration finds expression in what appears to be a harsher line being taken in the admission of certain 'health concern' non-citizens. In order to gain a visa, most migrants must show a clean bill of health. However, there are a few humanitarian and family-related categories that allow the entry of individuals who have a disease or condition that may either require medical treatment or otherwise represent a cost for the Australian community. The grant of a visa in such cases is a matter for the Minister's discretion in 'waiving' the relevant health test. The waivable classes include close family members and those identified as 'interdependent persons': non-relatives with whom an Australian citizen or permanent resident has a permanent relationship of 'interdependence'. The visa class is the one available to persons in a homosexual relationship who in other circumstances might be termed 'spouses'. In recent years controversy has arisen over the blanket refusal of visas to 'interdependent' applicants who have tested positive for the Human Immunodeficiency Virus (HIV). The totality of this ban is a new development. Under the Labor administration there appears to have been a quiet policy to admit such persons on humanitarian grounds and in the interests of fostering strong and permanent relationships. Anecdotal evidence suggests that while no HIV-positive applicant for an interdependency visa has been granted a visa since March 1996, HIV-positive children have been admitted over the same period. If the health rules are being administered in a discriminatory fashion so as to disadvantage gay and lesbian couples, this is a matter of deep regret and concern.

Carer visas

For Australian citizens and permanent residents suffering from disability, or illness, or who otherwise have special needs, it has become much more difficult to sponsor an overseas relative to come in as a carer. On 1 November 1998 the law was changed so as to tie the grant of 'carer' visas to the same criteria used to determine eligibility for a disability pension. The scheme replaces what was known previously as the 'Special Need Relative' visa category that enabled Australians with 'special needs' (as defined) to sponsor overseas relatives to assist them. The present regime is no longer confined to overseas relatives. However, a major change is in the nature and level of disability the Australian party is required to suffer before being eligible to sponsor a foreign carer. Under the Table of Maims set out in federal social security legislation, eligibility for a disability pension is achieved where a score of 24 points is obtained. To sponsor a foreign carer, the Australian party must score 30 points on the same table. As the table is focused specifically on disability, it is noteworthy that persons suffering emotional or psychological distress would receive no points.

migration law and policy 267

To provide concrete examples, applicants like the emotionally disturbed woman in *Fuduche v. Minister for Immigration and Ethnic Affairs* (1993) or the mother with infant children in *Chen v. Minister for Immigration and Ethnic Affairs (No. 2)* (1994) would no longer be eligible as sponsor or visa applicant respectively. For the Minister, this is deliberate, the rationale for the changes being the desire to reduce 'rorting' of this beneficial or compassionate visa category. Given the modest number of persons who benefited from the old concessions, it is a matter of debate whether this clampdown was warranted. Once again, the message is of a hard-edged immigration system.

Controlled compassion: the growth in ministerial power in the review of Migration Rulings

Ministerial power and 'bad aliens'

If the sharper economic focus of the migration program is a hallmark of the present administration, another dramatic change has been in the nature of the Minister's power to intervene personally so as to determine the final outcome of a whole range of matters. The Minister's power to control the intake through the institution of numerical 'caps' is not a recent invention. Neither is the concept of a 'non-compellable, non-reviewable' power to override an (adverse) ruling by a review authority (Crock 1998a, pp. 274–6). What is new is the extraordinary powers that have been given to the Minister to deal with matters relating to character and conduct.

Under section 501 of the *Migration Act 1958* (Cth), the Minister has power to either refuse or cancel a visa where a person is 'reasonably suspected' of failing the 'character test'. This test applies to all non-citizens who are in Australia or who seek a visa to come into the country. It deems a person to be of bad character in specified circumstances, throwing the onus onto the applicant to prove that they are fit and proper 'types' to enter or remain in the country. The disqualifying factors include identifiable matters such as prior criminal record, but also more general criteria, such as a person's association with an organisation which the Minister 'reasonably suspects' has been involved in criminal activities (s 501(6)–(12)). The powers given to the Minister are such that he or she can determine whether the 'rules of natural justice' do or do not apply in making a decision; and whether or not a character ruling is to be appellable to the Administrative Appeals Tribunal (ss 501(3) and 501A(3) (Crock 1998b).

Temporary safe haven

Other changes which have concentrated the Minister's personal powers include the special provisions introduced to enable the grant of temporary 'safe haven' (TSH) to refugees from the crisis in Kosovo. The distinctive features of the new visa class 448 begin with the manner in which people are chosen for safe haven. One cannot 'apply' for these visas. Rather, you are selected by immigration officials and deemed to apply if you 'indicate' to an authorised officer that you accept the Australian Government's offer of temporary stay in Australia and the officer 'endorses' the acceptance (according to the Migration Regulations 1994 (Cth)). While some interesting concessions are made to delay the health processing of TSH visa holders, those found to be of bad character (as defined) face expulsion under the regime that provides no room for argument or appeal — the rules of procedural fairness do not apply.

The most restrictive aspect of the TSH scheme, however, is that visa holders are not permitted to change their status while they remain in Australia. As the legislation stands, the visas are of three months duration, and can be renewed only once. The legislation achieves these objectives by providing that non-citizens who either hold a TSH visa or who have not left Australia since ceasing to hold a TSH visa cannot make a valid application for a visa (new ss 91J and 91K). The blanket exclusion extends to protection visas, the immediate vehicle for persons wishing to seek protection as refugees. The only exception is made where the Minister acting personally determines that section 91K is not to apply to a person. Regulations have been made that allow for a more general TSH visa, suggesting that this mechanism will be used henceforth to cover all persons whose presence in Australia is the result of events in their country of origin that make their immediate return impossible.

Although the major parties have agreed to a bipartisan approach to the treatment of the Kosovar refugees, Amnesty International and others have expressed their concern about the lack of independent safeguards against the possible refoulement of a genuine refugee to a place where she or he may face persecution under the TSH scheme. The matter is viewed with such seriousness that it has been made part of the terms of a major Senate inquiry into the operation of Australia's refugee and humanitarian system.

Ministerial interventions: the non-compellable, non-reviewable discretions

Perhaps the most remarkable feature of the present administration, however, is the personal nature of the current Minister's stewardship. He is on the record for intervening in many more cases than his Labor predecessors, both to benefit and to penalise applicants. Although the Administrative Appeals Tribunal still has a nominal power to override a departmental decision to deport a criminal permanent resident or to permit the admission of a person of 'bad character', the present Minister seems to be using his overriding powers under section 501 in virtually every case. The Minister has been a vocal critic of tribunal members who are seen to be too lenient in their interpretation of the law. In one celebrated incident the Minister was reported to have issued a public warning to members of the Refugee Review Tribunal who had held certain women victims of domestic violence to be refugees. The Minister is reported to have said that members who purported to rewrite the definition of refugee should not expect to be reappointed to the tribunal (*Canberra Times* 1996).

The Minister has also attracted criticism from the legal profession for his attack on judges whom he has perceived as being too 'activist' in their review of migration cases, finding errors of law and grounds for review where the Minister considers none exist.[2]

The way forward

The present Minister is an avowed supporter of multiculturalism in Australia and of the concept of immigration. He also prides himself on being a member of Amnesty International and of the International Commission of Jurists. In this light, it is unfortunate that the cumulative effect of all the legal and policy changes outlined in this essay, together with the strident rhetoric about the need to stamp out all manner of abuses, leaves a very negative impression of Australia's immigration system. It is my opinion that the rhetoric is in part political; that it reflects the government's desire to be seen to be responding to the anti-immigration mood reflected in the policies of groups like the One Nation Party. On the other hand, the totality of present laws and policies also seems to be solidly economic and 'rationalist' in its focus, to the detriment of compassion and to the detriment of family. It is my view that the present laws and policies envisage the extended family as a burden on society, captured neatly in the description of family or 'chain' migration as the 'chains that bind' society in its efforts to betterment (Birrell 1989). Australia's immigration laws and policies favour the wealthy, the educated, the healthy and the articulate. They also celebrate the individual. Herein lies the catch. As Lindsay Tanner has observed, it is the cult of the individual in our society that has led to the modern plague of isolation and alienation in our communities. Tanner said in his address to the Sydney Institute in May 1999:

Our new social objective should be to ensure that all individuals have a capacity to participate in our society ... This offers a philosophical foundation for social institutions that counteract the dominance of individualism. Society has an obligation to ensure that all of its members are able to belong ...

Building a new community framework to counter alienation, social exclusion and loneliness should start with a renewed commitment to community organisations. Their intrinsic value is far greater than the sum total of the services they provide. It is time we rediscovered compassion and recognised that dollars are not necessarily the primary currency of social inclusion and belonging.

Tanner was speaking in this instance of the breakdown in the sense of community within Australian society. In the present context, it is well to remember that the essence of community is family. As the International Covenant of Civil and Political Rights acknowledges, the family is the fundamental group unity of society. When we lose sight of the importance of family in the creation and sustenance of community, we lose sight of the most vital ingredient that turns a group of individuals into a society. Indeed, some might venture that we lose sight of the most important attribute of our humanity.

chapter 17

From here to equality: the voice of disability rights in the twenty-first century
by Steve Hurd and Peter Johnston

PAID TO CARE
John had no sight
but his mind was great
But they still sold his soul
to a welfare state —
Where they said you have problems
your voice cannot hide —
And though we can't love you,
we will still be your guide.

But his hardship was feelings
they just couldn't know
The need for the warmth
they were taught not to show
And he tried to tell them
but they said don't you dare —
just thank GOD for the wisdom
of those paid to care.

He met with a man saying he knew the truth,
A specially trained friend they bought for their youth;
But when John asked 'Can we go out for a drive?'
He said 'I'm sorry I can't, as I leave work at five.'

He said 'Son, you have more problems than I can put right.'
John said 'You have less vision than I have got sight
for if I really have problems, can you show me where?'
He said 'I wouldn't know, I am just paid to care.'

His teachers said 'John, there's no future for you,
for you can't perceive things the way that we do —
you'd be a good student, if you could just see.'
John said 'You'd be good teachers if you could learn about me.
Oh please could you teach me what love is about,
why you get it so easily and I must do without;
teach me how to feel needed, how to give and to share.'
They said 'Sorry my dear, we are just paid to care.'

One hot summer's night on a dune by the beach
away from the crowds he just couldn't reach;
while young men and women walked along holding hands,
he felt the thorns that grew under the sands.

He thought what is this love so easily won,
bought by the moonlight and sold by the sun.
So he went to a woman who said lie over there —
you'll still have to pay me, but I'll give more than care.

He met with a woman who said 'I'll always be near,
I'll calm all your anger and soothe all your fear.'
But he said 'Sorry my love, I can't ask for your hand,
for I keep getting a feeling you just won't understand;
though I've dreamed of this time which will always be ours,
even rain in the desert won't always bring flowers.
For the thought that brings love to the depths of despair
is that you like the others are just paid to care.'

    (by Steven D. Hurd (1999) — All rights reserved
    and reproduced with permission of the author)

You see I think that their problem
is just not dramatic enough
Three Mile Island and melt downs
are really grit hardened stuff
Seal cubs are cute
and whalers are dumb ugly brutes.

    (Dave Warner)

The above quotation from singer-songwriter and now author Dave Warner highlights the reason hordes of university students and activists are not storming the gates of sheltered workshops, institutions and the corridors of power to prosecute the cause of people with disabilities. The fact is that disability is not 'cute': the cause of disabled people does not have broad appeal, because it is not immediately conducive to mainstream awareness-raising, the issues are not so black and white, and the suffering of people with disabilities is visually less evident and more ambiguous to students and activists and the like. Unlike beautiful forests, lovely animals and gorgeous children, disability is often as different and strange to John Howard's 'mainstream Australia' as people from another planet out of some 1950s' science fiction movie. Like John in the poem 'Paid to Care', those who have been educated in segregated schools, who were taken away from their families at an early age (a practice which occurred up until the early 1970s), who are still institutionalised in sheltered workshops, and those who need to be assisted by those paid to care, have endured, and continue to endure, severe forms of emotional deprivation.

Furthermore, there are many barriers to people with disabilities leaving institutional care and being integrated into the community. From the very practical matter of physical access to buildings at which decisions are made to the more systemic issues such as conceptions of productivity. From the very inability of a person who has an intellectual disability to read their telephone bill to the fact that he or she cannot write a cheque or get a credit card from a bank to make payment of the bill possible over the phone. From the difficulty facing any one disadvantaged person in gaining respect and power due to societal conditioning and the propensity of care to be contingent on payment (again, see 'Paid to Care'), to the general unwillingness of employers to take on people with disabilities despite their overtures of support for the rights of disabled people.

There are numerous attitudinal barriers with regard to employment, for instance. Common complaints are that employers can only see what people with disabilities *cannot* do instead of what they can; that they are concerned about how clients and co-workers might react to a disabled person in the workplace; that they assume people with disabilities can only do boring repetitive tasks; and finally that they are cautious when dealing with an unknown quantity and conclude that it would be safer for them to employ non-disabled people (Tyler 1993, p. 205). Even in the public/community sector, very few people with disabilities have been employed. There are countless organisations advocating for disabled people but very few of these actually employ people with disabilities, claiming that a lack of resources precludes their being able to afford necessary technology or pay co-workers to assist disabled employees (for example, installing TTY telephones for people who are deaf, or having co-workers type and read for people who are blind or who have poor motor skills).

In the media, people with disabilities have been consistently reported as a marginalised group. Disability issues are more often than not reported in the media as tragic tales about the need to give people with disabilities charity, or about parents leaving children with disabilities on the steps of Parliament House because they don't have the money to provide for them. The story of perhaps one out of every hundred (at very best) disabled people who complete a university degree or who win a prize will be reported in a 'man bites dog' manner — as an unusual and outstanding achievement to be sensationalised and condescendingly praised. This type of reporting does very little to constructively raise mainstream awareness of the genuine hardships and suffering faced by people with disabilities.

The treatment of disabled people raises very difficult but compelling issues of social justice in relation to community attitudes, institutional care, media coverage and employment and social opportunities, as touched on here. In this essay we examine, albeit very briefly, the complexities of these issues, and consider how effective present disability legislation is in achieving greater substantive equality for people with disabilities and promoting a more just and humane society. We also seek to outline the issues and highlight the tension between the capitalist motive of productivity and the ethic of democratic participation. However, it is necessary to first define the meaning of disability.

Defining disability

Social and functional constructs of disability

In order to meaningfully discuss the way in which the modern state interacts with people with disabilities, it is useful to consider some of the ways in which disability is defined and constructed. Traditionally, there have been three main groupings of disabilities: physical, intellectual and psychiatric. Within these broad parameters there can be numerous subgroups or classifications. The taxonomies may be arbitrary and inappropriate, and will depend on who is doing the classifying and who is being classified. On the other hand, it is somewhat misleading to talk about 'the disabled' or the 'disability community' in generalised ways as there are profound differences and disagreements, and indeed, discrimination between various groups who are ostensibly disabled in some way.

Whether or not an individual is classified as 'disabled' may be dependent upon an attitudinal context. For example, a person temporarily in a wheelchair as a result of a broken leg caused by a fall during a skiing holiday may not necessarily be viewed as disabled by his or her fellow workers in the same way as a colleague who is wheelchair-bound by reason of cerebral palsy or some other congenital condition. Similarly, a person with a one-off case of pneumonia may not necessarily be stigmatised to the same extent as a person whose pneumonia is a symptom of being HIV positive or part of an AIDS-related illness.

Definitions of disability mainly describe the barriers people with disabilities face in terms of personal inadequacies or functional limitations. This approach reinforces the notion that disability is the result of personal dysfunction and ignores the social causes of disability. It fails to acknowledge the need for infrastructural change and flexibility, and to appreciate the need to provide for greater accommodation of people with disabilities via parallel disability services instead of generically accessible services (Banks & Kayess 1998, p. 157). As we shall discuss later in the context of employment and employment services, the focus is more on what a disabled person cannot do rather than what they can.

Administrative and political constructs of disability

Another way of viewing disability, which is of particular relevance to this chapter, is as an administrative construct or category (Davis 1998). Drawing from the earlier work of Stone (1984), Fulcher (1989) and Oliver (1990), Davis describes how the modern welfare state establishes an administrative category called 'the disabled' so as to determine and allocate benefits and resources depending on whether particular individuals are in or out of that category. People who are predetermined as disabled according to some arbitrary medical and/or legal classification are then placed into this homogenous category, notwithstanding any clear differences between types of disability. Therefore, in order for individuals to receive aid (read: charity) from the state, they must fit themselves into this state-sanctioned and -produced category.[1] Be it in education, employment, recreation, health services or housing, 'The way in which people with power respond to what they perceive as disability actively constructs the nature of disability' (Davis 1998, p. 15).

Furthermore, and as with many other social movements, this state-mediated construction of disability, through legislation, funding and service provision, has tended to form the dominant basis for the as yet embryonic movement of disability rights (see Fulcher 1989, p. 41). Identifying oneself as a person with a disability is fundamentally different, however, from identifying oneself as being indigenous or gay, or even a woman. This is because to identify yourself as disabled is more hazardous and has more negative connotations than the other categories mentioned, and also because, as illustrated above with the wheelchair examples, the category of disabled can be quite fluid. There are many people who have disabilities who simply want to live their lives in a normal way and who dismiss any calls to fight for their rights as part of any group on a collective basis. People who receive a benefit such as WorkCover for example, who may well also have a disability, may prefer to perceive their problems as related to the WorkCover system in particular, as opposed to systemic disability issues more generally, and will therefore not align themselves with any disability rights movement in a broader sense. Compounding these categorisation and identification issues is the fact that often when a person with a disability questions the way they are being inappropriately treated by an agency or relative who regards them as 'disabled', they are often referred to as 'just bitter' or 'having a chip on their shoulder' because of their disability. This view is largely the product of a regime of thinking which is derived from the Victorian sense of philanthropy, whereby individuals are treated in a certain largely condescending and impersonal manner because they fall into a formal category, rather than on a individualistic substantive basis.

Existing legislative measures to counter disability discrimination

The law, whether in the form of legislation or through the decisions of the courts, has certainly been commonly used as a tool for change by various human rights movements. Indeed, the use of the law and the courts as a means of fighting for and achieving human rights is a growing phenomenon (Parsons forthcoming, p. 34). Yet the law and the legal process have proven a limited and often unsatisfactory strategy for achieving justice and human rights for people with disabilities. The legislative measures introduced under the previous Labor Government and maintained and modified by the present Coalition Government were meant to ameliorate the disadvantaged position of people with disabilities, in contrast to the problematic approach of philanthropy which prevailed beforehand and which served merely to maintain the status quo. The two major federal Acts which concern people with disabilities are the *Disability Discrimination Act 1992* (Cth) and the *Disabilities Services Act 1986* (Cth). Both however are arguably flawed in their ability to meet the high expectations that people with disabilities had of them when they were enacted.

The Disability Discrimination Act

While the definition of disability for the purposes of the *Disability Discrimination Act 1992* (Cth) (DDA) is very wide-ranging, the DDA has provided only a narrow right for an individual to bring an action against a discriminator for a perceived incident of discrimination, usually in a court or tribunal setting. Whilst there may have been some small successes for disabled people in using anti-discrimination legislation and processes, such examples are indeed:

> *[f]or the most part scattered and it is much more common for people concerned with human rights issues to come away from their day in court — or more commonly from their day in the solicitor's office — disappointed at how ineffective the law has been in achieving change.* (Parsons forthcoming, p. 37)

With the lack of funding for the Human Rights and Equal Opportunity Commission (HREOC) to administer the Act, and the effect of High Court decisions which have rendered decisions of the HREOC unenforceable against anyone other than the Commonwealth, there is widespread disappointment with the DDA (*Brandy v. Human Rights and Equal Opportunity Commission & Ors* 1995). Complaints often take over three or four years to resolve and very often are declined by the HREOC (HREOC 1998). There is and has been much criticism of the HREOC as being overly political and intimidated by the Howard Government, and it has been argued that it is not sufficiently independent to fulfil its proper functions.

Also, the Howard Government is, at the time of writing, proposing to amend the DDA. These amendments would see applications go to the Federal Court for full hearing rather than to the HREOC. Whilst this would improve the enforceability of the DDA, it would create other kinds of difficulties for potential disabled applicants. People with disabilities who lack adequate legal representation would very often not be able to prosecute their complaints without the assistance of a lawyer — currently, however, the DDA legal services network is only funded to have one lawyer in each capital city and one part time in Cairns. Another deterrent would be the spectre of heavy costs orders being made against unsuccessful applicants in the Federal Court. These factors combined would effectively render any claims to fairness under the DDA absurd, especially as those individuals trying to survive on Disability Support Pensions would find these expenses fairly preclusive.

The government, however, would argue that combined with the *Disability Services Act 1986* (Cth) and State legislation, the issues are well covered. Whereas in fact the abolition of the Disability Discrimination Commissioner and the administrative merging of disability discrimination with other areas such as race discrimination only evidences a view in the Howard Government that these issues are not important enough to merit special and independent consideration.

The Disability Services Act

The *Disabilities Services Act 1986* (Cth) (DSA) primarily operates from a 'service provider framework' and buttresses the process of professionalisation or 'welfarisation' of human need. Despite drawing its principles and objectives from international covenants such as the Declaration on the Rights of Disabled Persons 1975, it is fair to state that 'the DSA is essentially a funding mechanism' (Rose 1998). It supports an administrative arrangement whereby the Commonwealth Health Department can support and fund organisations and services aiding people with disabilities both at State and federal level. Under the scheme the DSA establishes, people with disabilities are classified according to a medical model perspective, and individuals must fit into a prescribed bureaucratic category in order to take advantage of funding or benefits. Through this type of systemisation, people's needs are understood in terms of programs, schemes, eligibility criteria, outcomes, outputs, and so on — it represents the professionalisation of human need, which only serves ultimately to let the broader community 'off the hook' (Parsons forthcoming).

The Australian Law Reform Commission (ALRC), in its review of the DSA, concluded that:

> [T]he legislation falls short of providing services that meet and apply the legal and social justice objectives that Australia has set itself with respect to people with disabilities. The ALRC considers that new disability services legislation should be fairer and based upon a rights model. The present Australian position, far from recognising the rights of people with disabilities, is largely the result of the presumption, apparent in the legislation, that government and service providers know what is in the best interests of people with disabilities and necessarily will act accordingly.
> (Rose 1998, p. 99)

The basic right that activists campaigned for in the mid-1980s, which was an independent complaints tribunal to deal with dissatisfaction with 'charitable organisations', was not provided. Furthermore, whilst the DSA does require 'consumer participation' by way of client evaluation, it is often felt by DSA auditors and disability rights activists that the consumers who are invited to offer feedback and opinions are carefully selected according to whether they are likely to hold positive views of the agency being audited under the DSA.

The failure of the DDA and DSA to adopt a rights-based approach

At the time the DDA was passed, disabled people felt that it, more so than its predecessor (the DSA), would effectively be their Bill of Rights. In recent years, however, that hope has given way to disillusionment. It needs to be understood that the DDA is not a human rights charter or bill for people with disabilities, even if, as with much social legislation, it has laudable aims couched in the language of human rights. The DDA certainly outlines the areas in which disability discrimination is unlawful and actionable, but it does not positively and directly proclaim human rights for those who experience such discrimination. Nor, as the Law Reform Commission pointed out, does the DSA adopt a rights-based perspective.

The Howard Government's disability policies fail disabled people

The Howard Government has done little to assist people with disabilities, and has in fact contributed to the social, economic and political disadvantage of those people. The Howard Government views service provision for people with disabilities as a matter of needs rather than rights. According to such a view, such service provision is only possible through a strongly functioning capitalist economy and an adherence to traditional (family) values. Lynne Davis analyses particularly well the tension that is reflected in the conservatives' move away from a rights-based disability policy to a needs-based one. Quoting extensively from a speech given by Prime Minister Howard to the Australian Council of Social Service, she writes:

> *According to [Howard], 'a fair and compassionate society has a basic responsibility to assist the genuinely needy and disadvantaged through the provision of a strong and secure social welfare safety net'. Neeedless to say, under the Coalition's policy, 'genuine need' is never defined by the recipients of social welfare themselves. The Coalition Government views the welfare state in terms of welfare pluralism, whereby 'Government, the community and the tremendous voluntary welfare organisations [are] all working together'. The family is seen as the linchpin of this system because '[a] stable functioning family provides the best welfare support system yet devised'. Economic growth is said to be the necessary condition for a system of welfare provision — 'We take it as fundamental that sustaining and maintaining a fair and compassionate society in which individuals have the opportunity to succeed and prosper through their own initiative and endeavour requires a productive, competitive and growing economy.'* (Davis 1998, p. 22)

The belief held by the Howard Government is that the 'care of people with disabilities rightly belongs in the private sphere, particularly the family', according to traditional family values of caring. These traditional values suggest 'that the needs of people with disabilities should and can be met primarily through the unpaid labour of family members (mainly women). The implications of this ideology on government expenditure on services for people with disabilities are obvious' (Hauritz, Sampford & Blencowe 1998, p. xvi). This type of attitude divests the government and the market of any form of responsibility for making disabled people truly inclusive members of society.

Family Services Minister Judi Moylan reveals the essence of the conservatives' approach to disability funding and policy when she states that the government's policy 'is to assist [disabled people] to develop their skills and independence and to ensure they are able to contribute to society through productive employment' (Davis 1998, p. 23). Such a statement may seem innocuous on the surface, but in combination with cutbacks to the HREOC's funding and general health services provision,[2] its deeper implications are revealed. In short, under conservative governments, 'There has been a retreat from a framework of citizenship rights and an embrace of such themes as the market, radical individualism, a minimal role for the state and assistance for the (genuinely) needy' (Davis 1998, p. 23).

Whilst former Labor administrations may not have always matched their rhetoric of rights with concrete action or adequate funding levels, the present Coalition Government does not even attempt to use this rhetoric — or rather it has replaced the rhetoric of rights with the language of self-help, compassion and need. People with disabilities are having these paradigms imposed upon them by the Howard Government. Increasingly over the last couple of decades, however, many disabled people have reacted by regarding themselves as political actors with political interests, and disability community groups are consistently invoking the language of human rights, disability rights and equality. The way forward is therefore a political solution incorporating a new legislative rights regime, and fostering new social attitudes. What is needed is a new sense of government and corporate responsibility, not a return to public or private charity, with its ethic of beneficence without obligation and concomitant perpetuation of stereotypes.

Proposals for the future

The major criticism then of disability legislation by those who advocate in the disability area is that it remains in the form of either a narrow complaints-based mechanism, in the case of the DDA, or in a service-delivery framework, in the case of the DSA. A major failure is that neither the DDA nor the DSA adopts a rights-based approach. Furthermore, since the passage of the DSA and the DDA, little has changed in terms of the real socio-economic position of people who have disabilities. The legislation does not even begin to address the emotional, psychological and social deprivation suffered by disabled people through institutionalisation, as illustrated by the poem 'Paid to Care', nor does it redress the ways in which the democratic power of people with disabilities is tacitly undermined. The DDA or the DSA in themselves will not stimulate attitudinal change towards people with disabilities so long as socially acculturated discriminatory attitudes and practices are allowed to thrive (Thornton

1990, p. 7). Whether 'social' legislation can change discriminatory behaviour, or indeed any form of behaviour, is a difficult issue and a somewhat circular issue: is the law capable of promoting that kind of attitudinal and social change, or must societal attitudes change before such laws can be introduced and prove effective? Thornton, for one, is somewhat sceptical as to whether individual complaints mechanisms can have a 'more generalised educative effect'. She argues that such laws may merely serve to disguise discrimination or drive it underground (Jones & Marks 1998, p. 77).

Despite such criticisms, we believe that laws such as the DDA are necessary, although not sufficient, measures to promote social justice and equal rights for people with disabilities. We believe that discriminatory attitudes can be best broken down through integration based on a rights-oriented framework. The kinds of ways in which this integration might take place are through the enhancement of community-type facilities, a more open public-service entrance policy, and perhaps subsidisation for employers schemes.

Certainly in our work we believe by 'spreading the message' we hope to change people's misconceptions and ignorance as to what being disabled means. Whether we are talking to students, business people or local government officers, we stress the *abilities* of the disabled person — what he or she can do rather than what they cannot. Certainly attitudes can be changed in positive ways when a person actually meets or interacts with a disabled person in school, at the club or in the workplace. For this reason alone, laws which oblige an employer to employ a disabled person, all other things being equal, are to be welcomed. As one writer has written elsewhere, in the case of gays and lesbians, '[The disabled] can only fulfil symbolic roles of the "other" or the "not-self" if they are abstract synecdoches rather than flesh and blood loved ones, co-workers, etc.' (Johnston 1996, p. 1155).

Even assuming that the participation rate of disabled people could be increased, it is evident that once a disabled person gets a job or is accepted into a class or club, new problems then arise. Many teachers and co-workers regard with suspicion and uncertainty a person who must do their tasks in a different way from their peers. Discrimination or even unfair treatment which may not (in the legal sense of the term) be discrimination is so inherent that the process of attitudinal adjustment that must occur in order for true participation to be possible is still a long way off.³

Yet attitudinal change will also be harder to achieve in a political climate where, despite the inclusive and positive rhetoric, government policy has fundamentally shifted from a rights-based focus and an accommodation of difference to a revisionist, charity-based reflection of upper-middle-class guilt.

If politicians, policy-makers and economists continue to withdraw support for social justice and affirmative action policies, we run the real risk that the wider public will not view the disabled as people with the right to participate fully in community life, even if this would require extra taxation. True citizenship cannot be reduced to individual contractual relations. In order for rights to be effective and more than just window dressing, they must transcend the '[p]otentially partisan limitations of legislation and government policy in Australia' (Banks & Kayess 1998, p. 162).

In writing this brief essay, we are mindful of the magnitude of the changes required to create a social framework in which people with all types of needs can feel included and wanted. No 'five-point plan', nor any single legislative act, would be capable of achieving the depth and breadth of change necessary. Such change would require a multidisciplinary task force to form a systemic basis upon which to begin fostering a culture of inclusion. As stated earlier, being with, working with and knowing a person with a disability is often the best way to change things. Ultimately, the paramount issue is the ability of people to feel 'relaxed and comfortable' in the company of disabled people. This will only happen when a framework is established with adequate funding by the state. Once people have the opportunity to learn about a disabled person individually, they will undoubtedly feel less strange or uncomfortable about them and will begin to realise that people with disabilities are like everyone else: they have qualities and faults, they have good days and bad days — and, above all, like anyone, they feel pride and derive meaning from being a productive part of society.

chapter **18**

Difference in an age of homogeneity: feminism, democracy and the illusion of consensus
by Anne Schillmoller

The emergence of a single world market has engendered a superficially convergent global culture dominated by Western iconography. Both economic globalisation and the corporate entertainment and media industries ride roughshod over local diversity and authenticity, with the result that cultural identities become commodified. Some futurists predict that within a 'globalised' culture, all of the world's subcultures will collide, with the result that individual differentiation and points of divergence will increasingly diminish. Accompanying such cultural uniformity, it is said, will be the emergence of a 'transcendent global consciousness'.

The role played by industrial capitalism and neo-liberal economic orthodoxy in driving globalisation has been considered at length by William Greider, who notes that two-thirds of the world's trade is controlled by transnational corporations. Greider contends that while it might be observed that economic globalisation imposes uniformity where there is diversity, it also seems incapable of solving the problems of the ever-increasing disparity between the world's rich and the world's poor, and may even be responsible for aggravating it (Greider 1997, p. 7).

Uniformity has been further fostered by the custodians of the information revolution in which English, the *lingua franca* of cyberspace, has emerged as the predominant global language. Indeed, Margaret Wertheim notes that much of the rhetoric used by cyberspace champions is drawn from the language of colonisation. She suggests that the technological media function to reproduce the structures of domination and subordination which characterise social systems as a whole and that the colonisation of cyberspace by the American West is an ongoing form of cultural imperialism, geared toward the erasure of all non-Western histories (Wertheim 1999, p. 296).

Using contemporary feminist critiques, this essay will challenge some of the assumptions underlying the vision of global homogeneity. It attempts to expose the fictive nature of such a representation, and to reveal how the rhetoric of globalisation and the neo-liberal democratic orthodoxy supporting it operate to entrench authoritative cultural representations which suppress differences of culture and of gender. It will be argued that the homogenising imperative, while superficially convincing, is a continuing form of cultural imperialism which reinforces existing economic and political privilege while marginalising difference within a heterogeneous global culture. It will also demonstrate the ways in which uniformity has been facilitated by the rhetoric of democratic discourse, the exclusionary effects of which will be considered. Finally, a number of strategies will be outlined that may more effectively provide for inclusive and open-ended democratic structures which recognise heterogeneity and diversity and which enable active participation by hitherto silenced voices in democratic decision-making processes.

Feminism and the politics of representation

Aware of the importance of recognising women's heterogeneity, most contemporary feminists know that the way in which women represent themselves and other women for political purposes is fraught with peril. Indeed, it might be observed that a number of predominantly white, Western feminists share the homogenising rhetoric of globalisation. The tendency of some feminists to speak about and on behalf of others without those voices being present to arbitrate, complicate or contest such claims is a troubling one. Where any group of women become the 'custodians' of feminism there emerges a privileged elite promulgating a type of evangelical secularism which, through a process of appropriation, purports to represent the interests of all women. As noted by Anna Yeatman: 'Historically the custodians of feminism drew discursive legitimacy from the universal civilising mission of the middle class in extending to their less fortunate sisters a matronizingly appropriative embrace' (Yeatman 1993, p. 238).

An increasing number of contemporary critics, recognising that feminism has moved beyond the search for an authoritative speaking position, and concerned at the complacency with which some feminists have arrogantly exported a feminism which is destructive of local experiences and knowledges, have brought feminism to account and have interrogated its claims to authority.

Such critics argue that in a context of multiple oppressions based on factors such as ethnicity, race and economic circumstances, feminist theory and practice can no longer be predicated upon the assumption that gender is the only, nor the most salient, basis of oppression. It follows from this that women cannot be regarded as a coherent class since their oppression transcends the limits of their gender. Certainly, for example, the struggles of middle-class women for professional recognition and advancement have not always struck a responsive chord among non-Western women. There is also a difficulty in trying to locate the 'cause' of women's oppression, since any attempt to identify one aspect of human experience, such as economic status, sexuality or child-rearing as the ultimate factor in women's oppression, is overly reductionist. And, as Sandra Berns has observed, among a myriad of voices 'it is difficult to find a core which might be held up as a universal, identified as a need rather than a bare preference' (Berns 1993, p. 97).

The danger, then, in contemporary political movements is that through strategies of inclusion, universal interests are cast in a way which preserves a privileged identity, while excluding other, 'marginalised' identities. As Gayatri Spivak has argued, within feminist political movements, it has traditionally been hegemonic individuals who have monopolised the agenda-setting. These political custodians then construct a representational politics out of a dichotomy of 'sameness' and 'difference'. The result is that participants either share a common agenda, in which case no space is created for difference, or they are relegated as 'other', in which case they are required to speak on behalf of all the others, all minorities, all differences (Spivak 1988).

Essentialism, universalism and pluralism

The tension within feminism between describing women's experiences collectively as a basis for political action (essentialism) and respecting differences among women (pluralism) is unlikely to go away. Indeed, in the face of profound cultural differences among women, how feminist strategies might effectively combine collective political action while avoiding charges of cultural imperialism is a continuing issue.

Some feminists have suggested that women have much to lose in any movement away from universal standards in favour of deference to pluralism. There is a continuing dialogue concerning the degree to which women's conditions transcend boundaries of race, culture and class which parallels the struggle between universal and culturally specific visions of human rights. The anti-essentialist stance demands that feminists pay attention to the particularities of women's condition, especially those women who are relatively less powerful, by constantly questioning the validity of cross-cultural assumptions. However, despite its theoretical and political vulnerabilities, the practical appeal of essentialism, like the appeal of universalism, persists.

One argument put forward in favour of essentialist strategies is that essentialist assumptions offer the promise of uniting women in a way that transcends or precedes politics and that an emphasis on differences rather than commonalties threatens political alliances among women. Another argument is that highlighting difference rather than sameness may encourage provincialism and justify isolationism among feminists. Similarly, if cross-cultural intervention is seen as imperialist or coercive, feminists may be reluctant to intervene in support of women globally, and respect for difference may be used as a justification for inaction. Finally, proponents of essentialist strategies argue that the assumption that moral standards are necessarily local dismisses the possibility that cross-cultural oppression in fact exists. It is argued that although its particular manifestations may vary from culture to culture, oppression on the basis of sex is not a local phenomenon. So while feminist method generally exhibits a wariness towards generalisations which transcend the boundaries of culture and region, some feminists contend that it's only by putting differences aside, by recognising common political goals, that political action can be effective.

While 'strategic essentialism' may have a certain pragmatic appeal, it may also, as Diane Elam suggests, demand that women join together, in the name of 'identity' and 'identification', on the basis of what they have in common, so that their differences are not only ignored, but erased: 'The question that arises is: must feminism always seek to erase difference by giving birth to a family of identical daughters who all fight for the same causes, who all pretend to share the same feminist goals?' (Elam 1994, p. 72).

Certainly there is a danger in the common oppression argument in which a singular identity functions as the standard around which political action is organised. Identity politics tends to ignore the complexity of the relationship between identity and difference. This is so even when it tries to become more nuanced by allowing for a set of purportedly inclusive identities. It is a gross oversimplification, Elam argues, to suggest that all women are oppressed equally. The identification of categories of difference, such as the 'black woman', the 'lesbian', the 'migrant women', is similarly problematic since it homogenises identities, leads to stereotyping and sets up hierarchies of oppression. As Vietnamese film-maker Trinh Minh-ha has noted, we have all become entwined in the centre of cultural production. She relates how when women like her were first asked to speak to a Western audience, they felt that they were expected to take up certain positions and were treated variously as exotic, dangerous and/or endangered (Bulbeck 1998, p. 207).

A heterogeneous difference

With regard to the above dialogues, it is argued that we should attempt to conceive of difference as a truly heterogeneous difference. This position is predicated upon an ambivalent separation of sex from gender in which the former is a biological category and the latter the cultural interpretation of biological existence. It is a vision which rejects the social, cultural and legal homogenisation of women's specificities into models produced in the interests of universalism. It is one which comprehends the way in which homogenised representations frequently disguise an affinity with hegemonic frameworks of knowledge.

Such a standpoint does not, however, involve the total abandonment of essentialist strategies for political purposes. It is argued that one can resort to essentialist strategies without also making an overall commitment to universalism. As Gayatri Spivak has suggested, women should remain vigilant about their practice and use essentialist strategies where appropriate, rather than resorting to the totally counterproductive gesture of repudiation (Harasym 1990, p. 11).

The exclusionary effects of homogenisation in contemporary processes of power

In his seminal work, *Voltaire's Bastards*, John Raulston Saul notes that women were not part of the formulation and creation of the 'age of reason', but were the symbol of the irrational. He suggests that it would be a great error to assume that our society has had or has within it today the basic flexibility to allow real female participation. Women who occupy positions of power and influence, he says, are obliged to hold onto their power by deforming themselves into honorary men or into magnified archetypes of the female who manipulates men. It is still not clear, Saul argues, if women can successfully enter or become part of established structures without accepting such deformations (Saul 1992, p. 35).

Iris Young has similarly observed that 'a homogeneity of citizens has been forced on the civic public' (Young 1987, p. 124). She argues that modern normative reason and its political expression in the idea of the civic public only has unity and coherence by its expulsion and confinement of everything that would threaten to invade the polity with differentiation: the difference of gender, race and culture, the heterogeneity of needs, goals and desires, and of ambiguity and changeability.

One might also observe the tendency of some emancipatory political movements to deploy the historically achieved democratic features of an established political discourse in an irresponsible way. Anna Yeatman suggests that there is too often a utilitarian acceptance of what already exists by way of democratic institutional process and guarantees of rights, a concern shared by Pauline Johnson:

Any attempt to interpret women's objectives in terms of principles and formulations directly borrowed from political liberalism is a limited ambition, since it is one which merely demands the end of discriminatory practices which thwart the access of women to the range of life choices already made available by contemporary socio-political institutions. (Johnson 1994, p. 73)

Indeed, the individualistic underpinnings of liberalism, predicated upon the notion of the autonomous individual in pursuit of self-chosen goals, is inimical to many people, most frequently women, for whom relationships of care and inter-relationship are often paramount. The tension between the liberalist rhetoric of the self-legislating subject and the realities of women's interdependencies and affective ties renders entry into sites of political power problematic, frequently compelling women to submit to the imperatives of a culture which historically was adapted for men alone. The liberalist notion of formal equality, predicated on the myth of the 'level playing field', fails to acknowledge the need for a radical alteration of values within institutional and political culture in order to effectively incorporate differences of gender and of culture.

Recent feminist analyses of modern political theory and practice suggest that appeals to shared values, the bedrock of liberalism, obscure differences amongst political subjects. Margaret Thornton, for example, argues that the deliberative processes of democracy assume a neutral citizen, one who has shed particularities and conforms to the normative standards of 'benchmark man' (Thornton 1995, p. 200).

Within such frameworks, Thornton says, women and differentiated others have been expected to adapt in order to be included within the society of equals, despite the structural impediments.

Similarly, Nancy Fraser contends that androcentric ideological constructs have been built into the conception of the public sphere and have functioned to legitimate an emergent form of class rule (Fraser 1994, p. 77). Liberalist discourse, she notes, is predicated on a separation of the 'public' from the 'private', a dichotomy much critiqued by feminists who recognise that these spheres are not neutral designations but are cultural classifications and rhetorical labels. It is argued that in political discourse, 'public' and 'private' are powerful terms that are frequently deployed to delegitimate some interests and to valorise others. The way in which the 'privacy' argument, for example, has been used to reinforce inequality has been the subject of much feminist dialogue. It is argued that the domestic realm and the internal inequalities of the family have always been largely ignored by politicians and political theorists because of a fundamental assumption that the separation of the private sphere from the public realm is irrelevant to theories of justice and to political life.

Many feminists would agree that the lifting of formal restrictions to 'public' sphere participation does not suffice to ensure inclusion in practice. Even after women and other marginalised groups have been formally licensed to participate, their participation may be hedged by notions of domestic or economic privacy that limit the scope of debate. The notion of public and private, then, is a vehicle through which gender and economic disadvantage may continue to operate informally even after explicit formal restrictions have been rescinded. For this reason, a tenable conception of the public sphere should include interests and issues that liberalist ideology labels 'private', and thereby treats as inadmissible.

In discussing the formal and informal impediments to participatory parity and the way in which societal inequality infects the formally inclusive public sphere, Nancy Fraser argues that there is no single public arena, and that a proliferation of a multiplicity of publics would be an advance towards democracy rather than a departure from it, as assumed to be the case in the liberal state. She argues that in societies where social inequality persists, full parity of participation in public debate and deliberation is not possible. In such societies, she says, deliberative processes in the public sphere will tend to operate to the advantage of dominant groups and to the disadvantage of subordinates. This is because, Fraser suggests, modes of deliberation mask domination by absorbing the less powerful into a false 'we' that reflects the interests of the more powerful.

The way forward

A number of contemporary political theorists have recognised the need to develop more inclusive and open-ended democratic structures which recognise heterogeneity and diversity. Katherine O'Donovan, for example, considers how a concern for difference might be realised in political practice. She suggests that such a project is not simply a matter of incorporating the hitherto powerless into existing institutional forms. She suggests also that we must abandon unitary notions of citizenship and civil society and give voice to claims made on the basis of difference. Responses to claims will then be agreed upon as a form of compromise (O'Donovan 1985).

She argues that, in heterogeneous societies, public life cannot consist exclusively in a single, comprehensive public sphere. Such an arrangement, she says, privileges the expressive norms of one cultural group over others, thereby making assimilation a condition for participation in public debate. The idea of an egalitarian society only makes sense if we suppose a plurality of public arenas in which groups with diverse values and rhetoric may participate. Such a proliferation of publics assumes the demise of orthodox democratic processes and the increasing marginality of centralised political institutions such as parliaments. Such arrangements would result not in fragmentation, but in the development of a strong civic culture, beyond markets and orthodox government. It would give rise to a greater involvement by people in groups and associations, and enable single-issue groups to influence orthodox political institutions.

Gayatri Spivak uses the expression 'subaltern counterpublics' to describe this multiplicity of public spheres (Spivak 1988). A proliferation of 'counterpublics', she says, gives rise to a widening of discursive contestation, thereby reducing the gap in participatory parity between dominant and subordinate groups. Fraser and Spivak agree that the ideal of participatory parity is most realisable by arrangements that permit deliberation among a plurality of different, and sometimes competing, publics. They argue that there is no reason to rule out the possibility of a society in which social equality and cultural diversity coexist within participatory democracy and that the ideal of participatory parity is better achieved by a multiplicity of publics than by a single public. It is a view in which democratic values are understood as the realisation of equal value in the constitution of identity and difference.

Deliberative models such as those suggested above are not, however, predicated on consensus, a notion which conceals the fact that groups, and individuals within groups, may be differentially empowered. Nancy Fraser, for example, suggests that consensus is usually only reached through deliberative processes tainted by the effects of subordination and domination. Fraser is also suspicious of the notion of 'community' because, she argues, it suggests a bounded and fairly homogenous group. Similarly, Anna Yeatman argues that referents such as 'we Australians' will always be specific to a particular and exclusive political community whose identity establishes unambiguous boundaries between those who belong and those who do not (Yeatman 1993, p. 235).

Emphasising that democracy is much more than a formal theory of political organisation — it is a potent way of daily life — Yeatman has been critical of the tendency of some theorists to criticise the inadequacies of existing institutions and the culture of democracy without also developing a sufficient and positive contribution to contemporary policy debates about how these institutions and the democratic culture might be changed so as to become more inclusive (Yeatman 1993, p. 232).

Mindful of these concerns, it is upon a consideration of inclusive strategies for participation in democratic processes that the final part of this essay will now focus.

Towards a communicative democracy

The challenge for contemporary political practice is to be able to effectively challenge multiple oppressions within an organisational framework that does not relegate any of its participants to an exclusionary status. What is required is an organisational form which does not result in one interest overcoming and silencing other interests, a form which does not give rise to arrested dialogue nor imprison its participants within its own organisational framework. At the same time, however, it is recognised that effective political action requires the identification of an 'interest' or 'interests' around which to organise. This is not always a simple task, since the notion of 'interest' frequently surrenders a vision of the world we might share to a project of individual development that repudiates inter-subjectivity and interdependence. The other danger is that individual interests may be translated into categorical and universalistic prescriptions for human activity. A more useful organising principle, then, may be found in the idea of a non-foundational 'ethics' that recognises that our prevailing moral outlooks are not absolute, but finite.

But as Anna Yeatman observes, we are still responsible for arguing the value of our ethics in a logically coherent manner (Yeatman 1993). This pragmatic realisation poses a challenge for contemporary theorists who reject the existence of a universal or transcendental ethical truth and are committed to a representational politics that recognises a plurality of perspectives.

Mindful of these concerns, Christopher Falzon's suggestion of a 'dialogical ethics', may provide a useful concept around which to organise (Falzon 1998, p. 57). Such an ethics stands in direct opposition to the foundationalist, prescriptive ethics that seek to establish ultimate, universal rules to which all practices must conform. Recognising the exclusionary effects of a transcendentally conceived ethics, Falzon suggests that we should instead turn to a 'dialogical picture' that understands human beings as embodied, active beings in the midst of dialogue with others. Such a conception, he says, does not preclude the development of organisational principles in terms of which we judge and act. What it means, however:

> ... *is that there is no pre-existing, transcendental set of principles which forms the basis for a proper organisation of practices. Rather, normative principles and forms of practice emerge historically out of human activity, out of the play of dialogue, to the degree that some forces are able to bring others under control.*
> (Falzon 1998, p. 60)

The animating principle of this interplay, Falzon suggests, is the freedom to transgress constraints imposed by other forces, to create new forms of thought and action, and to transform those other forces in turn. Falzon suggests that such a recognition allows for 'openness to the other', a willingness to take the claims of the other seriously and a refusal to reduce the other to a mere function of prevailing categories. Dialogical ethics does not preclude the engendering of organising principles; however, as an ongoing dialogue, such an ethics allows for the continual transformation and creative transgression of these principles. What the attitude of openness opposes is not forms of order or organisational activity as such, but rather the absolutism of particular forms of order and the establishment of fixed states of closure and domination. It thereby avoids the exclusionary rigidity of a closed, dogmatic ethics. Such an organisational ethics also avoids a teleological tendency to understand outcomes in terms of intentional, preconceived purposes and instead focuses on the particularity and specificity of events. In this way, differences of culture, gender, and socio-economic circumstances, for example, may be recognised and accommodated by decision-making processes.

As Falzon points out, however, such an attitude of openness also means an abandonment of the security and comfort which comes with an all-embracing view of the world and will necessarily involve an element of risk, uncertainty and instability.

It has been recognised by Iris Young that contemporary democracies tend to discourage deliberation and encourage in citizens a 'privatised consumer orientation' towards politics (Young 1995, p. 136). She notes the way in which current models of deliberative democracy tend to assume that deliberation is both culturally neutral and universal, disguising the fact that the norms of deliberation are culturally specific and may operate as forms of power that silence or devalue the speech of some people. The norms of deliberation, Young suggests, privilege speech that is assertive and confrontational, formal and general, dispassionate and disembodied. The deliberative model, Young says, assumes unity and consensus and regards difference as something to be transcended, rather than regarding it as a resource, a way to reveal the partiality of one's own perspectives, interests and cultural meanings. As argued above, one problem with the deliberative model is that, under the guise of consensus, it may harbour another mechanism of exclusion. When participants in a discussion strive for unity or consensus, there is usually an appeal to a 'common good' which requires the participants to leave behind their particular experiences and interests. The result of this may be that privileged perspectives are likely to dominate the definition of that common good. The corollary of this is that within a deliberative process in which some participants have greater material or symbolic privilege than others, appeals to the common good may have the effect of further entrenching this privilege.

As Jean Baudrillard has observed:

> *[T]he reconciliation of antagonistic forms in the name of consensus and conviviality is the worst thing we can do. We must reconcile nothing. We must keep open the otherness of forms, the disparity between terms; we must keep alive the forms of the irreducible.* (Baudrillard 1996, p. 123)

Young's strategy, reminiscent of Falzon's 'dialogical ethics', is for the development of a 'communicative democracy' which attends to social difference and to the way in which power enters speech itself. Such a democracy, she suggests, is able to recognise the cultural specificity of deliberative practices and to incorporate a more inclusive model of communication. It is a model which provides for an equal privileging of any forms of communication where people attempt to reach understanding, and allows for speaking across differences of culture, social position and need, which are preserved in the process. This type of deliberative process demands substantial institutional and attitudinal shifts. While consciousness-raising is rarely a sudden phenomenon, Young envisages that within a communicative democracy, the exposure of participants to differently situated knowledge will add to their overall social knowledge and engender critical reflection.

As Jacques Derrida has remarked: 'Justice is not a matter of neutralising differences but rather, requires us constantly to maintain an interrogation of the origin, ground and limits of our conceptual, theoretical or normative apparatus surrounding justice' (Derrida 1992, p. 27).

Open endings

Within the contemporary information economy, we are continuing to witness a struggle over meaning in which challenges to traditional knowledge require no less than a major change in forms of democratic participation. It has been argued that the vision of a consensual global order ought to be resisted and its exclusionary effects recognised.

Civil society is the arena in which democratic values are fostered. The development of more inclusive and open-ended democratic structures, together with a proliferation of publics, can lead to an enlarged and more diverse democratic polity which can, within its diversely constituted and multiple sites of influence, challenge the hegemony of imperialist representations. Such 'subaltern' publics may, as this essay has suggested, be able to transgress the constraints imposed by dominant representations and to create new, more inclusive, forms of thought and action.

Jean Baudrillard has observed that within a consensual universal order in which singularity is obliterated, every representation is a servile image. His prediction, however, is that singularity will one day rebel:

> [A]nd then our whole system of representation and values is destined to perish in that revolt. This slavery of the same, the slavery of resemblance, will one day be smashed by the violent resurgence of otherness. Violent singularities will well up reflecting the extent of the inadmissibility of the consensual universal order. (Baudrillard 1996, p. 149)

endnotes

Chapter 2

1. Or 'statism' in Castells' (1996) formulation, perhaps a more useful term given the rather distant resemblance that Soviet-style societies bore to a generally accepted conception of socialism.
2. Rather contradictorily, neo-liberals argue that large salaries are needed as an incentive for good managers, while ordinary workers are supposed to feel enthused by wage cuts, the elimination of penalties and unpaid overtime.

Chapter 3

1. Although the reader should note that the essay is not intended to be a statement of party policy.

Chapter 5

1. For a discussion of strategic planning, see Weil (1997).
2. It should be noted that the data used in figures 1 to 3 is from the Australian Bureau of Statistics' catalogue 6323.0 'Trade Union Statistics' series (ABS 1998d), which is based on a survey of union officials and includes financial and non-financial members. This series was discontinued by the ABS in 1997; the remaining series is catalogue 6325.0, 'Trade Union Members' (ABS 1998e), which is based on a survey of employees and excludes non-financial members.
3. For a discussion on comparative union density, see Blanchflower and Freeman (1992).
4. For a discussion of 'Laborism' versus 'socialism' and other ideological influences in the Australian labour movement, see Easson (1990).

endnotes 301

5. See Schwartz (1991) for a discussion of scenario planning in corporate strategy.
6. Many of my senior union colleagues have emphasised to me the importance of the Eureka Youth League in their own education and interest in art and culture when educational opportunities were limited.
7. I benefited from comments by Dennis Glover and Evan Thornley on the 'youth' question.

Chapter 6

1. A search of the Melbourne *Age* database for 1998–99 yielded only two instances of the terms 'industrial democracy', 'employee participation', 'employee representation' or 'workplace democracy'. By contrast, the term 'Workplace Relations Act' produced 140 scores.
2. Trade union membership Australia-wide was 51.1 per cent in 1976 and 31.1 per cent in 1996 (ACIRRT 1999, p. 58).
3. For helpful descriptions of the Australian industrial relations system, see Mitchell (1998), Vranken (1998) and Creighton and Stewart (1994).
4. See also ACIRRT (1999, pp. 55–6) for statistics on the extent to which change is dominated in a unilateral manner by management. At workplaces where there had been a significant change that had affected workers, workers had either made the decision or had significant input into the decision in only 20 per cent of cases; in 10 per cent of workplaces, management made changes without even informing the workers. A clear majority of workers (58 per cent) felt they had little or no influence over decision-making, and only 13 per cent felt they had a lot.
5. Both the Coalition and the Labor Party are still significantly influenced by the neo-liberal agenda described and criticised in other chapters in this volume. Furthermore, the major parties have given very little consideration to alternative models of government and private sector decision-making. The participatory model provides a viable and exciting alternative prototype of democratic decision-making.
6. In this chapter I am describing the opportunities for widespread popular participation rather than dealing with the apparent problem of political apathy.
7. It is worth noting that the participatory model provides a blueprint to promote and enhance democratic decision-making in all aspects of society. Examples of legislation promoting the participatory vision include the enlargement of freedom of information legislation to cover government commercial dealings; the liberalisation of legal standing requirements that

restrict community organisations' ability to bring public interest litigation; and the introduction of legislation that promotes democratic decision-making in government and private-sector employment, private clubs and societies, schools and universities. While I believe the adoption of legislation incorporating such a model would have profound and beneficial consequences, this important discussion falls outside the scope of this paper.
8. This seems to be the crucial difference between the participatory model and, say, the protective model of representative government, which places a primary value on good government — that is, government in the interests of the mass of citizens (see Patmore 1998, p. 100; Bentham 1843/1961, pp. 155–8).
9. Various other proposals have been advanced as extending employee participation beyond collective representation by unions, including: (i) employee representation on company boards; (ii) employees voting side-by-side with shareholders in the election of directors; (iii) directors' duties to recognise and consider employee interests in enterprise decision-making; (iv) employee share-ownership schemes; (v) performance-based payment systems — payment of workers to vary according to the profitability of the enterprise — thus employees share in extra profits; and (vi) worker cooperative democracy.
10. The EWCD (1994) and EWCD (1997) are forms of law binding on European Union and European Economic Area countries. Norway, Liechtenstein and Iceland are members of the European Economic Area. The EWCD must be implemented by a member country enacting legislation or by other appropriate methods, such as implementation through collective agreements.
11. See article 2 for calculation of number of employees.
12. By contrast, at the national level in Europe, works councils operate in large, medium and smaller enterprises. For example, in Germany works councils may be established in private-sector enterprises with five or more permanent employees (Muller-Jentsch 1995, p. 55). It is estimated that about 35 per cent of the enterprises (covering 70 per cent of the workforce) that are eligible to establish works councils have done so. Typically the enterprises that do not have works councils are small businesses of fewer than 50 employees (Muller-Jentsch 1995, p. 56). See also Hansmann (1993, p. 604), who contends that around 80 per cent of workers in Germany are represented by works councils.
13. Note also that the commission will examine whether the current size thresholds are appropriate before 22 September 1999 (European Works Council 1994, EC art. 15).

14. This discussion draws upon the work of Streeck (1995, pp. 331–3), Rogers and Streeck (1995) and Freeman (1994).
15. Works councils also exist in the United States and Canada, Japan (Nitta 1996), South Korea and the Philippines. See the brief case study of works councils in Rogers and Streeck (1994).
16. It is notable that Ireland has passed legislation to implement the EWCD — the *Transnational Information and Consultation of Employees Act* of 1996. Section 14 provides that employees' representatives shall be elected or appointed as determined by employees, or appointed by agreement between employees and management. The Irish Act thus leaves open the possibility of the democratic election of employees.
17. The EWCD has a number of significant implications for Australia, most obviously, the EU directive's universal application to otherwise very different national industrial relations systems, including common law countries such as Britain and Ireland. The EWCD thus provides a prototype for the adoption of works councils in a common law country such as Australia. The directive also provides:
    (i) a model of a works council (in the annex) that could be established in Australian corporations;
    (ii) a procedure to establish works councils, namely, by initially encouraging voluntary negotiations followed by mandatory requirements;
    (iii) a recognition that mandatory requirements are necessary if works councils are to be established; and
    (iv) a realisation that works councils are a vital response to the process of globalisation.

    It is noteworthy that EU directives have already been used as a model for reform in Australia in the case of the creation of a new cause of action for products liability in the *Trade Practices Amendment Act 1992* (Cth), part V, division 2A. Also, it is not necessary to reinvent the wheel. The spokes of the wheel of reform are supplied by the EWCD.
18. Although works councils are formally independent of the union movement, most council members in Europe are active union members.
19. It is noteworthy that the Australian Democrats introduced the Industrial Democracy Bill on 24 May 1983 into the Senate to create a form of works councils for Australia, but the Bill lapsed.
20. In Europe, attempts to introduce voluntary schemes as union substitutes have either failed, or worse, have been inimical to economic efficiency and to the development of harmonious workplace relations (see Streeck 1995, pp. 317–19).

Chapter 8

1. For the sake of the argument, I accept poverty measures that use 'income' to stand in for living standards more generally, and by 'living standards' I mean 'more stuff'. For more nuanced and interesting ways to measure the standard of living and deprivation, see the papers collected in Eckersley (1998) and the discussion in chapter 1 of Travers and Richardson (1993). I also use the Organisation for Economic Cooperation and Development (OECD) measure of poverty as income below 50 per cent of the national equivalent median family income (see Harding and Mitchell (1992) and ABS (1998) for figures). The Henderson Poverty Line, the measure most commonly used in Australia, is calculated on a different basis and updated according to rises in household disposable income per capita. The number of people below the Henderson line increased from 8.2 per cent to 14.4 per cent between 1973 and 1996. Anthony King, in discussing these figures, comments: 'Instead of seeing solid evidence of a dramatic increase in poverty over the period, a safer conclusion is that the proportion of the population in poverty in 1996 was somewhat higher than in 1973, though within the same broad order of magnitude' (King 1998, pp. 78–9).
2. For example, in 1993–4 the average young-couple family without dependant children had an average weekly income of $951 which, after taxes and transfers, dropped to a final income of $741. By contrast, the average weekly market income of couples with a child aged between five and fourteen was $765, which, after taxes and transfers, was bumped up to $823 (ABS 1996, p. 119). I have described a simple point-in-time analysis of the Australian tax-transfer system that might too easily support an 'us-and-them' outlook. If you think about it, it in fact suggests that many people will move from being net contributors to the tax-transfer system to being net beneficiaries, depending on life cycle circumstance. Around 40 per cent of the redistribution effected by the system is redistribution of income across individuals' own lifetimes.
3. This occurs not just in Australia; some Western European welfare states do an even better job of reducing inequality and lifting the poor out of poverty (see the studies in McFate, Lawson and Wilson (1995)).
4. Garrett and Mitchell admit that it is unclear what the causal relationship is here. A government that spends money on the welfare of its citizens might be creating the kind of investment climate that attracts international capital or, conversely, increased integration in world markets might create the kind of social dislocation and disruption that would require govern-

ments to increase welfare spending to ameliorate the damage.
5. Here I follow the schema suggested by Froud et al. (1997, pp. 365–71). For an extended discussion of these issues see Howe and O'Donnell (forthcoming).
6. Myles glosses his comment with the observation that it becomes politically more difficult because when earnings inequality is high, large amounts have to be taxed from the few in order to provide for the many, leading to a more intense distributional conflict than taxing small amounts from the many to benefit the few in need, the option that presents itself when inequality is low. I am not sure about this. As the political adviser in Robert Penn Warren's *All the King's Men* put it, the massive wealth at the top of the scale offers good prospects for 'soaking the fat boys'. For example, in Australia it might mean reinstating a top marginal tax bracket of 60 per cent (abolished by Labor in the 1980s) on incomes over $75 000. This would raise an extra $1.5 billion per year. Again, Australia is one of the few OECD countries without a tax on accumulated wealth. The reintroduction of estate duties could raise another $1.5 billion per year. Abolition of family trusts and other tax avoidance schemes that favour the most well-off could raise another $4 billion (see Quiggin (1998) for an extended discussion of these issues). Politically, Australians do not seem to mind paying a bit more tax as long as it is to fund extra services, rather than merely making up for deficiencies in policing evasion by the rich (Withers, Throsby & Johnston 1994). The other argument against higher marginal tax rates and wealth taxes is that they stifle saving and investment, but Australia already has low taxes by OECD standards and yet still has low levels of saving and investment.
7. The assumption behind the 'top-up' prescriptions seems to be that if we want higher employment, we will have to accept lower wages. The contrasting fortunes of Australia and the United States are often trotted out to justify this argument. In fact, internationally there seems to be no simple correlation between high minimum wages and high unemployment (see Hancock (1999) for a review of the evidence). Even the United States, with a much greater incidence of low pay than Australia and Western Europe, still has similar levels of non-employment amongst working-age males: in 1996, nearly 24 per cent compared with the Australia's 23 per cent and around 24 per cent for Austria and the Netherlands (OECD 1998, pp. 9–11). This suggests that the low US unemployment rate is a statistical artefact, and also that incarceration of working-age males operates as a disguised but particularly brutal form of labour market regulation. Rather than there being a clear choice between either low wages or unemployment, the fiercest neo-liberal

economies — such as Britain in the 1980s — managed to secure themselves both low wages and high unemployment.
8. For example, productivity gains could be taken as shorter hours rather than as wage rises, a return to the type of union strategy that characterised labour struggles earlier this century (Cross 1993). An 'equitable reduction' of paid working time means it should be directed primarily at those in full-time work who are, on average, working longer hours than twenty years ago, and not at those on low incomes. I am not promoting shorter hours as a precondition for job-sharing and hence as a means of solving unemployment. After all, part-time work, as we have seen, has blossomed in the past fifteen years without a commensurate decline in the unemployment rate. Instead, as Doug Henwood has argued, a good argument for promoting shorter working time is not the spread of underwork in a supposed 'post-work' society but that there is already too much overwork, under debilitating and alienating conditions, producing nothing but toxins and consumer schlock (Henwood 1997).
9. See Cass and Cappo (1995) for an exploration of the idea of a 'participation income' in an Australian context.
10. As I have tried to show, it is useful to think of the tax-transfer system as a whole as either progressive or regressive. Many people tend to concentrate on whether taxation alone is progressive. Up until now, the Australian tax system overall has been more or less neutral, with mildly progressive direct taxes offset by mildly regressive indirect taxes and greater scope for the well off to avoid tax, but as I have argued, the distribution of the kitty has been skewed towards the less well off (see McClelland and Krever (1993) for a more detailed discussion of redistribution and the tax-transfer system). Some Western European social democracies have had much more progressive taxes with a relatively neutral transfer system focusing on universal rather than targeted benefits and services, which is another way of achieving a progressive or redistributive tax-transfer system. The folly of focusing solely on taxation can be seen in the case of the United States pre-Reagan, which displayed a nominally progressive tax system, yet failed to provide adequate benefits or services for its poor, instead spending the money on arms and fomenting bloodbaths in the Third World — hardly a 'progressive' system in any sense of the word.

Chapter 10

1. The interpretative framework for this essay is taken from that established by a number of writers associated with the Australian journals *Arena* and *Arena Journal*. Key sources include:

Sharp (1985), Hinkson (1993) and (1997), Caddick (1992) and Gill (1984).
2. This form of new social category definition has superficial similarities with theses of the 'new class' and the 'symbolic manipulators' of less critical theorists. The limits of the latter should be clear. The 'new class' is no such thing, merely an identified stratification group which had some minimal usefulness in the transition to postmodernity in the 1960s. Robert Reich's symbolic manipulators fails to differentiate between the secretary who word-processes letters and the quantum physicist (see Reich 1991).
3. The World Health Organization's *Global Burden of Disease* estimates that clinical depression will be the greatest health problem of advanced capitalist societies by 2020 (WHO 1999).
4. The example is Graham Little's.
5. Latham (1998) makes the most thorough attempt to theorise Australian social democracy to date, yet does not break out of that framework in any significant way.

Chapter 12

1. The use of the masculine pronoun is deliberate in this passage. The sites of sex commerce I am examining here are primarily directed to male consumers of sex product. Though contemporary culture is increasingly accommodating women as consumers of sex product, the economies of sex are still largely predicated on a traditionally patriarchal system of division where the consumer is identified as masculine. Though this is shifting, at least within Western spheres, it strikes me that the contemporary sex industries are still precariously navigating this shift.
2. This is not to argue that even within highly technological late-capitalist societies there are not collectives and individuals struggling against this postmodern citizen, but ultimately the rhetoric of this reactionary struggle is largely couched in anti-democratic and anti-secular terms.
3. Not that I am deliberately setting up an opposition between the liberal agendas of many gay and lesbian organisations and a commitment to a more radical sexual political critique. Civil and legislative work is crucial and important, but for me that arises from a commitment to a civil democratic culture which is assimilative and encouraging of difference. Sexual difference is in itself, however, no more important (nor less so) than any other forms of struggle within the general framework of something called 'human rights'.

Chapter 13

1. The following statistics are noted by the Federal Race Discrimination Commissioner (1997):
   - The life expectancy of Aboriginal people is fifteen to twenty years less than that of the general population.
   - Indigenous mortality is still more than three to five times higher than that for other Australian children. Infectious diseases are twelve times higher than the Australian average. 2.2 per cent of indigenous people have tertiary degrees compared with 12.8 per cent of all Australians.
   - The unemployment rate is 38 per cent for indigenous people, compared with 8.7 per cent for the general population.
   - The mean individual income is 65 per cent of that of the general population.
   - Indigenous peoples are 17.3 times more likely to be arrested; 14.7 times more likely to be imprisoned; and 16.5 times more likely to die in custody than non-indigenous Australians.
2. The Australian Bureau of Statistics in the 1996 census figures placed the indigenous population at 352 970 out of the total population of 17 892 423 (ABS 1996).
3. The court in *Cooper v. Stuart* (1889) held that the British claim to sovereignty over Australia was justified on the basis that it was an uninhabited territory. Blackstone stated that where land was acquired by settlement, British law prevailed (see Blackstone 1765–69/1979). The view was that the British had annexed parts of Australia in 1788, 1824, 1829 and 1879. The Crown had become both absolute and beneficial owner of the land. Aborigines had no property interests.
4. In *Milirrpum v. Nabalco Pty Ltd* (1971), Blackburn J held that given Australia was settled rather than conquered, its common law did not recognise native title.
5. Radical title was vested in the Crown of the 'discovering' nation — or the subsequent independent government — but the indigenous people retained the right of occupancy although they could dispose of their interest in the land to the Crown.
6. The court also held that native title exists in the manner in which it is defined by the Aboriginal community, that is, the laws and customs of the community will determine the parameters of the native title. It is a communal right. It can be extinguished by legislation that has a clear and plain intent to do so (the grant of a fee simple interest by the Crown will extinguish native title: see *Fejo v. Northern Territory* (1998)). The High Court also stated that where native title rights are extinguished, they

cannot be resuscitated. Brennan J, with whom McHugh J and Mason CJ agreed, said that native title could be extinguished if there is an intent shown by the legislature or the executive which would contradict the common law. Deane and Gaudron JJ said that if this was the case in certain circumstances, it may be done wrongfully and would give rise to compensation.

7. A right to compensation was found under section 7 of the *Racial Discrimination Act 1975* (Cth). That section prohibits the deprivation of property on the basis of race. The court found (by a 4:3 majority) that any extinguishment after the Act was passed breached section 7. Repealing the Act would eradicate the need to pay compensation.

8. One example is the following statement by Hugh Morgan:
    As far as the campaigners are concerned, they have made it crystal clear that their endeavours, extending over two generations, will only be concluded when a separate, sovereign state is carved out of Australia. We can reasonably predict that this Aboriginal state will have all the trappings of sovereignty, but will rely almost entirely on subvention from Australia for its continuing existence. (Morgan 1992, p. 13)

9. The court held that a native title holder cannot exclude the holder of a pastoral lease from the area covered by the pastoral lease or restrict pastoralists from using the lease area for pastoral purposes. Nor can a native title holder interfere with: the pastoralists' ability to use land and water on their leasehold; the pastoralists' privacy; or the pastoralists' right to build fences or make other improvements to the land. In fact, coexistence of the native title interest and the leasehold interest reflects arrangements informally created by pastoralists who allowed indigenous people access to traditional sites and whose properties had supported communities of indigenous people as a pool of cheap labour.

10. The passing of the 10 Point Plan in the *Native Title Amendment Act 1998* (Cth) meant that 80 of the 115 claims before the Native Title Tribunal in New South Wales were dismissed. Section 51(xxvi) of the Constitution states that:
    The Parliament shall, subject to this Constitution, have power to make laws for the peace, order, and good government of the Commonwealth with respect to ... (xxvi) The people of any race, for whom it is deemed necessary to make special laws.

    The 1967 Referendum facilitated changes to this section that allowed it to include indigenous Australians.

    This move from special rights to an individual rights-based framework involves what Nancy Fraser refers to as the 'decoupling of cultural politics from the social politics of redistribution' (Fraser 1997). Northern Land Council Chairman Galarrwuy

Yunupingu is quoted as saying: 'Our people are living in conditions which no other Australian would accept ... We don't accept it either, and we are now demanding our citizenship rights' (Berger 1988). Contemporary observers continue to believe in the importance of an active public sphere for the efficient workings of a democracy. Habermas believes that in multicultural societies, the citizenry can no longer be held together by consensus on values, but rather by consensus on procedures for the legitimate enactment of laws and exercise of power. Citizens integrated in this way share the rationally based conviction that unrestrained freedom of communication in the political public sphere, a democratic process for settling conflicts and the constitutional channelling of political power together provide a basis for checking illegitimate political power. This is used in the equal interest of all (Habermas 1994, p. 135).

The right to self-determination is recognised in the International Covenant on Civil and Political Rights, opened for signature on 19 December 1966 (999 UNTS 171, 6 ILM 368, art. 1 (entered into force 23 March 1976)). It states that self-determination is a right of all 'peoples'. Indigenous nations from all over the world assert that they are 'peoples' for this purpose but states have resisted this claim (see Anaya 1996).

Chapter 14

1. The documentary was 'Nobody's Children', directed by D. Goldie and written by J. Holmes and T. Moore.
2. This topic was also covered in the 1994 ABC television documentary, 'Growing Up Fast', directed by I. Cumming and written by T. Barrell.
3. As shown in 'Bohemian Rhapsody, Rebels of Australian Culture', 1996 ABC television documentary, written and directed by T. Moore.

Chapter 15

1. Australian citizens were, until the *Nationality and Citizenship Act 1948*, not Australian citizens, but British subjects.
2. From Hanson's letter to the *Queensland Times* in the lead-up to the 1996 election, quoted in Brunton (1998, p. 40).

Chapter 16

1. See his speeches and statements to this effect in: *Hansard*, House of Representatives, Wednesday 2 December 1998, p. 1134; press

release of 13 February 1999, 'Failed protection visa applicants cost Australia millions'; and press release of 7 March 1999, 'Taxpayer foots rising asylum seeker litigation costs'.
2. See, for example, statements made by Minister Ruddock in *Hansard*, House of Representatives, Wednesday 2 December 1998, pp. 113, 1246.

Chapter 17

1. This observation has long been made in the writings of theorists such as Offe (1988) and Foucault (1980).
2. Not only did the HREOC receive a 40 per cent funding cut in the 1997 Federal Budget, but the position of disability commissioner was not replaced after former commissioner Elizabeth Hastings resigned due to illness. Currently, the functions of the Disability Commissioner have been 'incorporated' into the position of the general Human Rights Commissioner, Chris Sidoti.
3. In a sheltered workshop in Melbourne, there are employees who have university degrees.

bibliography

Introduction

Australian National Audit Office (1999), *Staff Reductions in the Australian Public Service*, audit report 1998–99, no. 49, Australian National Audit Office.
Bordieu, P. (1998), *Acts of Resistance Against the New Myths of Our Time*, Polity Press.
Davis, M. (1997), *Gangland: Cultural Elites and the New Generationalism*, Allen & Unwin.
Giddens, A. (1998), *The Third Way*, Polity Press.
Gray, J. (1997), *False Dawn: The Delusions of Global Capitalism*, Granta.
Hage, G. (1998), *White Nation: Fantasies of a White Supremacy in a Multicultural Society*, Pluto Press.
Hutton, W. (1996), *The State We're In*, Vintage Press.
Martin, H-P. (1997), *The Global Trap*, Pluto Press.
Productivity Commission (1999a), *Impact of Competition Policy Reforms on Rural and Regional Australia*, Commonwealth of Australia.
Productivity Commission (1999b), *Productivity and the Structure of Employment*, Commonwealth of Australia.
Tanner, L. (1999), *Open Australia*, Pluto Press.
Thompson, M. (1999), *Labor Without Class*, Pluto Press.
Wark, M. (1999), *Celebrities, Culture and Cyberspace: The Light on the Hill in a Postmodern World*, Pluto Press.

Chapter 1

Boix, C. (1998), *Political Parties, Growth and Equality: Conservative and Social Democratic Economic Strategies in the World Economy*, Cambridge University Press.

Giddens, A. (1998), *The Third Way*, Polity Press.
Mackay, H. (1993), *Reinventing Australia: The Mind and Mood of Australia in the 90s*, Angus & Robertson.
White, S. & Cummings, S. (1997), *Silent Majority III: The Everyday Problems of the Average Australian*, Clemenger/BBDO.
Wiseman, J. (1998), *Global Nation: Australia and the Politics of Globalisation*, Cambridge University Press.

Chapter 2

Castells, M. (1996), *The Rise of the Network Society*, Blackwell.
Doyle, T. (1998), 'Sustainable development and agenda 21: the secular bible of global free markets and pluralist democracy', *Third World Quarterly*, vol. 19, no. 4, pp. 771–86.
Giddens, A. (1971), *Capitalism and Modern Social Theory: An Analysis of the Writings of Marx, Durkheim and Max Weber*, Cambridge University Press.
Giddens, A. (1984), *Beyond Left and Right: The Future of Radical Politics*, Polity Press.
Harvey, D. (1990), *The Condition of Postmodernity*, Blackwell.
Martins, M.R. (1982), 'The theory of social space in the work of Henri Lefebvre', in Forrest, R., Henderson, J. & Williams, P., *Urban Political Economy and Social Theory*, Gower.

Chapter 3

Alder J. (1994), *Constitutional and Administrative Law*, 2nd edn, Macmillan.
Batchelor, A. (1992), 'Referendums and initiatives', *Politics Review*, vol. 6, no. 3, February.
Carlton, J. (1994), 'How to break parliament's monopoly', *Independant Monthly*, February, pp. 34–5.
Haigh, C. (ed.) (1985), *The Cambridge Historical Encyclopaedia of Great Britain and Ireland*, Cambridge University Press.
Hughes, R. (1987), *The Fatal Shore*, Pan.
Kernot, C. (1994), 'Direct democracy', address delivered by Senator Cheryl Kernot, Leader of the Democrats, Ted Mack, Member for North Sydney, and Peter Reith, Shadow Defence Minister, to the National Press Club, Canberra, 28 July 1994.
Kirner, J. & Rayner, M. (1999), *The Women's Power Handbook*, Penguin.
Padfield, C.F. (1977), *British Constitution Made Simple*, 4th edn, W.H. Allen.
Reith, P. (1994), *Direct Democracy: The Way Ahead*, autumn, Department of the Parliamentary Library.
Wright, R. (1992), *A People's Counsel: A History of the Parliament of Victoria*, Oxford University Press.

Chapter 4

ACTU/TDC (1987), *Australia Reconstructed*, AGPS.
Alexander, M., Green, R. & Wilson, A. (1998), 'Delegate structures and strategic unionism', *Journal of Industrial Relations*, vol. 40.
Australian Labor Party (1996), *National Consultative Review Committee Report*, ALP.
Australian Labor Party (1998), *Platform*, ALP.
Australian Manufacturing Council (1990), *The Global Challenge*, AMC, Melbourne.
Beilharz, P. (1994), *Transforming Labor*, Cambridge University Press.
Bobbio, N. (1996), *Left and Right*, Polity Press.
Crean, S. (1999), 'Tax credits can't be dismissed', *Australian Financial Review*, 23 March.
Crosland, C.A.R. (1956), *The Future of Socialism*, Cape.
Dawkins, P., Freebairn, J., Garnaut, R., Keating, M. & Richardson, S. (1998), letter to the Prime Minister, 21 October.
Evatt Foundation (1995), *Unions 2001*, Evatt Foundation.
Finn, D. (1999), 'From full employment to employability: a new deal for Britain's unemployed?', paper presented at the 6th National Conference on Unemployment, University of Newcastle, 23–24 September.
Genoff, R. & Green, R. (1998), *Manufacturing Prosperity: Ideas for Industry, Technology and Employment*, Federation Press.
Giddens, A. (1998), *The Third Way: The Renewal of Social Democracy*, Polity Press.
Green, R. & Wilson, A. (1997), *The Accord and Industrial Relations: Lessons for Political Strategy*, ESC.
Hall, S. & Jacques, M. (1983), *The Politics of Thatcherism*, Weidenfeld & Nicholson.
Hindess, B. (1971), *The Decline of Working-Class Politics*, MacGibbon & Kee.
Kelly, P. (1992), *The End of Certainty*, Allen & Unwin.
Latham, M. (1998), *Civilising Global Capital*, Allen & Unwin.
Latham, M. (1999a), 'Politicians, take heed of new Machiavelli', *Australian Financial Review*, 30 August.
Latham, M. (1999b), 'Why it is vital to break the cycle of welfare dependency', *Australia Financial Review*, 9 August.
Lipset, S.M. (1960), *Political Man*, Heinemann.
McEachern, D. (1991), *Business Mates: The Power and Politics of the Hawke Era*, Prentice Hall.
Moore, D. (1998), *The Case for Further Deregulation of the Labour Market*, Council of Labour Ministers.
Pilger, J. (1989), *A Secret Country*, Cape.
Reich, R. (1991), *The Work of Nations*, Knopf.
Reith, P. (1998), 'Employment initiatives canvassed', letter to the

Prime Minister, 3 December.
Reith, P. (1999), 'Getting the outsiders inside', address to the National Press Club, 24 March.
Tanner, L. (1999), *Open Australia*, Pluto Press.
Thompson, M. (1999), *Labor Without Class: The Gentrification of the ALP*, Pluto Press.
Watson, I. & Buchanan, J. (1999), 'Beyond impoverished visions of the labour market', paper for the Creating Unequal Futures Project of the Academy of Social Sciences, May 1999.
Wooden, M. (1999), *The Future of Australian Industrial Relations*, National Institute of Labour Studies, Flinders University, Adelaide.

Chapter 5

ABS (1998a), *Population Projections: 1997 to 2051*, cat. no. 3222.0, Australian Bureau of Statistics.
ABS (1998b), *Population Projections: 1997 to 2051*, cat. no. 6203.0, Australian Bureau of Statistics.
ABS (1998c), *Population Projections: 1997 to 2051*, cat. no. 6310.0, Australian Bureau of Statistics.
ABS (1998d), *Population Projections: 1997 to 2051*, cat. no. 6323.0, Australian Bureau of Statistics.
ABS (1998e), *Population Projections: 1997 to 2051*, cat. no. 6325.0, Australian Bureau of Statistics.
ACIRRT (Australian Centre for Industrial Relations Research and Teaching) (1998a), *Agreements Database and Monitor Reports*, Prentice Hall.
ACIRRT (1998b), *Australia at Work*, Prentice Hall.
ACTU (1993), *Partners for Justice*, doc. no. 151, Australian Council of Trade Unions.
ACTU (1997), *A Note on Australian Trade Union Membership Data and ACTU Affiliation*, doc. no. 62, Australian Council of Trade Unions.
ACTU (1998), *The Benefits of Belonging: A Comparison of Union and Non-Union Wages and Benefits — No. 4*, doc. no. 77, Australian Council of Trade Unions.
Blanchflower, D. & Freeman, R. (1992), 'Unionism in the United States and other advanced OECD economies' in Bognanno, M. & Kleiner, M. (eds), *Labor Market Institutions and the Future Role of Unions*, Basil Blackwell.
Callus, R. et al. (1991), *Industrial Relations at Work: The Australian Workplace Industrial Relations Survey*, Department of Industrial Relations, AGPS.
Dunlop, J. (1980), *The Management of Labor Unions: Decision Making with Historical Constraints*, Book Tech.

Easson, M. (1990), 'What it means to be Labor' in Easson, M. (ed.), *The Foundation of Labor*, Labor Council of NSW, the Lloyd Ross Forum & Pluto Press.

Garrett, G. & Lange, P. (1995), 'Internationalization, institutions and political change', *International Organization*, no. 49, pp. 627–55.

Grattan, M. & Gruen, F. (1993), *Managing Government: Labor's Achievements and Failures*, Longman Cheshire.

Harcourt, T. (1997), 'The economics of the living wage', *Australian Economic Review*, no. 30, pp. 194–203.

Isaac, J.E. (1993), 'How important is industrial relations reform to economic performance?' in Bryce, M. (ed.), *Industrial Relations Policy under the Microscope*, ACIRRT working paper no. 40, Prentice Hall.

Isaac, J.E. (1998), 'Australian labour market issues: an historical perspective', *Journal of Industrial Relations*, no. 40, p. 690.

Labor Council of NSW (1996), *IR News*, winter, Labor Council of NSW.

Labor Council of NSW (1997) *Labor Council Industrial Relations Survey*, Labor Council of New South Wales.

Latham, M. (1998), 'Economic policy and the third way', *Australian Economic Review*, no. 31, pp. 384–98.

Morehead, A. et al. (1995), *Changes at Work: The 1995 Australian Workplace Industrial Relations Survey*, Longman.

Peetz, D. (1998), *Unions in a Contrary World*, Cambridge University Press.

Rodrik, D. (1997), *Has Globalization Gone Too Far?*, Institute for International Economics.

Ruthven, P. (1996), 'Changing economy — changing workforce', *IR News*, winter, Labor Council of NSW.

Schwartz, P. (1991), *The Art of the Long View*, Doubleday.

Stilwell, F. (1986), *The Accord and Beyond*, Pluto Press.

Weil, D. (1997), *Turning the Tide: Strategic Planning for Labor Unions*, Book Tech.

Chapter 6

ACIRRT (1994), *Agreements Database and Monitor Report*, Australian Centre for Industrial Relations Research and Training.

ACIRRT (Australian Centre for Industrial Relations Research and Training) (1999), *Australia at Work: Just Managing?*, Prentice Hall.

ACTU (1999), *Unions@Work: The Challenge for Unions to Create a Just and Fair Society*, report of the Australian Council of Trade Unions Overseas Delegation.

Australian Democrats (1998), *Issue Sheet '98: Industrial Relations*, http://www.democrats.org.au/issue/industrialrelations.htm.

bibliography 317

Australian Government Publishing Service (1986), *Industrial Relations and Employee Participation* ('the Green Paper'), AGPS.

Australian Green Party (1999), *Society: Industrial Relations*, http://www.peg.apc.org/~ausgreen/pol-soc.html.

Australian Labor Party (1999), *Platform Chapter 7 — Income, Job and Social Security for Working Age Australians: A Fair Industrial Relations System*, http://www.alp.org/policy/plat1_8.html#fair.

Barnard, C. (1999), 'The changing shape of worker representation in the United Kingdom: the influence of European Community law', *Australian Journal of Labour Law*, vol. 12, p. 1.

Bellace, J. (1997), 'The European Works Council Directive: transnational information and consultation in the European Union', *Comparative Labour Law*, vol. 18, p. 325.

Bentham, J. (1843/1961), *The Works of Jeremy Bentham*, Bowring, J. (ed.), Russell & Russell.

Callus, R. et al. (1991), *Industrial Relations at Work: The Australian Workplace Industrial Relations Survey*, Department of Industrial Relations, AGPS.

Cole, G.D.H. (1921), *Guild Socialism Re-Stated*, Leonard Parsons.

Conference on the Practical Application of the European Works Council Directive (1999), Brussels, 28–30 April 1999, organised by the ETUC, UNICE and CEEP (supported by DG5), http://europa.eu.int/index-en.htm.

Creighton, B. & Stewart, A. (1994), *Labour Law: An Introduction*, 2nd edn, Federation Press.

Davis, A.M. & Lansbury, R.D. (eds) (1996), *Managing Together*, Longman.

Department of Employment, Education and Training (1995), *Report of the Industry Task Force on Leadership and Management Skills*, AGPS.

European Works Council (1994), Council Directive 94/45, 1994 OJ (L 254).

European Works Council (1997), Council Directive 97/74, 1998 OJ (L 010).

Evatt Foundation (1995), *Unions 2001. A Blueprint for Trade Union Activism*, Evatt Foundation.

Finkin, M.W. (1994), *The Legal Future of Employee Representation*, ILR Press.

Flynn, P. (1999), 'European Works Councils: Practices and development', speech by the European Commissioner with responsibility for Employment and Social Affairs, Brussels, 28 April.

Freeman, R.B. (ed.) (1994), *Working Under Different Rules*, Russell Sage Foundation.

Hamburger, J. (1962), 'James Mill on universal suffrage and the middle class', *Journal of Politics*, vol. 24, p. 167.

Hansmann, H. (1993), 'Worker participation and corporate governance', *University of Toronto Law Journal*, vol. 43, p. 589.
Held, D. (1987), *Models of Democracy*, Stanford University Press.
Hutton, W. (1998), *The Stakeholding Society: Writings on Politics and Economics*, Polity Press.
Kelty, B. (1991), *Together for Tomorrow*, ACTU, Melbourne.
Liberal Party (1999), Department of Employment, Workplace Relations and Small Business, http://www.dewrsb.gov.au/group_wra/other/btrpay.htm#registorg.
Lively, J. (1975), *Democracy*, Blackwell.
Mathews, R. (1999), *Jobs of Our Own: Building a Stake-Holder Society — Alternatives to the Market State*, Pluto Press.
Mill, J.S. (1963), *Essays on Politics and Culture*, Oxford University Press.
Mill, J.S. (1975), *Three Essays*, Oxford University Press.
Mitchell, R. (1998), 'Juridification and labour law: a legal response to the flexibility debate in Australia', *International Journal of Comparative Labour Law and Industrial Relations*, vol. 14, p. 113.
Mitchell, R., Naughton, R. & Sorenson, R. (1997), 'The Law and employee participation: evidence from the Federal Enterprise Agreements', *Journal of Industrial Relations*, vol. 39, p. 196.
Morehead, A. et al. (1997), *Changes at Work: The 1995 Australian Workplace Industrial Relations Survey* ('AWIRS'), Longman.
Muller-Jentsch, W. (1995), 'Germany: from collective voice to co-management' in Rogers, J. & Streeck, W. (eds), *Works Councils: Consultation, Representation, and Co-Operation in Industrial Relations*, University of Chicago Press.
Nitta, M. (1996), 'Joint labour-management committees in Japan: theory and practice' in Davis, A.M. & Lansbury, R.D. (eds), *Managing Together*, Longman.
Pateman, C. (1970), *Participation and Democratic Theory*, Cambridge University Press.
Pateman, C. (1983), 'Feminism and democracy' in Duncan, G. (ed.), *Democratic Theory and Practice*, Cambridge University Press.
Patmore, G. (1998), 'Making sense of representative democracy and the implied freedom of political communication in the High Court of Australia: three possible models', *Griffith Law Review*, vol. 7, p. 97.
Phillips, A. (1991), *Engendering Democracy*, Polity Press.
Rogers, J. & Streeck, W. (1994), 'Workplace representation overseas: The works councils story' in Freeman, R.B. (ed.), *Working Under Different Rules*, Russell Sage Foundation, New York.
Rogers, J. & Streeck, W. (eds) (1995), *Works Councils: Consultation, Representation, and Co-Operation in Industrial Relations*, University of Chicago Press.
Streeck, W. (1995), 'Works councils in Western Europe: from con-

sultation to participation' in Rogers, J. & Streeck, W. (eds), *Works Councils: Consultation, Representation, and Co-Operation in Industrial Relations*, University of Chicago Press.

Vranken, M. (1998), 'Labour law and deregulation and the Australian Workplace Relations Act 1996' in Engels, C. & Weiss, M. (eds), *Labour Law and Industrial Relations at the Turn of the Century*, Kluwer Law International.

Chapter 7

ALRC (1986), *Report No. 31: The Recognition of Aboriginal Customary Laws*, Australian Law Reform Commission.

ALRC (1994), *Report No. 69 Part II: Equality Before the Law — Women's Equality*, Australian Law Reform Commission.

Attwood, B. & Markus, A. (1997), *The 1967 Referendum, or When Aborigines Didn't Get the Vote*, in collaboration with D. Edwards & K. Schilling, Australian Institute of Aboriginal and Torres Strait Islander Studies.

Charlesworth, H. (1993), 'The Australian reluctance about rights', *Osgoode Hall Law Journal*, vol. 31, p. 195.

Constitutional Centenary Foundation (1999), *'We the people of Australia ...' Report on the Preamble Quest*, http://www.centenary.org.au/preamble/index.html.

Constitutional Commission (1988), *Final Report of The Constitutional Commission*, vol. 1, AGPS.

Constitutional Convention (1998), 'Communique', in *Final Report of the Convention*, vol. 1, http://www.dpmc.gov.au/convention/report.html.

Eisenstein, Z. (1981), *The Radical Future of Liberal Feminism*, Longman.

Frazer, A. (1987), 'Conceptions of law and industrial arbitration in New South Wales 1880–1901', in Kirkby, D. (ed.), *Law and History in Australia*, vol. IV, LaTrobe University Press.

Hage, G. (1998), *White Nation: Fantasies of White Supremacy in a Multicultural Society*, Pluto Press.

Hand, G. (1987), *Foundations for the Future*, AGPS.

Hawke, R. (1956), 'The Commonwealth Arbitration Court — legal tribunal or economic legislature?', *University of Western Australia Annual Law Review*, no. 3, p. 422.

Higgins, H.B. (1915), 'A New Province for Law and Order', *Harvard Law Review*, vol. 29, p. 13.

HREOC (1997), *Bringing Them Home: Report of the National Inquiry into the Separation of Aboriginal and Torres Strait Islander Children from Their Families*, Human Rights and Equal Opportunity Commission.

Krever, R. (1991), 'The slow demise of progressive income tax', in

O'Leary, J. & Sharp. R. (eds), *Inequality in Australia: Slicing the Cake*, William Heinemann Australia.

Macintyre, S. & Mitchell, R. (eds) (1989), *Foundations of Arbitration: The Origins and Effects of State Compulsory Arbitration 1890–1914*, Oxford University Press.

Markus, A. (1979), *Fear and Hatred: Purifying Australia and California, 1850–1901*, Hale & Iremonger.

Morgan, J. (1994), 'Equality rights in the Australian context: a feminist assessment', in Alston, P. (ed.), *Towards an Australian Bill of Rights*, HREOC and Centre for International and Public Law.

O'Donovan, K. & Szyszczak, E. (1988), *Equality and Sex Discrimination Law*, Blackwell.

Oldfield, A. (1992), *Woman Suffrage in Australia: A Gift or a Struggle?*, Cambridge University Press.

Royal Commission into Aboriginal Deaths in Custody (1991), *Final Report*, AGPS.

Thornton, M. (1990), *The Liberal Promise: Anti-Discrimination Legislation in Australia*, Oxford University Press.

Watts, R. (1987), *The Foundations of the National Welfare State*, Allen & Unwin.

Wilcox, M.R. (1993), *An Australian Charter of Rights?*, Law Book Company.

Willard, M. (1978), *History of the White Australia Policy to 1920*, Melbourne University Press.

Yarwood, A.T. (1964), *Asian Migration to Australia: The Background to Exclusion, 1896–1923*, Melbourne University Press.

York, B. (1995), *Admissions and Exclusions: Asiatics and Other Coloured Races in Australia: 1901 to 1946*, Centre for Immigration and Multicultural Studies.

Chapter 8

ABS (1998), *Australian Social Trends 1998*, cat. no. 4102.0, Australian Bureau of Statistics.

ABS (1999), *Children, Australia: A Social Report*, cat. no. 4119.0, Australian Bureau of Statistics.

Burgess, J. & Campbell, I. (1998), 'The nature and dimensions of precarious employment in Australia', *Labour and Industry*, no. 8, pp. 5–20.

Cass, B. & Cappo, D. (1995), *Social Justice and the Life Course: Work, Social Participation and the Distribution of Income*, occasional paper no. 4, Australian Catholic Social Welfare Commission.

Cross, G. (1993), *Time and Money: The Making of Consumer Culture*, Routledge.

Crosland, C.A.R. (1956), *The Future of Socialism*, Cape.

Dawkins, P. (1996), 'The distribution of work in Australia', *Economic Record*, vol. 72, pp. 272–86.
Deakin, S. & Wilkinson, F. (1991), 'Labour law, social security and economic inequality', *Cambridge Journal of Economics*, no. 15, pp. 125–47.
Eckersley, R. (ed.) (1998), *Measuring Progress: Is Life Getting Better?*, CSIRO.
Fraser, N. & Gordon, L. (1994), 'A genealogy of "dependency": a keyword of the welfare state' in James, P. (ed.), *Critical Politics: From the Personal to the Global*, Arena Publications.
Freeland, J. (1993), 'Reconceptualising work, full employment and incomes policy', *The Future of Work*, Australian Council of Social Service.
Froud, J. et al. (1997), 'From social settlement to household lottery', *Economy and Society*, vol. 26, pp. 340–72.
Garrett, G. & Mitchell, D. (1995), *Globalisation and the Welfare State: Income Transfers in the Industrial Democracies, 1965–1990*, discussion paper no. 330, Australian National University Centre for Economic Policy Research.
Goldblatt, D. (1997), 'If at first you don't succeed ...', *Economy and Society*, vol. 26, pp. 147–56.
Gregory, B. & Sheehan, P. (1998), 'Poverty and the collapse of full employment' in Fincher, R. & Nieuwenhuysen, J. (eds), *Australian Poverty: Then and Now*, Melbourne University Press.
Hancock, K. (1999), 'Economics, industrial relations and the challenge of unemployment', keynote address to the Association of Industrial Relations Academics of Australia and New Zealand, Adelaide, 4 February.
Harding, A. (1997), 'The suffering middle: trends in income inequality in Australia, 1982–93/94', *Australian Economic Review*, vol. 30, pp. 341–58.
Harding, A. & Mitchell, D., 'The efficiency and effectiveness of the tax-transfer system in the 1980s', *Australian Tax Forum*, no. 9, pp. 277–303.
Henwood, D. (1997), 'Response to Stanley Aronowitz', *Left Business Observer*, vol. 76.
Hobsbawm, E. & Rudé, G. (1969), *Captain Swing*, Lawrence & Wishart.
Howe, B. & O'Donnell, A. (forthcoming), 'Working life, families and the welfare state' in Weeks, W. & Quinn, M. (eds), *Issues Facing Australian Families*, 3rd edn, Pearson Educational Publishers.
King, A. (1998), 'Income poverty since the early 1970s' in Fincher, R. & Nieuwenhuysen, J. (eds), *Australian Poverty: Then and Now*, Melbourne University Press.
Latham, M. (1998), *Civilising Global Capital: New Thinking for Australian Labor*, Allen & Unwin.

McClelland, A. & Krever, R. (1993), 'Social security, taxation law and redistribution: directions for reform', *Osgoode Hall Law Journal*, vol. 31, pp. 63–135.

McFate, K., Lawson, R. & Wilson, W.J. (eds) (1995), *Poverty, Inequality and the Future of Social Policy: Welfare States in the New World Order*, Russell Sage Foundation.

McIntosh, M. (1998), 'Dependency culture? Welfare, women and work', *Radical Philosophy*, vol. 91, pp. 2–5.

Murray, C. (1984), *Losing Out: American Social Policy 1950–1980*, Basic Books.

Myles, J. (1997), 'When markets fail: social policy at the turn of the century' in Saunders, P. & Eardley, T. (eds), *States, Markets, Communities: Remapping the Boundaries*, proceedings of the National Social Policy Conference, SPRC, University of NSW.

OECD (1998), *Employment Outlook*, Organisation for Economic Co-operation and Development.

Pahl, R. (1988), 'Some remarks on informal work, social polarisation and the social structure', *International Journal of Urban and Regional Research*, vol. 12, pp. 247–67.

Pfaller, A., Gough, I. & Therborn, G. (1991), *Can the Welfare State Compete? A Comparative Study of Five Advanced Capitalist Countries*, Macmillan.

Quiggin, J. (1998), *Taxing Times: A Guide to Australia's Tax Debate*, University of NSW Press.

Saunders, P. (1998), 'The distribution of work and the distribution of welfare' in Cass, B. & Couch, R. (eds), *Divided Work, Divided Society: Employment, Unemployment and Income Distribution in 1990s Australia*, University of Sydney.

Schmid, G. (1995), 'Is full employment still possible? Transitional labour markets as a new strategy of labour market policy', *Economic and Industrial Democracy*, vol. 16, pp. 429–56.

Shaver, S. (1998), 'Poverty, gender and sole parenthood' in Fincher, R. & Nieuwenhuysen, J. (eds), *Australian Poverty: Then and Now*, Melbourne University Press.

Travers, P. & Richardson, S. (1993), *Living Decently: Material Well-being in Australia*, Oxford University Press.

Withers, G., Throsby, D. & Johnston, K. (1994), *Public Expenditure in Australia*, Economic Planning Advisory Commission, paper no. 3, AGPS.

Chapter 9

Ball, D. (1996), *The Road to Nowhere? Urban Freeway Planning in Sydney to 1977 and the Present Day*, working paper no. 51, Urban Research Program, Australian National University.

Battellino, H. (1997), 'Mode choice for non-work trips', *Papers of the*

Australasian Transport Research Forum, no. 21, pp. 219–34.
EPA (1994), *Victorian Transport Externalities Study*, vol. 4, Environment Protection Authority, Victoria.
Gilbert, A. (1988), 'The roots of anti-suburbanism in Australia', in Goldberg, S. & Smith, F. (eds), *Australian Cultural History*, Cambridge University Press.
Glazebrook, G. & Johnson, D. (1995), *Timetabling for Tomorrow: An Agenda for Public Transport in Australia*, Australian Urban & Regional Development Review, Canberra.
GVRD (1993), *A Long Range Transportation Plan for Greater Vancouver*, Greater Vancouver Regional District.
IRTP (1997), *Integrated Regional Transport Plan for South-East Queensland*, Government Printer, Brisbane.
Mees, P. (1996), 'Do public choice and public transport mix? An Australian-Canadian comparison', working paper no. 58, Urban Research Program, Australian National University.
Mees, P. (1999), *A Very Public Solution: Transport in the Dispersed City*, Melbourne University Press.
Ministry of Transport (1982), 'Future context for transport: Metropolitan Transit Authority', unpublished, Melbourne.
MMBW (Melbourne and Metropolitan Board of Works) (1953), *Melbourne Metropolitan Planning Scheme 1954*, 2 vols, Government Printer, Melbourne.
Mogridge, M. (1990), *Traffic in Towns*, Macmillan.
Newman, P. (1991), *The Rebirth of the Perth Suburban Railways*, working paper, Murdoch University, Perth.
NGGIC (National Greenhouse Gas Inventory Committee) (1996), *National Greenhouse Gas Inventory 1988 to 1994, Vol. 8: Summary of Trends*, AGPS.
SACTRA (1994), *Trunk Roads and the Generation of Traffic*, Standing Advisory Committee on Trunk Road Assessment, London.
SACTRA (1998), *Transport Investment Intensity and Economic Growth*, Standing Advisory Committee on Trunk Road Assessment, London.
Sandercock, L. (1975), *Cities for Sale*, Melbourne University Press.
Scrafton, D. & Skene, P. (1998), *On the Right Track: Railway Development in South Australia 1968–1998*, ATRF paper, vol. 22, pp. 259–75.
Stevenson, G. (1987), *Rail Transport and Australian Federalism*, research monograph no. 48, Centre for Research on Federal Financial Relations, Australian National University.

Chapter 10

Anderson, P. & Mann, N. (1997), *Safety First: The Making of New Labour*, Granta.
Bloom, A. (1988), *The Closing of the American Mind*, Touchstone.

Caddick, A. (1992), 'Feminist and postmodern: Donna Haraway's cyborg', *Arena*, nos 99/100.
Castells, M. (1996), *The Rise of the Network Society*, Blackwell.
Drucker, P. (1994), *Post-Capitalist Society*, HarperBusiness.
Fromm, E. (1998), *The Essential Fromm: Life Between Having and Being*, Continuum.
Fukuyama, F. (1992), *The End of History and the Last Man*, Hamish Hamilton.
Gates, B. (1996), *The Road Ahead*, Penguin USA.
Gill, G. (1984), 'Post-structuralism as ideology', *Arena*, no. 69.
Hebdige, D. (1989), *Hiding In The Light: On Images and Things*, Methuen.
Hinkson, J. (1993), 'Postmodern economy: value, self-formation and intellectual practice', *Arena Journal*, no. 1 (new series).
Hinkson, J. (1997), 'The postmodern market', *Arena Journal*, no. 9.
Illich, I. (ed.) (1989), *Celebration of Awareness*, Heyday Books.
Krugman, P. (1997), *The Age of Diminished Expectations*, MIT Press.
Latham, M. (1998), *Civilising Global Capital*, Allen & Unwin.
McKay, G. (ed.) (1998), *DIY Culture: Party and Protest in Nineties Britain*, Verso.
Marcuse, H. (1992), *One Dimensional Man*, Beacon.
Reich, R. (1991), *The Work of Nations*, Knopf.
Sharp, G. (1985), 'Constitutive abstraction and social practice', *Arena*, no. 70.
Showalter, E. (1998), *Hystories: Hysterical Epidemics and the Modern Media*, Columbia University Press.
Toffler, A. (1991), *Powershift: Knowledge, Wealth and Violence at the Edge of the 21st Century*, Bantam.
WHO (1999), *Global Burden of Disease*, World Health Organization.

Chapter 11

Andersen, K. (1998), 'Entertainer-in-chief', *New Yorker*, 16 February, p. 34.
Connolly, W. (1995), *The Ethos of Pluralization*, University of Minnesota Press.
Donovan, R.J. & Scherer, R. (1992), *Unsilent Revolution: Television News and American Public Life*, Cambridge University Press.
Fallows, J. (1996), *Breaking the News: How the Media Undermine American Democracy*, Vintage Books.
Fraser, N. (1990), 'Rethinking the public sphere' in Robbins, B., *The Phantom Public Sphere*, University of Minnesota Press, pp. 1–32.
Hartley, J. (1992), *The Politics of Pictures: The Creation of the Public in the Age of Popular Media*, Routledge.
Hartley, J. (1996), *Popular Reality: Journalism, Modernity, Popular Culture*, Arnold.

Hitchens, C. (1998), 'It's not the sin. It's the cynicism', *Vanity Fair*, December, pp. 50–7.
Kinsley, M. (1998), 'In defense of Matt Drudge', *Time*, 2 February, p. 39.
Lippman, W. (1922), *Public Opinion*, Macmillan.
Lippman, W. (1927), *The Phantom Public*, Macmillan.
Robbins, B. (ed.) (1993), *The Phantom Public Sphere*, University of Minnesota Press.
Steinem, G. (1998), 'America's sexual obsessions', *Sydney Morning Herald*, 24 March, p. 19.

Chapter 12

Lacan, J. (1992), *The Ethics of Psychoanalysis 1959–1960: The Seminar of Jacques Lacan — Book VII*, ed. J-A. Miller, trans. D. Porter, UK edn, Tavistock/Routledge.

Chapter 13

ABS (1996), *1996 Census of Population and Housing: Selected Social and Housing Characteristics*, cat. no. 2015.0, Australian Bureau of Statistics.
Anaya, S.J. (1996), *Indigenous Peoples in International Law*, Oxford University Press.
Behrendt, J. (1995), 'So long and thanks for all the fish', *Alternative Law Journal*, vol. 20, no. 1, p. 11.
Berger, J. (1988), *Aborigines Today: Land and Justice*, Anti-Slavery Society.
Blackstone, W. (1765–69/1979), *Commentaries on the Laws of England*, (originally published in 4 vols by Clarendon Press) 1979 edn, University of Chicago Press.
Cohen, F.S. (1960), 'Anthropology and the problems of Indian administration' in Cohen, L., *The Legal Conscience: Selected Papers of Felix S. Cohen*, Yale University Press.
Cooper v. Stuart (1889) 14 App Case 285.
Federal Race Discrimination Commissioner (1997), *Questions and Answers about Aboriginal People and Torres Strait Islanders*, AGPS.
Fejo v. Northern Territory (1998) 156 ALR 721.
Fraser, N. (1997), *Justice Interruptus: Critical Reflections on the 'Postsocialist' Condition*, Routledge.
Goodall, H. (1996), *Invasion to Embassy: Land in Aboriginal Politics in New South Wales, 1770–1972*, Allen & Unwin.
Habermas, J (1994), 'Struggles for recognition in the democratic constitutional state' in Taylor, C., *Multiculturalism: Examining the Politics of Recognition*, Princeton University Press.

Jopson, D., Verrender, I. & Vass, N. (1997), 'Wik winners', *Sydney Morning Herald*, 10 May, p. 35.
Kartinyeri v. Commonwealth (1998) 152 ALR 540.
Kingston, M. (1998), 'Racing towards an election', *Sydney Morning Herald*, 11 April, p. 29.
Mabo v. Queensland (No. 2) (1992) 175 CLR 1.
Milirrpum v. Nabalco Pty Ltd (1971) 17 FLR 141.
Minister of State for the Army v. Dalziel (1944) 68 CLR 261.
Morgan, H. (1992), 'The dangers of Aboriginal sovereignty', *New Weekly*, 29 August.
Ramsay, A. (1997), 'Conflict of interest? So what?', *Sydney Morning Herald*, 10 May, p. 45.
Reynolds, H. (1982), *The Other Side of the Frontier: Aboriginal Resistance to European Invasion of Australia*, Penguin.
Reynolds, H. (1987), *Frontier: Aborigines, Settlers, and Land*, Allen & Unwin.
Reynolds, H. (1992), *The Law of the Land*, Penguin.
Savva, N. (1997) 'The sooner we get this debate over, the better off for all of us', *Age*, 1 December.
Wik Peoples v. Queensland; Thayorre Peoples v. Queensland (1996) 187 CLR 1.
Woodford, J. (1997), 'PM's apology draws protest', *Sydney Morning Herald*, 27 May, p. 1.
WSGAL Pty Ltd v. Trade Practices Commission (1994) ATPR 41-314, 42,175-7, 585, 678.

Chapter 14

Alomes, S. (1983), 'Cultural radicalism in the sixties', *Arena*, no. 62, pp. 35-42.
Bowles, S. & Gintis, H. (1976), *Schooling in Capitalist America: Educational Reform and Contradictions of Economic Life*, Routledge & Kegan Paul.
Connell, R.W. (1983), *Which Way is Up?: Essays on Sex, Class and Culture*, George Allen & Unwin.
Connell, R.W., Ashenden, D.J., Kessler, S. & Dowsett, G.W. (1982), *Making the Difference: Schools, Families And Social Division*, George Allen & Unwin.
Davis, M. (1997), *Gangland, Cultural Elites and the New Generationalism*, Allen & Unwin.
Dusseldorp Skills Forum (1999), *Australia's Young Adults: The Deepening Divide. A National Perspective on Developments that have Affected Young Adults during the 1990s*, Dusseldorp Skills Forum.
Dwyer, P., Wilson, B. & Woock, R. (1984), *Confronting School and Work: Youth and Class Cultures in Australia*, George Allen & Unwin.
Eckersley, R. (1988), *Casualties of Change — The Predicament of Youth*

in Australia, Australian Commission for the Future.
Eckersley, R. (1989), 'Social and economic issues affecting youth', *Bulletin of the National Clearinghouse for Youth Studies*, vol. 8, no. 1, February.
Freeland, J. (1986), *The Political Economy of Schooling*, Deakin University Press.
Freeland, J. (1987), *Teenage Unemployment: A Description and Explanation*, NSW Parliamentary Library.
Gerstner, R. & Bassett, J. (1991), *Seizures of Youth, 'The Sixties' and Australia*, Hyland House.
Hall, S. & Jefferson, T. (eds) (1976), *Resistance Through Rituals: Youth Subcultures in Post-War Britain*, HarperCollins Academic.
Howe, B. (1989), *Reform of Social Security Policies and Administration 1983–90*, AGPS.
Human Rights and Equal Opportunity Commission (1989), *Our Homeless Children: Report of the National Inquiry into Homeless Children*, AGPS.
Irving, T., Maunders, D. & Sherrington, G. (1995), *Youth in Australia: Policy, Administration and Politics*, Macmillan Education Australia.
Mass, F. (1990), 'The effects of prolonged dependence on young people becoming adult', *Youth Studies*, February, pp. 24–9.
Moore, T. (1988), *Counting the Costs*, Developmental Youth Services Association.
National Inquiry into Racist Violence (1991), *Racist Violence: Report of the National Inquiry into Racist Violence in Australia*, AGPS.
Pisarski, A. (1987), 'Rivers of babies', *Undercurrent*, no. 1.
Polk, K. & Tait, D. (1990), 'Changing youth labour markets and youth lifestyles', *Youth Studies*, February.
Sherrington, G. & Irving, T. (1989), 'Youth policies in twentieth century Australia', *Bulletin of the National Clearinghouse for Youth Studies*, vol. 8, no. 3, August.
Stilwell, F.J.B. (1986), *The Accord and Beyond: The Political Economy of the Labor Government*, Pluto Press.
Trethewey, J. & Burston, O. (1989), 'Changing entitlements for the young unemployed', *Bulletin of the National Clearinghouse for Youth Studies*, vol. 8, no. 2, May, pp. 45–9.
Tsiolkas, C. (1995), *Loaded*, Vintage.
Van Ryke, P. (1986), 'Whatever happened to class?', *Youth Work: Grappling with Politics*, Developmental Youth Services Association, pp. 42–5.
Walker, J.C. (1988), *Louts and Legends: Male Youth Culture in an Inner-City School*, Allen & Unwin.
Williams, R. (1961), *The Long Revolution*, Greenwood Press.
Willis, P.E. (1977), *Learning to Labour: How Working Class Kids Get Working Class Jobs*, Saxon House.

Chapter 15

Abbott, T. et al. (1998), *Two Nations: The Causes and Effects of the Rise of the One Nation Party in Australia*, Bookman Press.
BIR (1991), *Australian Citizenship: Statistical Report No. 1*, AGPS.
Brunton, R. (1998), 'Keating's Legacy' in Abbott et al., *Two Nations: The Causes and Effects of the Rise of the One Nation Party in Australia*, Bookman Press, pp. 38–47.
CAAIP (1988), *Immigration: A Commitment to Australia*, AGPS.
Castles, S. et al. (1992), *Mistaken Identity: Multiculturalism and the Demise of Nationalism in Australia*, 3rd edn, Pluto Press.
Castles, S. et al. (1998), *Immigration and Australia: Myths and Realities*, Allen & Unwin in conjunction with the Housing Industry Association.
CIE (1988), 'The relationship between immigration and economic performance' in CAAIP, *Immigration: A Commitment to Australia*, AGPS.
Clarke, H.R. et al. (1990), *Immigration, Population Growth and the Environment*, Bureau of Immigration Research, AGPS.
Clyne, M. & Kipp, S. (1997), 'Trends and changes in home language use and shift in Australia 1986–1996', *Journal of Multilingual and Multicultural Development*, vol. 18, no. 6, pp. 451–73.
Davidson, A. (1993), presentation in 'National Boundaries, Sovereignty and Citizenship', *Immigration Policy: The Moral and Ethical Dimensions. A Workshop*, Australian Catholic University, pp. 24–9.
de Bot, K. & Clyne, M. (1994), 'A 16-year longitudinal study of language attrition in Dutch immigrants in Australia', *Journal of Multilingual and Multicultural Development*, vol. 15, no. 1, pp. 17–28.
DILGEA (1988), *Australia and Immigration 1788 to 1988*, AGPS.
Doyal, L. & Gough, I. (1989), *A Theory of Human Need*, Macmillan.
Evans, M.D.R. (1988), 'Choosing to be a citizen: the time path of citizenship in Australia', *International Migration Review*, vol. XXII, no. 2, pp. 243–64.
Forsyth, P., Dwyer, L., Burnley, I. & Murphy, P. (1993), 'The impact of migration on tourism flows to and from Australia', discussion paper, Australian National University Centre for Economic Policy Research, p. 282.
Foster, L. & Stockley, D. (1988), *Australian Multiculturalism: A Documentary History and Critique*, Multilingual Matters.
Goot, M. (1998), 'Hanson's heartland: who's for One Nation and why' in Abbott et al., *Two Nations: The Causes and Effects of the Rise of the One Nation Party in Australia*, Bookman Press, pp. 58–73.
Gould, C. (1988), *Rethinking Democracy*, Cambridge University Press.
Grattan, M. (1998), 'Pauline Hanson's hijack of John Howard' in

Abbott et al., *Two Nations: The Causes and Effects of the Rise of the One Nation Party in Australia*, Bookman Press, pp. 75–88.

Human Rights and Equal Opportunity Commission (HREOC) (1997), *Bringing Them Home: The Report of the National Inquiry into the Separation of Aboriginal and Torres Strait Islander Children from their Families*, AGPS.

Jayasuriya, L. (1984), 'Whither multiculturalism?', 10th Annual Lalor Address, Human Rights and Equal Opportunity Commission.

Jayasuriya, L. (1988), *Asian Migrants in Australia: Fact and Fiction*, H.V. Evatt Research Centre.

Jayasuriya, L. (1996), 'Immigration and settlement in Australia: an overview and critique of multiculturalism' in Carmon, N. (ed.), *Immigration and Integration in Post-Industrial Societies: Theoretical Analysis and Policy Related Research*, Macmillan.

Jennings, M.K. & Niemi, R.G. (1974), *The Political Character of Adolescence*, Princeton University Press.

Jennings, M.K. & Niemi, R.G. (1981), *Generations and Politics*, Princeton University Press.

Junankar, P.N., Pope, D. & Withers, G. (1996), 'Immigration and the Australian macro-economy: perspective and prospective', *Immigration and Australia's Population in the 21st Century*, ANU–ASSA Workshop, October 1996, discussion paper no. 351, Australian National University Centre for Economic Policy Research, pp. 11–24.

Kelley, J. & McAllister, I. (1982), 'The decision to become an Australian citizen', *Australian and New Zealand Journal of Sociology*, vol. 18, no. 3, pp. 428–40.

Kerkyasharian, S. (1991), speech by the Chairman of the Ethnic Affairs Commission of NSW Mr Stepan Kerkyasharian to the NSW RSL State Council Meeting, 17 August.

Lack, J. & Templeton, J.W. (1995), *A Bold Experiment: A Documentary History of Australian Immigration Since 1945*, Oxford University Press.

Leser, D. (1998), 'Welcome to Australia', *Sydney Morning Herald*, 12 September, 'Good Weekend' p. 16.

Li, J. & Cockayne, J. (1999) 'W(h)ither multiculturalism?', unpublished manuscript.

Llinos, D. (ed.) (1992), *The Lesser Used Languages — Assimilating Newcomers: Proceedings*, Joint Working Party on Bilingualism in Dyfed.

Malouf, D. (1998), *A Spirit of Play: The Making of Australian Consciousness*, Boyer Lectures, ABC Books.

Martin, J. (1978), *The Migrant Presence*, George Allen & Unwin.

Nevile, J.W. (1990), 'Immigration and macroeconomic performance in Australia' in Nevile, J.W. (ed.), *The Benefits and Costs of Immigration*, CEDA study, Growth vol. 39.

Pan, B.A. (1995), 'Code negotiation in bilingual families: my body starts speaking English', *Journal of Multilingual and Multicultural Development*, vol. 16, no. 4, pp. 315–27.

Ruddock, the Hon. P. (1996), 'Opening speech', *Immigration and Australia's Population in the 21st Century*, ANU–ASSA Workshop, October 1996, discussion paper no. 351, Australian National University Centre for Economic Policy Research.

Sheehan, P. (1998), *Among the Barbarians: The Dividing of Australia*, Random House.

Smolicz, J.J. (1985), 'Multiculturalism and an overarching framework of values' in Poole, M., de Lacy, P. & Randawa, B. (eds), *Australia in Transition*, Harcourt Brace Jovanovich.

Stanton, P.J. & Lee, J. (1995), 'Australian cultural diversity and export growth', *Journal of Multilingual and Multicultural Development*, vol. 16, no. 6, pp. 497–511.

Sydney Morning Herald (1998), editorial, 24 June.

Tanner, L. (1999), *Open Australia*, Pluto Press.

Taylor, D. (1996), 'Citizenship and social power' in Taylor, D. (ed.), *Critical Social Policy: A Reader*, SAGE.

Thompson, J. (1993), 'Justifying immigration restrictions' in *Immigration Policy: The Moral and Ethical Dimensions. A Workshop*, Australian Catholic University, pp. 4–13.

Waas, M. (1993), 'Language attrition among German speakers in Australia: a sociolinguistic inquiry', unpublished doctoral dissertation, Macquarie University.

Walzer, M. (1983), *Spheres of Justice: A Defence of Pluralism and Equality*, Martin Roberston.

Wearing, R. (1985), 'Some correlates of choosing Australian citizenship', *Australian and New Zealand Journal of Sociology*, vol. 21, no. 3, pp. 395–413.

Withers, G. (1990), 'Immigration and Australia's development' in Nevile, JW.. (ed.), *The Benefits and Costs of Immigration*, CEDA study, Growth vol. 39.

Wooden, M. (1990), 'Economic aspects of immigration' in Sloan, J., Holton, R., Hugo, G. & Wooden, M., *Australian Immigration: A Survey of the Issues*, AGPS.

Yarwood, A.T. & Knowling, M.J. (1982), *Race Relations in Australia — A History*, Methuen.

Zubrzycki, J. (1977), 'Towards a multicultural society in Australia' in Bowen, M. (ed.), *Australia 2000: The Ethnic Impact*, University of New England.

Chapter 16

Baker, M., Sloan, J. & Robertson, F. (1994), *The Rationale for Australia's Skilled Migration Program*, AGPS.

Barker, G. (1997) 'Judges rebuke of refugee tribunal angers Ruddock', *Australia Financial Review*, 24 December.

Birrell, R. (1989), *The Chains that Bind: The Australian Experience of Chain Migration*, Department of Immigration and Ethnic Affairs, Canberra.

Birrell, R. & Rapson, V. (1998), 'The 1998–1999 Immigration Program', *People and Place*, vol. 6, no. 2.

Canberra Times (1996), editorial, 27 December.

Chen v. Minister for Immigration and Ethnic Affairs (No. 2) (1994) 51 FCR 322.

Crock, M. (1997), 'Migration law and the labour market: targeting the nation's skills needs' in Ronfeldt, P. & McCallum, R. (eds), *Labour Law Outlook*, ACIIRT.

Crock, M. (1998a), *Immigration and Refugee Law in Australia*, Federation Press.

Crock, M. (1998b), 'The relationship between the government and tribunals: politics, power and the exclusion or removal of "bad aliens"', paper to the NSW Chapter of the Australian Institute of Administrative Law Forum, 2 September 1998 (unpublished paper).

Cronin, K. (1993), 'A culture of control: an overview of immigration policy-making' in Jupp, J. & Kabala, M. (eds), *The Politics of Australian Immigration*, AGPS.

Fuduche v. Minister for Immigration and Ethnic Affairs (1993) 45 FCR 515.

Healey, E. (1991), 'Specialist temporary residents — what's happening?', *People and Place*, vol. 1.

Layman, L. (1996), 'To keep up the Australian standard: regulating contract migration 1901–1950', *Labour History*, no. 70.

O'Connor, M. (1998), *This Tired Brown Land*, Duffy and Snellgrove.

Parcell, W., Sparkes, L. & Williams, L. (1994), *A Brief Historical Outline of Skill Migration in Australia 1980–93*, BIPR.

Quinlan, M. & Lever-Tracy, C. (1990), 'From labour-market exclusion to industrial solidarity: Australian trade union reponses to Asian workers' in Easson, M. (ed.), *Australia and Immigration: Room to Grow?*, Pluto Press.

Rubenstein, K. (1997), 'Citizenship as democratic participation and exclusion: the High Court's approach to judicial review and refugees' in *'Retreating from the Refugee' Convention Conference Proceedings*, Northern Territory University, Darwin, 7–10 February.

Ruddock, P. (1997), 'Proposed changes to the Administrative Review Scheme', speech to the Australian Institute of Administrative Law Meeting (Victorian Chapter), 12 November.

Ruddock, P. (1998), 'Immigration reform: the unfinished agenda', address to National Press Club, Canberra, 18 March.

Chapter 17

Banks, R. & Kayess, R. (1998), 'Disability advocacy: Too much talk and not enough action' in Hauritz, M., Sampford, C. & Blencowe, S. (eds), *Justice for People with Disabilities*, Federation Press.

Brandy v. *Human Rights and Equal Opportunity Commission & Ors* (1995) 127 ALR 1.

Davis, L. (1998), 'Rights replacing needs: a new resolution of the distributive dilemma for people with disabilities in Australia?' in Hauritz, M., Sampford, C. & Blencowe, S. (eds), *Justice for People with Disabilities*, Federation Press.

Foucault, M. (1980), *Power/Knowledge: Selected Interviews and Other Writings 1972–1977*, ed. & trans. C. Gordon, Harvester Press.

Fulcher, G. (1989), 'Disability as a social construction' in Lupton, G. & Najman, J. (eds), *Sociology of Health and Illness: Australian Readings*, Macmillan.

Hauritz, M., Sampford, C. & Blencowe, S. (eds), *Justice for People with Disabilities*, Federation Press.

HREOC (Human Rights and Equal Opportunity Commission) (1998), *Annual Report 1997–98*, http:www.hreoc.gov.au/publications/a_reports.html .

Johnston, P. (1996), 'More than ordinary men gone wrong: can the law know the gay subject?', *Melbourne University Law Review*, vol. 20, p. 1152.

Jones, M. & Basser Marks, L. (1998), 'The limitations on the use of law to promote rights: an assessment of the Disability Discrimination Act 1992 (Cth)' in Hauritz, M., Sampford, C. & Blencowe, S. (eds), *Justice for People with Disabilities*, Federation Press.

Macalman, J. (1999), 'Why this prime minister makes me ashamed', *Age*, 17 February.

Offe, C. (1988), 'The divergent rationalities of administrative action' in Keane, J. (ed.), *Disorganised Capitalism*, Oxford University Press.

Oliver, M. (1990), *The Politics of Disablement*, Macmillan.

Oliver, M. (1996), *Understanding Disability: From Theory to Practice*, Macmillan.

Parsons, I. (forthcoming), *Human Rights and Social Movements*.

Rose, A.D. (1998), 'Australian Law Reform Commission Review of the Disability Services Act 1986 (Cth)' in Hauritz, M., Sampford, C. & Blencowe, S. (eds), *Justice for People with Disabilities*, Federation Press.

Stone, D. (1984), *The Disabled State*, Temple University Press.

Thornton, M. (1990), *The Liberal Promise*, Oxford University Press.

Tyler, M.C. (1993), 'The Disability Discrimination Act 1992: genesis, drafting and prospects', *Melbourne University Law Review*, vol. 19, p. 211.

Chapter 18

Baudrillard, J. (1996), *The Perfect Crime*, Verso.

Berns, S. (1993), 'Through the looking glass — gender, class and shared interests: the myth of the representative individual', *Law in Context*, vol. 11, p. 95.

Bulbeck, C. (1998), *Re-Orienting Western Feminisms; Women's Diversity in a Postcolonial World*, Cambridge University Press.

Derrida, J. (1992), 'Force of law: the mystical foundations of authority', in Cornell, D., Rosenfeld, M. & Carlson, D.G. (eds), *Deconstruction and the Possibility of Justice*, Routledge.

Elam, D. (1994), *Feminism and Deconstruction*, Routledge.

Falzon, C. (1998), *Foucault and Social Dialogue: Beyond Fragmentation*, Routledge.

Fraser, N. (1994), 'Rethinking the public sphere: a contribution to the critique of actually existing democracy', in Giroux, H. & McLaren, P. (eds), *Between Borders: Pedagogy and the Politics of Cultural Studies*, Routledge.

Greider, W. (1997), *One World: Ready or Not: The Manic Logic of Global Capitalism*, Simon & Schuster.

Harasym, S. (ed.) (1990*)*, *Gayatri Chakravorty Spivak, the Post-Colonial Critic: Interviews, Strategies, Dialogues*, Routledge.

Johnson, P. (1994), *Feminism as Radical Humanism*, Allen & Unwin.

O'Donovan, K. (1985), *Sexual Divisions in Law*, Weidenfeld Nicholson.

Saul, J.R. (1992), *Voltaire's Bastards*, Penguin.

Spivak, G. (1988), 'Can the subaltern speak?' in Nelson, C. & Grossberg, L. (eds), *Marxism and the Interpretation of Culture*, Macmillan.

Thornton, M. (1995), *Public and Private: Feminist Legal Debates*, Oxford University Press.

Wertheim, M. (1999), *The Pearly Gates of Cyberspace: A History of Space from Dante to the Internet*, Doubleday.

Yeatman, A. (1993), 'Voice and representation in the politics of difference' in Gunew, S. & Yeatman, A. (eds), *Feminism and the Politics of Difference*, Allen & Unwin.

Young, I. (1987), 'Impartiality and the civic public' in Behhabib, S. & Cornell, D. (eds), *Feminism as Critique*, Polity Press.

Young, I. (1995), 'Communication and the other: beyond deliberative democracy' in Wilson, M. & Yeatman, A. (eds), *Justice & Identity; Antipodean Practices*, Allen & Unwin.

index

Aboriginal Deaths in Custody 121
Aboriginal people 12, 14, 201–15
　Constitution and 202, 209–10
　Howard Government and 13, 121–3, 206–9
　Queensland voting system and 51
　property rights and 202–6, 210–15
　rights 116, 117, 118, 121–3, 124, 126, 238
　trade unions and 99
Accord 6–7, 63–5, 73–5, 93
　see also trade unions
accountability 38, 43, 49, 102
Adelaide transport system 142, 147, 151, 152
affirmative action 54
Alder, J. 56
aliens 267–8
Alomes, S. 221
Among the Barbarians (Sheehan) 240, 241, 243
Anderson, Kurt 179–80
Anderson, P. 160
arbitration system 79–80, 95, 116–17
Asian economic crisis 159
assimilation 234, 238–40
audiences, media and 182–8
Australia's Young Adults (Dusseldorp) 218, 224
Australia Reconstructed (ACTU/TDC) 67, 75
Australian Centre for Industrial Relations Research and Training (ACIRRT) 93, 101
Australian Democrats
　GST and 120
　migration policy 255
　preamble and 126
　workplace democracy and 112–13
Australian Greens 3, 112–13

Australian Head of State 252–3
Australian Industrial Relations Commission 79–80
Australian Labor Party (ALP)
　Aboriginal people and 122
　Accord and 63–5, 75
　alliances and 84
　charter for government 30
　deregulation and 73–82
　migration policy and law 265, 270–1
　1996 election 67, 76
　postmodern politics and 170
　Reith reforms and 80–1
　trade unions and 81–2, 83–4, 94
　workplace democracy and 113
　youth policies 216–17, 219–20, 225–6, 227–8
Australian Law Reform Commission 280
Australian Workplace Industrial Relations Survey (AWIRS) 91–2, 101

baby boomers 227–9
Banks, R. 276, 285
barbarism 171
Barnard, C. 104, 105
Batchelor, A. 59
Baudrillard, Jean 298, 299
Beazley, Kim 31, 80, 82
Beder, Sharon 40
Behrendt, Larissa 13–14, 201–15
Beilharz, Peter 68, 73, 75
Bellace, J. 105
belonging 34–5
　see also community
Berns, Sandra 288
Bill of Rights 116, 209
　see also rights

Birrell, Robert 255, 261, 262, 270
Bjelke–Petersen, Joh 51
Blainey, Geoffrey 126
Blair, Tony 23, 68, 70–1, 72, 129, 170
Bloom, A. 164
Bobbio, Noberto 68
Boix, C. 30
Boyd, Robin 153
Breaking the News (Fallows) 173–4
Brisbane 147, 151
  Gold Coast tollway 142
Brown, Gordon 71
Buchanan, John 78
Burgess, John 134
bus services 150–1, 152
  see also public transport
Business Council of Australia 73
business migration 256
  see also migration law

Calwell, Arthur 238
Campbell, Iain 134
capital markets 32
Carr, Bob 248
cars, dominance of and decline of public system 141–55
Castles, S. 246, 251
casual employment 27, 134
  see also employment
censorship 197, 227
Centre left parties 1, 160
Charlesworth, H. 116
Chinese communities 236
cities, sustainability and transport systems 154–5
citizen initiated referenda (CIR) 8, 55–60
citizenship 4, 9
  democratic rights and 43–7
  difference and 294
  disabled people and 283–5
  immigrants and 242, 246, 251–3
  workplace democracy and 102–3
  youth and 220–1, 224–5
City Link project 148
Civilising Global Capitalism (Latham) 75, 76–8, 81
class 11, 26–7, 76, 168
  feminism and 288, 293
  youth and 216–17, 220, 225–6
Clemenger 22
clinical depression 170
Clinton, Bill 69–70, 129, 174, 175, 178–81
Cockayne, James 12–13, 233–53
Cohen, Felix 215

commodification 4, 9, 37–41, 164–8
  of sex 16, 192–200
communality 192
communicative democracy 298
  see also democratic reforms
community 33–5, 228, 246, 270, 295
  decision making 213, 214
competitive tendering 3, 43
Connell, Bob 225, 226
Connolly, William 186
consciousness raising 298
Constitution
  Aboriginal people and 202–3, 209–10
  changes to 57–8
  equality and 115–18
  Head of State 252–3
  preamble 118, 123–7
Constitutional Convention 123–4
consumers 4, 9, 161–3, 165–6
  media and 174, 182–4
  political action and 168–9, 192–3
contracting out 3, 43
corporatism 219–23
Costello, Peter 25
counterculture 164
counterpublics 185, 295
Crean, Simon 80
creativity 227
  see also cultural diversity
Crock, Mary 13, 254–71
Crosland, Anthony 69, 70, 130
cultural difference 13, 16, 234–5
  feminism and 286–99
  media and 185–8
cultural diversity 124, 187, 233–4
  monoculture and assimilation 235–40, 243
  multiculturalism and 240–53
cultural homogeneity 25
  feminism 286–99
  youth and 219–22, 227
cultural politics 10, 227, 249–50
cultural production
  multiculturalism and 250
  youth and 14, 227, 231–2
cultural studies 164, 165
Curtin, John 238

Davis, Lynne 277, 281–3
Davis, Mark 219, 227
Dawkins, John 226
Dawkins, P. 134, 137
Deakin, Alfred 237
Deakin, S. 138
democratic reforms 8, 48–60

Aboriginal people and 212–15
women and 53–5, 295–9
workplace and 100–14
see also representative democracy
demography, economic restructuring and 97
dependency 133, 224–5
see also welfare state
deregulation 6
ALP and 64, 67–8, 73–82
labour market 136
New Labour and 65–8
Derrida, Jacques 299
disability
as administrative construct 277–8
as social construct 276
discrimination laws 278–81
Howard Government and 281–3
Disability Discrimination Act 278–80, 281, 284
Disability Services Act 283, 284
disabled people 281
migration laws and 266–7
rights of 272–85
disempowerment 213, 223
diversity 16, 219–22
see also cultural diversity
DIY culture 167, 168–70, 231–2
Dole, Bob 29
Dollar Sweets 74
Doyle, Timothy 40
Drucker, Peter 161
Drudge Report 178
drug abuse 218
Dunlop, John 86
Dunstan, Don 141, 147, 151
Dusseldorp Skills Forum 218, 224, 226, 229

earnings credits 138–9
Eckersley, R. 216, 218, 220, 224
economic efficiency
migration 256
transport systems 145–6
economic rationalism 2, 12, 76
migration law and 255
public transport and 153–4
economic restructuring 14, 39, 63–5, 74–5
demographics and 97
role of welfare state and 134
union membership and 92, 97
youth and 216–17, 220–1
education 30–1, 81
class and 225–6
postmodern economy and 162–3, 219

reform of 229–32
trade unions and 98
Elam, Diane 190
elites 187, 222–3
employers
anti–union strategies 92–3
wage subsidies 137–8
workplace democracy and 111–12
employment
disabled people and 274–5
households and 134–5
migration and 256–7
New Labour policies 71–2
restructuring and the state 134
see also unemployment
empowerment 222–3
environment 17, 40–2
migration policy and 255
transport systems and 143–4, 154
equal opportunity 127
equality 30
Aboriginal people and 121–3, 124, 126, 201–15
Constitution and 115–18
Constitution preamble and 123–7
cultural difference and 244–53
formal and substantive 12, 18, 119–20, 211–15, 241–2, 292
of opportunity 127
sameness and 236
taxation and 118–20
transport systems and 17, 144–5
see also inequality
essentialism 289–90
ethics 296–9
ethnicity, and feminism 288
see also cultural diversity; multiculturalism
Ethos of Pluralization, The (Connolly) 186–7
European Union 67, 160
Social Chapter (EU) 9, 128
Works Councils 9, 104–11
Evatt Foundation 111, 113
exchange value 37–8
exclusion 237–8

'Fairness and Work' (New Labour) 66, 72, 160
Fallows, James 173–4
Falzon, Christopher 296–7, 298
families 27–8, 33
disability policies and 282
income 135–6, 224
migration 255, 261–5, 270
farmers, Aboriginal people and 205,

208
federal elections
  1996 67, 76
  1998 21–2
Federation, equality and 116–18
  see also Constitution
feminists
  censorship issues and 196, 197, 198
  Clinton and 180–1
  difference and homogeneity and 286–99
  Taliban 189, 200
  see also women
Ferguson, Martin 81
Finkin, M.W. 100
Finlay, Edward 50
fishing rights 210–11
Five Economists plan 78, 80
Flowers, Gennifer 180
Flynn, Padraig 106, 107
formal equality 12, 18, 119–20, 212, 292
  see also equality
Frankfurt School 165
Fraser, Nancy 185, 293–4, 295
Frazer, A. 117
Freeland, John 225
freeways 141–2
  see also urban transport
Friedman, Milton 137
Fromm, E. 163
Fukuyama, Francis 159

Ganglands (Davis) 219, 227
Garret, G. 95
Gates, Bill 163
gay identity politics 16, 191
  see also identity politics
generationalism 221, 227, 228, 232
  One Nation and 247
genetically modified foods 168
Germany 160, 167
ghettoisation 246
Giddens, Anthony 6, 7, 17–18, 24, 28, 38, 41, 68–9, 71–2, 73, 77, 170
Gillard, Julia 4, 7, 9, 21–35
Glass, Hugh 50
Global Challenge (AMC) 75
globalisation 2, 4, 9, 24–6, 41
  difference and 16, 286
  regulation and 6, 75–82, 128
  social infrastructure and 95–6
  trade unions and 86–99
  welfare state and 132
  workplace democracy and 107–8
  youth unemployment 217–18
Goldblatt, David 135

Goodall, H. 203
Goods and Services Tax (GST) 22, 118–20, 139–40
Goot, Murray 243, 247
Goss, Wayne 142
gossip and news 178–81
Grattan, Michelle 94, 245
Green Party (Germany) 167
Green, Roy 6, 17, 63–85
greenhouse gases 143
Gregory, Bob 131
Greider, William 286
Gruen, Fred 94
guest workers 256, 259

Hage, Ghassan 13, 121
Haigh, C. 56
Hall, S. 72
Hamburger, J. 102
Hamer, Rupert 147, 148
Hand, Gerry 121
Hanson, Pauline 12–13, 122, 176, 187, 235, 241, 243, 245, 260
Harcourt, Tim 5, 8, 96–9
Harding, A. 131
Harradine, Brian 123
Hartley, John 176–7, 182–3
Harvey, David 38, 42
Hawke, Bob 64, 117, 129, 217–18
Hayek, Friedrich von 70
Head On (film) 222
health
  migration laws and 265–6
  post modern disorders 165, 170
Hebdige, D. 164
Henderson, Ronald 130–2, 136
Hewson, John 74, 178
Higgins, H.B. 117
Hindess, Barry 76
Hindmarsh Island case 209–10
Hitchens, Christopher 181
Hobsbawm, Eric 137
homosexuality 15–16, 189
  see also identity politics
hospitality industries 219
household earnings 134–5
Howard Government 30, 45, 160
  Aboriginal people and 13, 121–3, 206–9
  cultural difference and 242–3
  disability policies 279, 281–3
  migration law and 255–69
  trade unions and 5, 74, 79–80, 82–3
  young people and 216, 219, 223, 227

Howard, John 126, 160, 206–9
Hughes, Billy 238
Hughes, Robert 48
human rights 190
Hunter, Rosemary 9, 11, 115–28

identity politics 11, 12, 15–16
   disabled people and 277
   feminism and 290
   media and 186–7
   socialism and 190–200
   young people and 219–22, 232
Illich, Ivan 163
images, audience and the creation of 182–3
immigrants 13, 233–4, 239–40
   economics and 247–8, 256–7
   see also migration law; multiculturalism
income distribution 5, 46–7, 74, 97, 130, 134–5, 138
   see also inequality
income support 134–5, 138–9
incomes policy 74
inculturation 255
individualism 64, 161, 165–6
   cultural change and 249
   homogeneity and 292
   media and 186–8
industrial democracy 7, 100–14
industrial disputes 74
industrial relations 31, 79–80
   see also trade unions
inequality 5, 7–8, 12, 46–7, 97
   Aboriginal people and 117, 118, 121–3, 124, 126, 210–15
   Constitution and 115–18
   democratic reforms and 48–60
   GST and 118–20, 139–40
   welfare state role and 133–9
   see also equality
information rich and poor 4–5, 25
insecurity 22
integration 121, 239–40
   see also immigrants
interest groups 11, 58–9, 76, 213, 220, 241, 296
internationalism, response to globalisation 9, 32, 41–3
Internet 11, 16, 161, 178–9, 189, 231
   "pornography" and sexual commodification 193–200
   power relationships and 287
Irvine, William 51
Irving, T. 217, 218, 220, 222
Isaac, Joe 95, 96

Isaacs, Sir Isaac 56–7

Jacques, M. 72
Jayasuriya, L. 243, 245
Johnson, Pauline 292
Johnston, P. 284
Jones, Paula 180
Jopson, D. 207
journalists 176
   see also media
judicial review 49

Kayess, R. 276, 285
Keating, Paul 64, 122, 178
   interest groups and 76–7
Kelly, Paul 74
Kelty, Bill 67, 100
Kennedy, J.F. 177
Kennett, Jeff 38, 44, 148
Keynes, John Maynard 69
King, Anthony 130
Kingston, Margo 207
Kinsley, Michael 178
Kirby, Justice M. 210
Kirner, Joan 54, 148
knowledge economy 8, 161, 219, 230–1
Knowling, M.J. 238
Kosovar refugees 268
Krever, Rick 119
Krugman, Paul 159

Labor Council of NSW 93
Labor Without Class (Thompson) 76
labour market deregulation
   see deregulation; trade unions; *Workplace Relations Act*
Lacan, Jacques 191
Lafontaine, Oscar 160
land rights 121–2, 203–4
   see also Aboriginal people
Lange, P. 95
Latham, Mark 75, 76–8, 81, 96, 129–30, 227
Lee, Ivy 175
Leser, David 246
Lever–Tracy, Constance 254
Lewinsky, Monica 174, 175, 178–81
Liberal Party, workplace democracy and 113
   see also Howard Government
libertarianism 163, 190–1, 196, 197
lifestyle politics 167
   see also identity politics
Lippman, Walter 175
Lipset, Seymour Martin 65

Lively, J. 101, 102, 103
Loaded (Tsiolkas) 222
localism 42
    see also community
Long, Colin 4, 9, 17, 36–47
Lonie, W.M. 148
Lumby, Catherine 11, 173–88

McEachern, D. 73
McKay, G. 168
Mackay, Hugh 22
mad cow disease 168
Maddock, Diana 54
Magna Carta 56
Malouf, David 237
Mann, N. 160
manual work 226
manufacturing industry 74–5, 219
Marcuse, Herbert 163, 165
maritime dispute 74
market research 176
Markus, Andrew 117
Martins, M.R. 38
mateship 126
Mathews, Race 103
Maunders, D. 217, 220, 222
Max, Karl 37
Meany, George 86
media
    consumers and 175, 182–4
    difference and 185–8
    public opinion and 175–88
Mees, Paul 17, 141–55
Melbourne road and transport system 147–50–1
migration law 254–6
    bad aliens 267–8
    carers 266–7
    economics of 256–7
    families 261–5
    health concerns and 265–6
    ministerial discretion 269
    points test 257–9
    safe haven 68–9
Mill, John Stuart 70, 101, 102, 103
Mind and Mood Study (Mackay) 22
Minh-ha, Trinh 290
mining companies 207
minority groups, parliamentary representation and 55
modernity 160–1, 164–8
Mogridge, Martin 146
monoculturalism 234, 235–8, 243
Moore, Des 79
Moore, Tony 14–15, 216–32
Morris, Dick 70

motorways 141–55
Moylan, Judi 282
Mudginberri 74
Muller–Jentsch, W. 106
multiculturalism 233–4, 240–53
    difference and 244–53
    static 240–4
Multilateral Agreement on Investment (MAI) 43, 160
Murray, Les 126
Myles, John 136, 137

national identity 235, 248, 251–3
Native title 12, 121–3, 204–6, 207, 209
    equal protection and 210–11
    see also Aboriginal people
neo-liberalism 37–41, 45, 68
    social democrats and 69–70
    see also economic rationalism; globalisation
New Labour 63, 65–72, 160
New Right 73–4
New Zealand
    Closer Economic Relations 128
    union membership in 91
Newman, P. 152
news values 174, 182–4
    see also media
non–English speaking background people 233–4, 248
    see also multiculturalism
North American Free Trade Agreement (NAFTA) 43, 128

O'Connor, Mark 255
O'Donovan, Katherine 294
O'Donnell, Anthony 5, 7–8, 129–40
On the Right Track 152
One Nation Party 12–13, 122, 235, 241, 243, 244, 247, 252, 255, 260, 270
one vote one value 51, 55
Open Australia (Tanner) 75, 77, 80, 81

Padfield, C.F. 56
Pahl, R. 134
Paid To Care (Hurd) 272–3
Pankhurst, Emmeline 54
parental migration 263–5
    see also migration law
parliamentary reform 8, 48–60
    see also representative democracy
part-time employment 135
    see also employment
pastoral leases 205, 211
Pateman, Carole 101, 102, 103

Patmore, Glenn 7, 9, 100–14
Peetz, David 92–3
Perot, Ross 176
Perth transport system 151–2
    see also urban transport
Phantom Public, The (Robbins) 184
Phillips, A. 103
Pilger, John 73
pluralism
    feminism and 289–90, 294
    media and 186–8
political parties, postmodernism and 168
politicians, lack of trust in 173
Politics of Pictures (Hartley) 176, 182–3
Polk, K. 217, 218, 219, 224, 229
Poor Laws 137
Popular Reality (Hartley) 182–3
population density and public transport 153–4
population policy 255
pornography 193
postmodernism 9–10
    social democracy and 161–72
    youth and 220–1
poverty 130–2
    see also inequality
power
    CIR and 58–9
    homogeneity and 291–4
Priority One 217
    see also youth
private property, compulsory acquisition of 49
    see also property rights
private sphere
    disability policies and 282
    homogeneity and 293
    news and 180–2, 183–4
    participation and 297–9
privatisation 39
productivity, disabled people and 274
property rights 49
    Aboriginal people and 202–15
    see also rights
proportional representation 8, 52–3
    see also representative democracy
public broadcasters 184
    see also media
public opinion
    media and 175–88
    trade unions and 93
public relations 176
public sector 2–3
    see also welfare state
public sphere 174, 182, 293

public transport 17, 141–2
    bureaucrats 153–4
    importance of 143–7
    integration of systems 141, 149–53
    Melbourne case study 147–52
    road lobby and 149–50
    Toronto comparison 150–1

queer politics 199
    see also identity politics
Quinlan, Michael 254

race power 209–10
Racial Discrimination Act 1975 (Cth) 204
railways 151–2
    see also public transport
Ramsay, A. 207
Rapson, Virginia 255, 261, 262
Rayner, Moira 54
reason, male 291–2
reciprocity 35
    third way and 71, 80, 129–30
referendum (1967) 202
    see also citizen initiated referenda
refugees 268–9
regional disadvantage 27
regional unemployment 218–19
    see also unemployment
Reich, Robert 70
Reith, Peter 57, 59, 79–80, 84
representative democracy
    Aboriginal people and 212–15
    media and 176–7
    women and 8, 58, 103, 116
Reynolds, Henry 201, 203
rights 43–7
    Aboriginal people and 202–15
    disabled people 272–85
    sexual politics and 196–200
    marketisation 41
road lobby 148
Robbins, Bruce 184
Rodrik, D. 95
Rogers, J. 100, 109
Roosevelt, Theodore 58
Rousseau, Jean–Jacques 60
Ruddock, Phillip 234, 261, 269–70
Rudé, George 137
Rundle, Guy 10, 159–72
Russia 159
Ruthven, Phil 97

safe haven, migration law 268–9
safety net 94, 131
Sandercock, Leonie 141

Saul, John Raulston 291
Saunders, P. 135
Savva, N. 206
SBS 184, 241
Schillmoller, Anne 16
Schmid, G. 137
school reform 229–32
Schroeder, Gerhard 170
Senate 52
services sector growth 219, 230–1
sex industry 194–200
sexual politics 191–200
Sheehan, Paul 240, 241, 243, 245
Sheehan, Peter 131
Sherrington, G. 217, 218, 220, 222
Showalter, E. 165
Silent Majority (Clemenger) 22
Simpson, O.J. 179, 185–6
skilled migrants 257, 259, 261
small business, NESB immigrants and 248
Snowy Mountains Scheme 239
Social Chapter (EU) 9, 128
social cohesion 242–3
social democracy 1–2, 8
   communicative 297–9
   Europe 160
   young people and 14–15
social exclusion 82–3
social inclusion 13
social infrastructure 94, 95, 232, 276
social market 169–70
social movements 99, 167, 168–9, 277
social policy expenditure 25
social security *see* welfare state
social wage 94
socialism 36, 164–8
   identity politics and 190–200
society of the spectacle 169, 173
sole parents 135
Speemhamland System 137
Spivak, Gayatri 289, 291, 295
spousal migration 261–3
   see also migration law
stakeholderism 5, 70
Starr, Kenneth 180, 181
State upper houses 51–3
State, democratic rights and 43–7
Steinem, Gloria 181
Stevenson, G. 152
Stilwell, Frank 93, 225
Stolen Generation 121
'Street Trash' web site 192–5
Streeck, W. 100, 109
subjectivity and postmodernism 164
substantive equality 12, 18, 119–20

Aboriginal people and 211–15
multiculturalism and 241–2, 244–53
   see also equality
suburbia 153
sustainable development 40–1
Switzerland 59
Sydney roads 147
   see also urban transport

Tait, D. 217, 218, 219, 224, 229
Taliban 189–90, 198, 200
Tanner, Lindsay 75, 77, 80, 81, 227, 235, 270
tax credits 63, 71, 77–8, 80, 136–8
taxation system
   fiscal crisis and 129
   equity issues and 118–20, 139–40
technological change, work and 26, 98, 161, 219, 230
   see also knowledge economy
television, politics and 177–80
   see also media
Ten Point Plan 206, 208
   see also Aboriginal people
terra nullius 14, 203–5, 206, 209, 211, 214
Thatcherism 1, 65–6, 68, 70, 72, 129
third way 5–6, 7, 17–18, 23, 63, 68–72, 170
   attacks on the welfare state and 129–30
   Australian setting 72–81
Thompson, Michael 11, 12, 76
Thornton, M. 284, 292–3
Toffler, Alvin 161
Toronto 150–1
Townsend, Matthew 8, 48–60
trade unions 39–40
   Accord and 63–5, 73–5
   ALP and 81–2
   benefits of belonging 95
   employment by 98
   fee–for–service idea 99
   globalisation and 86–99
   membership 3, 5, 87–94
   New Labour and 66–7
   restructuring needs 93–9
   rights of 117
   workplace democracy and 111–12
   Workplace Relations Act and 79–80, 83–4
   young people and 229
Trades Union Congress 67
traffic congestion 142, 145–7
   see also urban transport
transport planning 142, 147

triangulation 70
Truman, Harry 177
Tsiolkas, Christos 15, 189–200, 222

underclass 5
  see also inequality; unemployment
Underwood, Robin 148
unemployment 14–15, 83–4
  intergenerational 7
  long term 26
  obligation and 71, 80
  tax credits and 77–8, 80
  youth 82, 216, 217–19, 225–6
Unions@Work 111, 113
United States of America 159
universities 226
urban transport 17, 141–55
  see also public transport
use value 37–8
user pays 39

value systems 10
Van Ryke, P. 224, 225
Vass, N. 207
Verrender, I. 207
Victorian Constitution 49–51
Victorian Fund 50
Victorian Legislative Council 50–3
Voltaire's Bastards (Saul) 291

wages 63–5, 78–9, 82, 84, 97, 131, 135–6, 218–19, 223, 228
Wark, MacKenzie 11
Warner, Dave 273, 274
Watson, Ian 78
wealth and power, CIR and 58–9
welfare state 6, 8, 118, 129
  disability policy and cuts to 282
  dependency 71, 78, 129–30, 132
  flexibility needs 137–40
  globalisation and 132
  history of 130–3, 136
  immigrants and 242, 243
  USA 159
welfare-to-work 71, 78, 80, 82
Wertheim, Margaret 287
White Australia policy 116–17, 237–8, 240, 254
Whitlam government 74–5, 240–1
Whitlam, Gough 201, 215
Wik decision 12, 121–3, 205, 207

Wilbur Smith & Associates 147
Wilkinson, F. 138
Williams, Raymond 222
Wilson, Andrew 6, 17, 63–85
Wilson, Woodrow 175
Wiseman, John 24
women
  difference and 16–17, 286–99
  employment and 80–1, 135
  equality, history of in Australia 116, 124
  parliamentary representation 8, 53–5
  representative democracy and 8, 58, 103, 116
  trade unions and 90, 95
Women's Power Handbook (Kirner and Rayner) 54
Wong, Geoff 235–6
Wooden, Mark 82
Woodford, J. 207
work, changing nature of 26, 27, 81–3
  workplace democracy and 108–10
work-for-the-dole 216
working hours 97
workplace democracy 100–3
  Australian possibilities 110–14
  Works Councils and 104–11
Workplace Relations Act 79–80, 82
Wright, Raymond 50, 51

Yarwood, A.T. 238
Yat Sen Li, Jason 12–13, 233–53
Yeatman, Anna 288, 292, 295, 296
young people 14–15
Young, Iris 291, 297–8
youth
  categorisation and marginalisation 216–32
  citizenship 220–1, 224–5
  creativity 227
  cultural production 14, 227, 231–2
  education system and 226
  homelessness 218
  Howard Government and 216, 219, 223, 227
  'problem' 218
  technological change and 8, 14–15, 98, 219
  trade unions and 229
  unemployment 82